CLASSIC
NEW ZEALAND
ADVENTURES

Jonathan Kennett
Johnny Mulheron
Greg Carlyon
Malcolm O'Neill

Dedicated to South Westland's Heritage Area. May it remain the largest unroaded wilderness in New Zealand

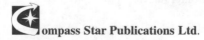

ompass Star Publications Ltd.

Published in 1997 by Compass Star Publications Ltd.
Kyre Park, Tenbury Wells, Worcs., WR15 8RP, UK.
Distributed in the USA by Hunter Publishing Inc., 300 Raritan
Center Parkway, CN 94, Edison, NJ 08810

2nd Edition

First published in 1992 by GP Publications Ltd (New Zealand)

British Library Cataloguing in Publication Data. A cataloguing record
for this book is available from the British Library

ISBN 0-9520900-2-3
—Cover photo: Mt Cook from Hooker Valley (Deanna Swaney).
—Back cover photos (from top to bottom): Jane Shearer; Jonathan
Kennett; Waiorau Nordic Ski Area.
—Photographer credits provided with captions for other photos.
—Maps: Sarah Drake
—Symbols: Simon Kennett
—Cover Design: Keith Jenkins & Marsh Design
—Production: CentrePrint/Hereford Repro

Printed & bound in Malta by Interprint Ltd.

★·K·E·Y·★ to Adventure Maps

•••••..»→	walking/single track	»→	coast
──~ »→	vehicle/4WD track	»→	rocks
── »→	road	»→	mudflat
─┼─ »→	foot bridge	⌂ »→	public hut/shelter
»→	native bush	⌂ »→	D.O.C info/private house
»→	exotic forest	★ »→	camping
»→	tussock/grass land	»→	cliff/terrace edge
»→	swamp	»→	cave
»→	stream/river	¥ »→	waterfall
»→	shingle	»→	lake

★·K·E·Y·★ to Regional Maps

★ »→	adventure site/area	»→	major road
~~ »→	river	● »→	town/city

Acknowledgements

For their support, information and encouragement while researching and writing this second edition the authors would like to thank:

DOC staff and adventure operators throughout the country; Dan Bolger, Barry Boyd, Sven Brabyn, Elise Bryant, Brian Dobbie, Peter Dymock, Maree Gurney, Simon Johnson, Jannette Kear, Paul Kennett, Geoffroy La Marche, Brent Love, Kirstan MacKay, Diana Parr, Adrian Syme, Bronwen Wall, and last but not least, all the people who helped with the first edition of Classic New Zealand Adventures. Thanks folks.

The Regions of
N·E·W Z·E·A·L·A·N·D

6. The Far North »»

8. East Cape AND Hawkes Bay

7. Auckland »»

9. Taranaki AND Tongariro »»

11. Nelson AND Marlborough

10. Wellington

12. The Wild West Coast »»

13. Canterbury

15. The Far South

14. Southern Lakes

Contents

Over the Tawhai Falls in an Inflatable
Kayak   (Plateau Guides)

The first edition of this book included a foreword by Rob Hall and
Gary Ball, intrepid adventurers from New Zealand. Sadly, both Rob
and Gary subsequently died in separate climbing accidents in the
Himalaya. We'd like to dedicate this new edition to their adventurous
spirits.

1. About the Book

What is Classic New Zealand Adventures?

It's the original guidebook to the best outdoor adventures in, under and over New Zealand.

Who is it For?

Classic New Zealand Adventures is for anyone and everyone who wants to enjoy the many outdoor activities packed into this small country.

We have combined our extensive outdoor experience to describe over 200 classics suitable for all adventurers, from the hesitant beginner right through to the adrenalin-crazed lunatic.

But remember: learning to venture safely into the outdoors takes time and experience. If your time, equipment or experience are limited then consider hiring a professional outdoors guide for the trips you plan to do. Most guides provide excellent instruction during their trips.

What is a Classic Adventure?

The adventures in this book are ones that we personally consider to be classics. They have been enjoyed in the past and will continue to be enjoyed in the future because they include the essential elements of adventure—challenge, commitment, adrenalin and excitement, discovery and reward—all bundled into a physical and psychological journey through an area of natural beauty. They needn't be absolutely death-defying tests of your technical abilities.

We'd like to think that even the hottest exponents in their particular fields would still find the beginner adventures worthwhile and enjoyable.

An Underlying Theme

We hope this book will inspire and motivate people to get out and enjoy New Zealand's wild places. The more people who do, the more there are to speak up for the future protection and preservation of our natural heritage.

This applies equally to New Zealanders and overseas visitors. We want to encourage tourism that will not destroy the very things travellers come to enjoy and many locals take for granted; unpolluted rivers, air and sea, untouched wilderness, and a sense of remoteness.

These qualities are under serious threat from developers of roads, monorails, gondolas, hotels, power stations and mining industries, all of which are proposed or occur in various wilderness areas of New Zealand.

New Zealand may at first seem a paradise of nature, but unfortunately New Zealanders are not always as conservation minded as we would like. Much of today's natural environment was preserved mainly because the early pioneers considered it useless land. That New Zealand retains so much wilderness land is attributable more to the short period of human settlement than a commendable conservation attitude in its people. Conservation battles here are as difficult as anywhere in the world.

Overseas visitors can help conserve our national heritage just as much as New Zealanders by respecting our wilderness and speaking up for its protection from such developments.

How to Use this Book

If you're new to the New Zealand outdoor scene, Chapters 2 to 5 tell you almost everything you need to know before setting off on an adventure.

If you're already an experienced adventurer and are looking for new things to try and places to go, start at Chapter 6. Chapters 6 to 15 describe classic New Zealand adventures, region by region. The location description beneath an adventure heading provides straight-line distances from the nearest well known landmark

One of the more common terms used in the adventure descriptions is true right (or left). This refers to the right (or left) of a river when you are facing downstream. For a more comprehensive list of the terms used, turn to the Glossary.

Unless indicated otherwise, all $ prices in the text refer to New Zealand dollars.

Gradings

'If at first you don't succeed, try, try again. Then quit. No use being a damn fool about it.'   (W C Fields)

Adventures rated 'beginner' are suitable for people who have little, if any, technical ability. All you need is a willingness to learn and a 'give it a go' attitude. 'Intermediate' adventurers need to have previous experience and a reasonable level of fitness.

'Experienced' adventurers need to be fit, have the relevant technical skills and be prepared for practically any contingency in the New Zealand wilderness.

The 'lunatic' adventures are inherently dangerous and should **not** be attempted by anyone. They are intended as humour only. If, in spite of this warning you still feel compelled to undertake them then you must take responsibility for your own actions. For further information about gradings, see the Grading Systems section at the end of the book.

Maps

Where appropriate, hobbit-style maps have been included. These maps, together with Department of Survey and Land Information (DOSLI) Terrainmaps and Topomaps, will provide you with the best information available, short of a personal guide. If maps are essential for a particular trip, we've said so and listed them at the end of the trip notes.

Part of the South Island is still in the process of being updated with new metric maps.

Maps can be bought from DOC centres, some information centres and most outdoors shops. Prices range from $10-$13.

Commercial or Not?

Many of the adventures in this book are done, or can be done, with a commercial operator. When this is the case, we have made it clear in the write-up. The operator's phone number, and the price of the trip at the time of writing, are also included.

However, this book is not a directory of commercial adventure operators. There may be other, just as reputable, clubs and non-commercial operators offering similar trips in the same area.

We have mentioned adventures which are human-powered only. Commercial trips which rely on the use of motorised transport, such as helicopters or jet boats, have been excluded because of their intrusiveness and unnecessary carbon dioxide emissions.

A Last Word

While revising this book we were amazed at how many things had changed in only four years. New huts, bridges and tracks were built, and some were damaged or destroyed by floods, landslides or earthquakes. A lot of prices went up (although a few dropped), the number of people heading for the hills greatly increased and many new adventure operators started up.

So...while following the trip descriptions in this or any other guide book, remember that things change, and look forward to a few surprises. We can point you in the right direction and give you plenty of tips to help out along the way, but in the end what makes an adventure 'classic' is up to you.

If you note any errors, please either contact the authors c/o Classic New Zealand Adventures, PO Box 11 310, Wellington, New Zealand or the publisher, Compass Star Publications, via post, phone/fax or e-mail (address details provided at the back of this book).

If you have access to the Internet, related World Wide Web sites include:

• http://www.kennett.co.nz

and

• http://www.mountainbike.co.nz

2. Information about New Zealand

The Story of the Land

The landscape of New Zealand is both diverse and dramatic. There are steep mountains, deep lakes, active volcanoes, and rugged coasts in a land that has been sculpted by glaciers, rivers, wind, sea (and bulldozers).

These erosional processes gradually etch their own signatures upon a basic landmass slowly emerging from the ocean as a result of continuous turmoil deep within the earth.

Flora & Fauna

Isolated from the evolutionary processes occurring on other continents, New Zealand developed a few of its own plants and animals.

Before humans arrived and introduced numerous noxious species, flightless birds and ancient tuatara were almost completely unchallenged and evolved many unique characteristics as a result. Unable to protect themselves adequately an estimated 73 native species were hunted to extinction by both humans and the animals they introduced. Species such as deer, possums, rats and rabbits pose an indirect, but very serious threat, by competing with native birds for food.

Today many of our rare and threatened species are confined to a handful of predator-free islands scattered around the country where the understaffed and underfunded Department of Conservation (DOC) desperately battles to save them.

On a positive note, New Zealand still remains free of many potential pests, such as snakes, scorpions, and nuclear ships.

People of Aotearoa

The Maori came to Aotearoa (Land of the Long White Cloud) between 800 and 1200 years ago from Hawaiki, land of legend somewhere in the Pacific. The majority lived in the warmer North Island, establishing a society based on hunting, gathering, fishing, agriculture and trading.

After European (Pakeha) explorers bumped into the country (Abel Tasman in 1642 and James Cook in 1769), a new wave of settlers gradually began arriving from the northern hemisphere, often travelling via Australia.

In 1840, when most, but not all, Maori chiefs signed The Treaty of Waitangi, New Zealand officially became a British colony.

Maori Land

From 1840 to 1940 much land was procured from Maori tribes around the country, often in very dubious ways. This led to considerable conflict at the time and was never forgotten by the Tangata Whenua (the people of the land).

In the mid 1980s the New Zealand government started listening seriously to land claims and grievances. Since then some land has been returned and financial compensation given, but in reality the problem is huge and we've only just begun solving it.

Travellers need to appreciate the importance that Maori place on the land they still own and show due respect.

Weather

Because New Zealand is a long, relatively small country surrounded by huge oceans, the weather often changes quickly and unpredictably. It also varies greatly from region to region.

While the far north of New Zealand is experiencing equatorial warmth, the south, 1600 km away, may be shivering in the blast of cold polar air. And the west coast, exposed to the moist westerly winds, is often wet, while the east side of the country is correspondingly dry.

Rain, snow, hail, and sleet can fall any time of year in the mountains. Winds from the south bring cold air and winds from the north are warm. Winter snows start falling in the mountains during May, but seldom reach sea level even on the South Island. Most cities rarely experience temperatures below 0° Celsius in winter (May, June, July and August) or above 30° Celsius in summer (December, January, February and March).

Remember, however, that the weather is extremely changeable—there are more exceptions than rules in New Zealand's climate. The main thing to keep in mind and be prepared for is that the weather can, and often does, change from great to terrible in just a few hours, especially in the mountains.

- For the national mountain weather forecast, phone ☎ 0900 99966, or listen to National Radio (AM band), at 1 pm daily. The standard five-day forecast is broadcast at 12.35 pm week days and 12.25 pm on weekends and public holidays.

- For an up-to-date weather forecast specific to any area in New Zealand, phone the MetPhone helpline on ☎ 0800 500 669.

Land Access

When undertaking the adventures described in this book, you'll encounter many different landowners. If permission is needed to cross land, we have said so.

To find out the current land access situation for adventures beyond this book, check with the Department of Conservation (DOC) or the local district council.

Respect people and their land—access is a privilege, not a right. If you get a hard time, it's probably because the last person did something stupid (like leaving a closed gate open or vice versa).

From Here to There

Without your own transport, getting to some of the more remote road ends can be a challenge exceeding the adventure itself. There are a surprising number of people, including small operators, who will take people to these remote road ends. Ask around, particularly at backpacker hostels.

Aside from the more conventional forms of public transport, there are several other options. Backpacker buses are cheap and will collect and dump you anywhere on their set tours around the country, although getting back on the next bus can be a problem if it is full. Mini-bus shuttles service most major cities and are cheap but a little cramped. Unless you're in a hurry, consider using the NZ Nature Safari transport (see Chapter 7, section 7.8). Hiring a campervan or car is convenient and good value for a group of people. Some backpackers hostels will sell you a cheap car and buy it back at the end of your trip. Cycling is a great way to get around and gives you the flexibility to go wherever you want. Bikes can be hired from bike shops or adventure companies in most New Zealand cities.

Hitchhiking is quite reasonable along the main routes of the North Island, but in the South Island, especially on the West Coast you can be left waiting for several hours.

Keep Left

Motorists drive on the left hand side of the road in New Zealand. This is easy to remember in the cities and on busy highways, but people sometimes forget when they are cruising along on remote back country roads. If someone drives towards you on the wrong side of the road stay left, slow right down and if practical pull off the road. Nine times out of ten, they'll swerve back onto the correct side of the road.

Unusual Laws

Cycle helmets must be worn while cycling on all public roads. It is compulsory for motorists and their passengers to wear seat belts.

Interisland Ferries

Ferries sail several times a day between Wellington and Picton and cost from $22 to $44 depending on discounts and time of year. The trip takes about 3 hours and is quite pleasant on fine days.

There are also a couple of fast ferries which cost more and take half the time. However, they may be ordered to slow down because of the environmental damage caused by their wake. For more information and bookings phone ☎ 0800 658 999.

A Roof over Your Head

There are hundreds of backpacker hostels, Bed and Breakfast houses and motorcamps with cabins scattered throughout the country. Most provide excellent-value accommodation priced between $10 and $18. Bed and Breakfast houses are usually more expensive, but they are also more comfortable and of course provide a huge breakfast. Some hotels are cottoning on to the backpacker market and now provide special backpacker accommodation at cheaper rates. During the peak months of December, January and February, it is advisable to book ahead.

Camping

Motorcamps spread around the country almost always have an area for camping and charge roughly $6-$10 per person. They also have facilities such as kitchen, TV room and showers, etc.

Out of the towns and cities the Department of Conservation (DOC) have camping areas scattered around most of their parks and reserves. In remote areas, away from the main tracks there are many informal 'no facility' campsites which make no charge. A 'low facility' camping area will probably have running tap water, toilets, rubbish bins and fireplaces, and it will cost $2-$6 per person per night. Their serviced camping grounds will have almost as many facilities as a motorcamp but be in a more scenic spot and cost $6-$9. DOC has a pamphlet listing all their campsites.

Free camping: the right to camp on private land does not exist in New Zealand, as it does in some countries. If you are discreet you can usually get away with camping on areas of public land; we've spent many happy nights at rest areas on the side of the road, under bridges and in railway stations. If you have to live cheaply, look on it as a challenge and do it with style.

Back-Country Huts

New Zealand has an extensive network of huts managed by DOC. The price is usually $4 or $8 per night depending on the standard of the hut. There is no charge for the really derelict huts and shelters. A $4 per night (one ticket) hut has four walls, a roof, bunks, a table and a pit toilet; anything extra is a bonus. An $8 per night (two ticket) hut will probably have extra luxuries such as tap water in the hut, a gas or coal stove, and mattresses, etc. An annual hut pass can be purchased for $58, and covers all DOC huts except those on the Great Walks and alpine huts in Mt Cook and Westland National Parks. Alpine huts are $12 per night and are equipped with kerosene cookers and mountain radios.

Hut tickets should be purchased in advance from DOC or local outdoor shops and then left at the huts you stay in. During summer there are hut wardens on all the popular tracks who, amongst other things, can help you pay should you have forgotten your hut ticket. All huts, except on the Milford and Routeburn tracks, operate on a 'first in first served' basis. Those who arrive to find a hut full may have to sleep on the floor.

Great Walks

For the 'Great Walks of New Zealand' you must purchase a 'Hut and Campsite Pass', which will cost $6-$14 per night. There are booking systems in place for the Milford and Routeburn tracks. These and the Tongariro Crossing and Abel Tasman tracks are the most popular and of course the most crowded as well. Expect the number of trampers, application of booking systems and prices of huts to continue increasing. Those looking for a wilderness experience can easily find one by tramping elsewhere or trying the Great Walks out of season.

☎ — Telephone Hints

A lot of companies offer toll-free telephone calls. Any number that starts with 0800 or 0508 can be dialled toll-free anywhere in the country. Any number that starts with 025 is a cell phone number and will cost the caller more than a local phone call.

Different pay phones will accept either coins, a pay phone card (which can be bought from most dairies, book shops, and service stations) or credit cards. Card phones are the most common.

☎ 111 for emergency services (police, fire, ambulance)
☎ 018 to find a New Zealand phone number
☎ 0172 to find an international phone number
☎ 010 to make operator-assisted calls in New Zealand
☎ 0170 to make operator-assisted calls overseas
☎ 00 + country code + area code + number... to dial direct overseas

Emergencies

Search and Rescue (SAR) operations take time and effort to extract people from wild places each year. To make their job easier, you should be well equipped, tell people where you're going, fill in hut intentions books, and perhaps hire a mountain radio (see Clubs & Contacts). Many national parks operate a 'sign in - sign out' system. It is **extremely important** to always sign out when you get out of the hills, otherwise a search and rescue operation will start. These operations cost thousands of dollars.

If things get out of control, SAR can be contacted through the police by phoning the national emergency number ☎ 111. When you venture into the wilderness, you have to accept responsibility for your own decisions and the risks that you take.

The Nature of Wilderness

'Wilderness is something that can only diminish, and future generations will only have what we leave of it for them.'
(Geoff Spearpoint, *Waking to the Hills*)

Nature is neither your friend nor enemy. The wilderness can be hard on people who venture beyond their ability, but is itself fragile when pressured by expanding humanity. Before people arrived, 80% of New Zealand was forested. Today, only 20% of our native forest remains.

At present there is an emerging conflict between tourism and environmental interests. Although tourist operators make our natural areas more accessible, they also have the potential to overpopulate and overdevelop them. If this happens then the initial get-away-from-it-all experience is lost. We suggest that you 'vote with your feet'; support operators who are the most environmentally clued-up and recommend them to others. As an adventurer you should plan your trip so that it is as unobtrusive as possible. Consider travelling in small groups, during off-peak times or into less crowded areas. Also consider your means of transport. By flying over certain areas or cycling on a popular walking track, you may be destroying other people's wilderness experiences.

If during your travels you discover a wilderness area under threat from development, then make yourself heard. Write a letter to the developer, the local newspaper, council or member of parliament. It does have an effect, especially in a small country like New Zealand.

Environmental Care Code

- **Protect plants and animals.** Treat New Zealand's forests and birds with care and respect. They are unique and often rare.

- **Remove rubbish.** Litter is unattractive, harmful to wildlife and can increase vermin and disease. Plan your trips to reduce rubbish and carry out what you carry in.

- **Bury toilet waste.** In areas without toilet facilities, bury your toilet waste in a shallow hole well away from waterways, tracks, campsites and huts. This helps to stop the spread of Giardia.

- **Keep streams and lakes clean**. When cleaning and washing, take the water and wash well away from the water source. Because soaps and detergents are harmful to water-life, drain used water into the soil to allow it to be filtered. If you suspect the water may be contaminated, either boil it for at least three minutes, filter it, or chemically treat it.

- **Take care with fires.** Portable fuel stoves are less harmful to the environment and are more efficient than fires. If you do use a fire, keep it small, use only dead wood, and make sure it is out by dousing it with water and checking the ashes before leaving.

- **Camp carefully.** When camping, leave no trace of your visit.

- **Keep to the track.** By keeping to the track, where one exists, you lessen the chance of damaging fragile plants.

- **Consider others.** People enjoy the back country and rural areas for many reasons. Be considerate of other visitors who also have a right to enjoy the natural environment.

- **Respect our cultural heritage.** Many places in New Zealand have a spiritual and historical significance. Treat these places with consideration and respect.

- **Enjoy your visit.** Enjoy your outdoors experience. Take a last look before leaving an area; will the next visitor know that you have been there?

- *Toitu te whenua. Leave the land undisturbed.*

Need to Know More?

For a wealth of well-written travel information we recommend the *New Zealand Travel Survival Kit* (Lonely Planet Publications), or for a very comprehensive encyclopedia-type book the *Mobil New Zealand Travel Guides* (Reed Methuen), North Island and South Island volumes (see the Further Reading section at the end of the book).

Foreign visitors can contact their closest New Zealand Tourism Board office—listings are given at the end of the book in the 'Overseas Information Sources' section.

For more specific adventure information ask at DOC or local council information centres. Outdoor clubs and specialist outdoor shops are good sources of information and advice. Local listings are given at the end of the book in the 'New Zealand Clubs & Contacts' and 'Local Information Centres' sections.

3. Equipment & Skills

The following information is relevant to all outdoor adventures in
New Zealand. Information about specific adventure sports is given in
Chapters 4 & 5.

Before You Go...

Before your trip get as much information as possible by reading guide
books and talking to the staff at the local DOC office or other people
who have done the trip.

Always take a good map—we have listed maps at the end of each
write-up. A compass and the ability to use it is essential for some of
the adventures in this book.

Leave your trip intentions, including where you are going, the
number of people in your party and when you are expected back, with
a DOC visitors centre or someone responsible at home. If you are
overdue then they can contact Search and Rescue through the police.
Always remember to let these people know you have made it back
from your trip, otherwise they will presume you are still in the hills
and contact the police. An unnecessary Search and Rescue operation
would then be started.

Mountain Radio or Cell Phone?

Many people are taking mountain radios or cell phones into the hills
these days as an emergency link with the outside world. Cell phones
are light and obviously easy to use, but they do not work in a lot of
New Zealand's back country, especially in valleys. Also, if people
know your number then you'll just be taking a big chunk of the city
into the hills with you.

Mountain radios are a bit heavier and only work once the 30 metre
long aerial has been strung out, but they will work anywhere in the
country. For more information see the Clubs & Contacts section,
Mountain Radio Services, at the end of the book.

First Aid

For every adventure take a good first aid kit. At the very minimum take a bandage, sterile gauze pads, adhesive tape, a needle, painkillers, sunblock cream, waterproof paper and pencil, and any special medication as necessary.

However, the most important thing of all to take is a good knowledge of First Aid. Go on an instruction course and buy a manual, such as the *Outdoor First Aid* manual (see Further Reading).

Exposure (Hypothermia)

New Zealand's weather is very changeable and difficult to predict compared with continental climates. Be prepared for extremes at any time of year, especially if heading above the bushline.

Hypothermia is caused by exposure to cold, wet or windy weather conditions. If a person in your party appears exhausted, uncoordinated or claims not to be cold when everyone else is freezing, they probably have hypothermia. You must act quickly to save his or her life.

Set up an emergency camp immediately. Get the person out of the wind and rain, dressed in dry clothes and placed inside a sleeping bag with someone else (not someone who is also developing the symptoms).

Do not massage, *do not* give alcohol, *do not* apply heat quickly, and, most important, *do not* push on to make it to a hut. The little heat the person has left must not be drawn away from the internal organs. If he or she is conscious, give warm sweet drinks. If there is no sign of improvement, go for help.

For more information read the *Bushcraft* manual (see Further Reading).

Rivers

Most New Zealand rivers rise and fall within a matter of hours during heavy rain.

Never attempt to cross, float or paddle down, a flooded river. Apart from their obvious swollen nature, flooded rivers can be recognised by their murky-brown colour and the faint rumbling sound of boulders being swept downstream. Crossing rivers even in normal flows can be a major danger in the back country. Rivers often require experience to cross safely and/or patience to wait until their level drops.

Camping

Choose a well drained camp site that isn't likely to become an island or a lake if it rains. Only light a fire in pre-established fire places or on river bed rocks, and make sure it's down wind of your tent because sparks easily melt nylon. In really wet conditions it may not be possible to light a fire so it is always advisable to take a portable stove.

Tents

Most tents for sale in New Zealand fall into two categories. Expensive but very high quality New Zealand-made and some foreign-made tents will last you through thick and thin for the rest of your travels. Cheap, Asian-made tents may not be insect proof (the insect mesh used is often too large to stop sandflies) and generally don't stand up to strong winds very well. The best NZ-made ones are of a dome or tunnel shape, made by companies such as Fairydown and Macpac, and cost $400-$800. The common Asian tent is a dome shape and costs $150-$300. All of the New Zealand tents are insect-proof, which makes life a lot more enjoyable in the sandfly and mosquito infested South Island forests.

The old A-frame type tents can still be found and are often quite cheap. They don't stand up so well in strong winds, are usually quite heavy and some are not insect-proof but otherwise they do the job.

A tent fly (large square of nylon with guy ropes attached) is perfectly adequate for camping below the bushline and costs around $100.

Sleeping Bags

Basically there are two types of sleeping bag: synthetic or down. Synthetic bags are cheap but bulky and heavy. Down bags (filled with fine duck or goose feathers) are very warm for their weight and compact well, but cost an arm and a leg (and a few ducks). Down bags are next to useless when wet; synthetic ones are better. To keep sleeping bags dry, always pack them in a plastic bag inside the stuff sac.

Sleeping Mats

A closed cell foam mat (snowfoam) is the most commonly used insulation between yourself and the cold ground. This costs about $15 and is light, waterproof and warm. A Therm-a-Rest, or similar self-inflating mattress is waterproof, warm, comfortable, and expensive (unless it gets punctured, in which case it's only expensive).

Clothes

For any trip into an isolated area you'll need a rainproof parka/jacket and warm clothes. Waterproof-breathable materials are comfortable but expensive. Japara (oilcloth) or PVC raincoats do the job almost as well, for a fraction of the cost.

Depending on the season and where you're going you'll need two to three warm tops and one or two warm bottoms, made out of materials such as wool, polypropylene, or polarfleece. There's not much difference in the performance of wool compared to synthetics. Wool is warmer in extremely wet conditions. Synthetics are light and fast drying (they also burn easily—be careful around camp fires). Most of the wool clothes you need can be bought for a few dollars at the local secondhand clothing shop. Cotton is next to useless when it's wet. Also take warm socks and a hat or balaclava. On trips above the tree-line or during winter add windproof over trousers, and gloves or mittens. Pack everything inside a plastic rubbish bag or pack liner to keep it dry.

Water Treatment

Although Giardia (a nasty parasite that causes giardiasis) is present in some New Zealand rivers, it is reasonably uncommon and most trampers drink the water untreated. To be on the safe side you should boil, filter or chemically treat water collected from popular tramping areas or when near farmland. Tap water is safe to drink.

Obviously people who have travelled through Giardia infested countries should be very careful not to spread the Giardia cysts here. See the Environmental Care Code in the previous chapter.

Food

Take whatever you want and eat as much as you can as long as you can carry it. Remember though that food is your fuel and it must have a high energy content. The following are some ideas for recommended meals.

—**Breakfast:** Muesli (soaked overnight), sandwiches or fruit bread, porridge with dried fruit, rice (or semolina) with milk and fruit, and if you can be bothered, bacon and eggs on toast. Low energy cereals such as cornflakes or weetbix are a waste of pack space.
—**Lunch:** your favourite types of bread, spreads, cheese, crackers, butter, fruit and any of the snacks listed below.
—**Dinner:** This is a basic lightweight formula; cook 100 grams per person of any carbohydrate base (includes rice, pasta, and potatoes) with vegetables of your choice (fresh or dehydrated). Add meat such as salami, bacon or TVP (textured vegetable protein) if you wish. Make it more edible by adding salt, pepper, herbs, spices and soup sachets.
—**Snacks:** for eating on the move take lots of food that doesn't require any preparation, for example, biscuits, energy bars, chocolate, your favourite sweets, fruit, and scroggin (trail mix of nuts, dried fruit, chocolate and seeds).
—**Drinks:** tea, coffee, drinking chocolate (with sugar and milk powder), cordial sachets, jellies, and soup sachets.

For short trips, when weight isn't such an issue, you can easily carry fresh fruit and vegetables and canned food. To lighten the load, however, pack things into lightweight containers and take dried or dehydrated fruits and vegetables. Complete freeze-dried meals can be bought from outdoor shops. The servings arc small though, so add rice or pasta to make a decent meal out of them. These, and dehydrated vegetables, need to be cooked or soaked for twice as long as the instructions on the packets say, and even then they are far from gourmet cuisine.

Cooking Equipment

Per group take: one or two billy cans or 'billies' (1.5 litres per person), a frying pan, cutlery, a sharp pocket knife, and either a plate and mug per person or a bowl which can double as both. Billy tongs, a big wooden spoon, and a pot scrubber help make camping life less of a chore.

Stoves

It is easier and more environmentally sound to cook on a camp stove than over a fire. There are several types of stoves on the market, including the three more common types mentioned here.
(i) Petroleum stoves give a high heat output, are lightweight, easily maintained, and operate at high altitude—some versions also offer multi-fuel options.
(ii) Methylated-spirits fuelled stoves are lightweight, low cost, and require low maintenance.
(iii) Propane/butane gas canister stoves are inexpensive and easy to use, but they don't work so well at high altitude and the canisters have to be thrown out after use.
Note: most of the huts on the 'Great Walks' have gas stoves available in the summer season .

Fuel

White spirit for camping stoves is sold at most petrol stations and comes under four different brand names: Shellite or Shell X55 (Shell), Calite (Caltex), Britolite (BP), and Pegasol AA (Mobil). Methylated spirits and kerosene are widely available. Gas canisters can be bought from most outdoor stores: the brands currently available in New Zealand are Primus, Gaz, Epi Gas and Kovea.

Other Essential Items

Always take a torch (with spare bulb and batteries), candle and matches, water bottle, pocket knife, toilet paper, map and compass.

For all outdoor activities, except caving, you should take good sunglasses and sunscreen (protection factor 15+). These are absolutely essential for sea kayaking and snow travel.

Survival Kit

In the event of being lost or trapped in the bush, this tiny little kit will become invaluable for your survival. Pack it into a plastic bag inside a waterproof container, and carry it in your bumbag or pack:

- Waterproof matches (packed inside a film canister)
- Waterproof paper and a small pencil
- Half a candle
- Pocket knife or razor blade
- Small roll of Leucoplast tape
- Fish hooks and a few metres of line
- Length of cord
- Survival bag or blanket
- Whistle

4. Land Adventures

 ## Tramping

Known outside New Zealand as trekking, hiking or backpacking, tramping is New Zealand's most popular adventurous activity. Tourist tracks, such as the Milford or Abel Tasman, are well known. However, there are hundreds of other, less developed tracks that also provide an escape from the city. Rather than being well maintained corridors through the bush, they are often little more than trampled paths, following small markers to fairly basic huts. The Department of Conservation (DOC) produce excellent pamphlets on the popular tramps. These provide all the information you need for any given tramp and are well worth the minimal charge of $1.

Skills

Most tramping skills are based on common sense. With a little effort even those with basic map reading skills should be able to follow the popular tramping tracks. Hypothermia and crossing rivers pose the two biggest dangers in New Zealand's back country. Always tramp with others: it's safer and a lot more fun. In summer it is easy to team up with other people on the 'Great Walks'. The definitive source of tramping information is the *Bushcraft* manual (see Further Reading).

Equipment

Apart from the equipment listed in the previous chapter, all you need is a pack and boots. Any pack that holds all your gear and is comfortable will be adequate. For serious trampers a large single-compartment internal-framed canvas pack is the ultimate. Packs can be hired from most large outdoor shops and many tramping clubs. To make it easier to carry, position the heavy stuff closer to your back.

Running shoes may suffice on the 'Great Walk' tracks in summer, but for anywhere else wear comfortable tramping boots. Also, take a roll of surgical tape—local brands include Sleek—and apply it to areas where your boots rub, well before blisters develop. For the

'Great Walks' take either a 'Trackmap' or a 'Parkmap', both published by DOSLI. In addition to being normal maps they provide a lot of useful information about the track and surrounding area.

The Learning Process   (Waiorau Nordic Ski Area)

 # Mountain Biking

From its fringe beginnings in California in the 1970s, mountain biking has boomed to become the No.1 recreational cycling activity throughout the world. With thousands of kilometres of gravel roads and 4WD tracks strewn throughout the country, New Zealand is a mountain biker's Mecca. All of the best rides which aren't covered in this book are described in *Classic New Zealand Mountain Bike Rides* (see Further Reading).

Skills

The best way to pick up skills and fitness is to ride. Watching other people crash helps a lot too. For downhill, shift your weight back as far as possible; for uphill, shift forward but don't get off the seat if your back wheel is likely to lose traction. Try and 'ride softly' (avoid skidding and sliding) especially on walking tracks which were not built with cycling in mind. It's safer and more fun to ride with a group.

Equipment

Buy or borrow a bike that can handle some punishment. The three main things to look for are cantilever brakes, a chromoly steel frame and fat knobbly tyres. Bikes with these features are usually $700 or more. Always ride with a helmet on, unless there's nothing up top worth protecting. Since 1994 cyclists have been legally required to wear helmets. Cycle shorts are in, mudguards are out. Take a tool kit and pump on all rides. Good quality mountain bikes can be hired in most cities and many towns for around $25 per day.

 # Back-Country Skiing

Skiing was developed in Scandinavia hundreds of years ago, as a practical and efficient way to travel on snow-covered terrain. In recent years many downhill skiers, in search of adventure, have turned away from the crowded skifields and headed into the back country. Mountaineers have also realised the advantages of skis for traversing large snowfields and glaciers.

Skills

For the absolute beginner, several weekends on a commercial ski field should give you the skills needed to traverse easy terrain on cross-country skis. A higher level of skill is required if you ski with a pack on your back or tackle steeper slopes. Mountaineering skills and an awareness of avalanche hazards and alpine weather are essential for safe travel in the New Zealand back country.

Equipment

All the normal skiing and mountaineering gear is needed, as well as special ski-mountaineering bindings. Skins, which enable you to travel uphill on skis, are also necessary. Long and skinny nordic or telemark type skis are gaining popularity in New Zealand. Avalanche transceivers may also be needed. For more information about skins see chapter 13, section 13.5 Ski-touring on the Two Thumb Range.

Mountaineering

Mountain climbing is a highly physical and mentally challenging activity. In New Zealand, unpredictable weather, loose rock, and frequent high avalanche danger make climbing as dangerous as anywhere in the world. New Zealand mountains are also amongst the most beautiful in the world; often lush forest reaches right up to the snowy slopes and the peaks are surrounded by stupendous scenery in all directions. In Mt Cook and Westland national parks, where most climbing activity occurs, DOC have a daily 'log-in' system for safety. All climbers notify the DOC park headquarters of their intentions and call in on the hut radios at a set time every night to update their plans.

Skills

Mountaineers usually build on a solid base of tramping skills. More recently, however, some have taken up mountaineering as their first outdoor activity—they often survive to become excellent climbers! Learning the skills to climb safely takes time and experience. Start by doing an alpine instruction course (AIC) with an alpine club or a professional alpine guide.

Equipment

There's lots of it, ranging from basic ice axe and crampons to more technical equipment, including ropes, harnesses, and karabiners. It's all listed in an excellent book called *Mountaincraft* (see Further Reading), which should be the first thing you buy. The basic equipment can usually be hired from major outdoor shops. Avalanche transceivers are becoming standard equipment for mountaineers and can be hired from several specialist climbing shops.

Rock Climbing

Originally developed because it was good training for mountaineering, rock climbing is now a sport in its own right. Essentially it involves the same mental and physical demands as mountaineering but there is less objective danger, much better weather and considerably easier access to the actual climbs. As a result its popularity has boomed in the past 10 years and indoor climbing walls have become commonplace.

Skills

Unless you know someone who is willing to teach you the ropes, as it were, the best way to learn is to do a course.

Climbing clubs and several adventure companies hold regular instruction courses and can give directions to the local crags (climbing areas).

Equipment

Much of the technical equipment used for mountaineering is also used for rock climbing. To get started with the minimum of expense, go bouldering or top-roping.

These terms and all the equipment are explained in the *Mountaincraft* manual (see Further Reading). The first things to buy are rock climbing boots, a chalk bag and a harness. Running shoes will suffice for beginners.

 # Caving

Caving and cavers have come a long way from their Neanderthal beginnings, a few thousand years ago. Nowadays it's called speleology and is one of the most varied adventure activities there is. A caving trip may involve climbing, crawling, squeezing, diving, abseiling, swimming, tramping, jumaring (using jumars or metal spring-loaded devices to ascend a rope) or tubing.

Skills

The only way to do more caving than the commercial circuit offers is to join a club, as it's almost impossible to find the caves by yourself, let alone know what experience and equipment is needed. They'll ask you if you'd like to do a 'sporty' cave, which involves squeezes, twists, drops and climbs; or a 'pretties' cave, which should be far less strenuous and offer a visual symphony of cave formations such as stalagmites, stalactites and organ pipes.

Equipment

A whole range of specialist caving equipment is usually needed, which is another good reason to join a club (see Clubs & Contacts). The basics include overalls, headlamps, SRT (single rope technique) gear, non-stretch ropes, and rigging gear similar to that used by climbers

 # Paragliding

Paragliding (or parapenting) is the cheapest and easiest way to learn how to fly. Within a few hours a qualified instructor can safely send you on a solo flight and after the initial fear of falling, an exhilarating sense of freedom takes over. Experienced fliers fly off mountains, soar for hours, and cover distances of more than 60 km.

Skills

Start with a one or two day course. It's very rewarding and teaches you how to take off and land, before completing up to half a dozen flights. After 40 flights you can sit a PG2 Pilots Rating exam which enables you to fly without an instructor's supervision.

Equipment

Paragliders are highly evolved parachutes designed to steer easily and glide efficiently. They weigh around 5 kg and fold away into a convenient backpack. The cost starts at $1000 for secondhand gliders and works way up to $5000 or more for the latest competition models, with glide ratios of 1:9 (1 metre fall for every 9 metres of travel).

5. Water Adventures

General River Safety

The following hazards apply to all river sports and can ultimately lead to death from exposure (hypothermia) or drowning. Reading about these hazards is easy. Recognising and dealing with them safely requires skills that take time and experience to develop. Beginners should do a commercial instruction course or join a club and go paddling with experienced people.

Whirlpools

A whirlpool has a downwards-moving vortex (spiral) of water in its centre. If you can't swim out of it then the theory is to follow the water down into the vortex, possibly by diving, to be spat out downstream a few seconds later.

Rocks

If you capsize in a rapid there is a good chance that you'll hit rocks while speeding along underwater. To avoid serious head injury, a helmet should always be worn. Being pinned against or wrapped around a rock (or log) by the current is a paddler's worst nightmare. Lean downstream, grabbing the rock, and allow the current to go under your boat. Try to work your way forwards or backwards off the rock always leaning downstream. This is a very serious situation— yell out to the others in your group straight away.

Trees & Log Jams

Trees and log jams are an insidious danger because they frequently change position in the river and can easily trap you. Trees that drag their branches in the river can easily be spotted, and should be avoided like the plague (never try to hold them). Logs carried down and jammed across the river by floods are often less obvious and therefore more dangerous hazards. At worst they form a submerged mesh that lets water pass through but sieves out paddlers.

Stoppers

Stoppers are large waves, formed at the bottom of a drop, that break back on themselves. As the name suggests they can stop you from moving down river. Approach them at full speed and you should break through. If not, then paddle sideways to the edge of the stopper or, as a last resort, dive deep. The water under a stopper will carry you downstream.

Approaching Rapids

Never paddle down a rapid 'blind'. If you can't see all of a rapid before entering it, then get out of the river and scout it out thoroughly. This will give you the best chance of avoiding the hazards mentioned above. If you have any doubts about the safety of the rapid you should portage it.

General Safety Equipment

Helmet

A helmet should always be worn in case you hit your head on an obstacle after capsizing or falling out. Bicycle helmets will do the job if you haven't got a proper one.

Life Jackets & Buoyancy Vests

Apart from keeping you floating the right way up, a well fitting life jacket is comfortable and provides some protection against rocks if you are swept down a rapid. You should attach a whistle to your life jacket.

Wetsuit

We recommend wearing wetsuits for all river sports: they keep you warm, buoyant and provide cushioning when bumping into rocks. Cheap ones can be bought secondhand. The armless and hoodless variety provide more flexibility for kayaking.

Throwline

A 20 metre length of rope is often essential for hauling people out of eddies, stoppers and whirlpools. Polypropylene rope is best because it floats. Ready made throwlines can be bought from specialist outdoor shops.

White Water Kayaking

Kayaking is New Zealand's most popular river sport. It's an individual's sport, involving a lot of fun challenges. Staying upright while trying to avoid boulders and punch through waves is enough to double anyone's heart rate. The more peaceful side of the sport involves gently gliding down beautiful rivers and through remote wilderness areas.

Skills

Kayaks have more speed and manoeuvrability than rafts. However, these are not positive attributes until you have the skill and judgement to be able to use them to your advantage.

Until the eskimo roll is mastered, any mistakes usually result in a 'swim' (being swept down a rapid while desperately clutching your canoe and paddle). New Zealand has an extensive network of canoeing clubs, many of which provide excellent instruction courses. As kayaking is potentially very dangerous, it is best to learn with a club or commercial canoe school.

Equipment

Currently one of the most highly rated all-purpose white water kayaks for those new to the sport is the Dancer. You'll also need a paddle, spray skirt and spray jacket (or nylon wind breaker), as well as the general safety equipment previously mentioned. Some outdoor stores and canoe clubs hire out equipment at very reasonable rates.

 # Tubing

Tubing is a lot of fun and has a strong appeal because it costs very little and requires few technical skills compared to kayaking. Also, a tube raft can easily be carried into remote rivers and constructed on site. After lashing a couple of over-inflated truck tyre inner-tubes together and making an improvised paddle, you're away. It's a hard-case sport that will probably never make it to the Olympics.

Skills

The main skill required is knowing how to read the river. Tubing itself is a piece of cake. A tube raft is stable (or at least it should be) and easy to climb back onto if you capsize. You also don't need to right it as it has no top or bottom. Picking the right line down the river and avoiding the obstacles mentioned above is not so easy. Tube rafts are difficult to steer and spin around quickly after bumping into rocks. They are very slow on long flat sections.

Equipment

For each rafter, beg, borrow, or steal two large truck tubes and 5 metres of rope, and the safety equipment previously mentioned. Each party needs at least one foot pump, a puncture repair kit, a valve tool and plenty of spare valves. You can get most of this stuff from a local garage and paddles can be improvised out of almost anything. The perfect craft has yet to be designed, so we'll leave that up to you. But make sure it's tied together tightly and there's nothing loose that could get snagged. To inflate a tube quickly, take the valve out, blow it up by mouth, screw the valve back in, then use the foot pump to inflate it the rest of the way.

 # Sea Kayaking

The kayak was originally designed and built by Eskimos to be used in the sea, and in recent years there has been a revival in its use for this purpose. Nowadays, well designed fibreglass and plastic, single or double kayaks can be hired at most of the best paddling spots. Both stable and fast, these kayaks can easily glide along at the same speed as a walker and carry twice as much gear.

Skills

Only basic kayaking skills and a moderate level of fitness are required. With a little common sense it's a very safe activity. A full briefing on kayaking techniques, safety procedures and the area you're paddling in should be given by the company you hire the kayaks from. If you're still hesitant, go on a guided trip. Companies do not rent kayaks to solo paddlers.

Equipment

Along with the kayak, a life jacket, spray skirt, paddle, and safety flares are provided. Often, camping equipment and snorkelling gear are also available. Take all the standard outdoor stuff (see Equipment & Skills), and an extra large sunhat and sunglasses. If you have soft hands then take a roll of surgical tape to avoid getting blisters.

 # Rafting

To raft down really rough rivers (grade IV and V) head for the nearest professional rafting company. Most guided trips are safe and well organised, and even for really big water no previous experience is required.

 # River Sledging

This exciting new sport involves swimming, with the aid of a glorified boogie board and flippers, down rivers and through rapids that would take years to master in a canoe. As yet the sledges cannot be bought in New Zealand, but a few adventure companies offer excellent trips on some of our most popular rivers.

 # Diving

Diving reveals an unimaginable world of strange creatures and bizarre plants—it's often difficult to tell which is which.

To skin dive you need three basic things: a mask to see, a snorkel to breathe and flippers to move. A wetsuit in cold waters enables you to dive without freezing to death. To go scuba diving you have to sit a course to obtain a scuba certificate. Shops will not fill your tanks unless you have one.

6. The Far North

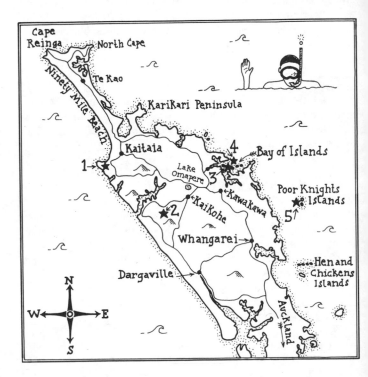

32

6.1 Erehwon Trail

Southern end of Ninety Mile Beach

For intermediate riders, 4-6 hours return; 27 km.

—Summary— Mountainous sand dunes fall steeply to the coast from a plateau of old kauri (a type of conifer) gum-fields behind Ahipara. There is excellent mountain biking around the rugged coast and throughout the area. Ahipara is reputed to be one of the best body surfing beaches in the Far North.

—How to Get There— Head 15 km southwest of Kaitaia to the small town of Ahipara.

—Description— You must return along the coast during low tide— ring Information Far North, ☎ (09) 408 0879, for tide times before departing.

From Ahipara Beach, ride southwest past the changing sheds and up the hill. Veer up to the left at the first Y-intersection and right at the second Y-intersection. After about 30 minutes you'll reach a plateau. Follow the metal Gumfields Road for another 30 minutes until you come to the first building (shack) on the left side of the road—it's a museum featuring relics from the gumfield days. Turn hard right onto a sandy clay track. After 2 km you'll reach a fork—go straight ahead (don't turn right).

This is the Erehwon Trail, cut by the owners of the yacht 'Erehwon' which stranded nearby in the late 1970s. They eventually hauled the boat up the track and over to Ahipara for repairs.

Follow the trail down through manuka scrub and out onto a farmland track. Cross the creek then ride on hard sand all the way to the beach. There's good camping around here.

At the coast turn right and ride firm sand, where you can find it, back towards Ahipara. Around Tauroa Point you'll pass some rough looking houses. The people living there gather seaweed to make agar and collect mussels to sell. As you get close to Ahipara you'll encounter flat patches of rock and the sea will force you to ride close to the cliffs. This section is only passable during low tide.

Weird Rock Patterns in the Ahipara Hills   (Jonathan Kennett)

—Track Conditions— 5% seal, 25% gravel, 25% 4WD and single track, 40% coastal rocks and hard sand, 5% unrideable sand.

—Notes— Water is scarce: take an extra bottle. If conditions are not right for this ride then check out the gum-fields; they're riddled with tracks. If you get lost, follow a stream west out to the coast. Clean your bike thoroughly after the ride—salt and sand are murder on metal components. Topomap N05 Herekino is useful for riding in the gum-fields.

6.2   Waoku Coach Road

40 km northwest of Dargaville

For intermediate/experienced riders, 4-7 hours; 30 km.

—Summary— This historical ride crosses the Mataraua State Forest on a 100-year-old stagecoach road. Most of the old road is now a rideable 4WD track, much of it through native forest, but there is a swampy section in the middle that demands considerable bike carrying.

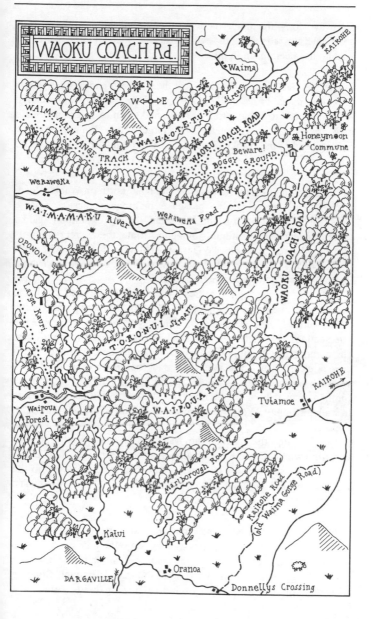

Halfway along the track there is a group of hippies living in a commune. Bird life abounds; even an unconfirmed sighting of the rare kokako has been made in this area.

—How to Get There— Tutamoe, at the southern end of the track, is 12 km northeast of Donnellys Crossing. Note that the Waima Gorge Road is closed to vehicle traffic, but it makes an excellent mountain bike ride (see 6.6 Cycling the Old Gorge Road). Waima, near the northern end of the Waoku Coach Road, is 25 km west of Kaikohe on Highway 12.

—Description— From Tutamoe School head north on Waoku Road. After 4 km, once   you've passed a picnic area beside a large 'Walkways' sign, the road becomes the seldom explored   Waoku Coach Road Track. Continuing along this route, the gravel road turns into a muddy, but rideable, 4WD track. Within an hour you will reach a gate bearing a 'Private Road...walking only' sign which you should ignore—this is definitely a public road!

Ride on up through the beautiful native bush and over the occasional stone culvert (built in the 1890s to carry away some of the 2500 mm of annual rainfall). When you reach a signposted intersection, turn left off the main track and skirt round past Honeymoon Hut (a public shelter) and Honeymoon Commune. You'll cross a clearing on a rideable 4WD track before entering the forest, where the walking begins. Those who don't fancy carrying their bikes for more than an hour should turn back at this point. It takes 1-2 hours to walk the boggy 2 km to the signposted Wekaweka Road turn-off on your left.

Continue past the Waima Main Range Track turn-off, also on your left, from where the riding gradually improves. Once you break out of the bush the single track becomes a rideable 4WD track. From the farmhouses, not far away, coast 3 km down to Highway 12. The 'Kruise in Cafe' is 1 km to your left.

—Notes— This ride is not recommended in wet conditions because of the boggy sections. Those not wanting to do the bike-carry section could ride back from the commune, and drive around to pick up the rest of the group at the northern end of the track. Although climbing to a height of 700 metres, the Coach Road never exceeds a grade of 1 in 12. This road has only been driven across once, in 1912, by the then Prime Minister, Sir Joseph Ward. There is a DOC camping ground and information centre at Waipoua Forest, ☎ (09) 439 0605. Topomap O06 Waipoua is essential.

6.3 Learning to Dive

 Paihia, Bay of Islands

For beginner adventurers (guided), 1 or 5 days.

—Summary— Only a privileged minority has explored the vast ocean world by scuba diving. In this world that can barely be imagined from the surface, adventurers can experience true weightlessness. An internationally recognised scuba diving certificate can be obtained in 5 days; there is also a 1 day option for non-certified divers who want to experience the underwater world for the first time.

—How to Get There— Contact Paihia Guide Shop ☎ (09) 402 7551, Pahia.

—Description— Learning to scuba dive is a challenge with many exciting rewards. When you first put on all the scuba gear, you'll probably think you've made a big mistake. The tank alone weighs 20 kg. Then there's the weight belt, a further 10 kg, and, to top it off, a 5 kg wetsuit. Who in their right mind would willingly jump into the ocean laden down with 35 kg of diving paraphernalia and a large 'dummy' stuffed in their mouth, that causes them to hyperventilate?

Once in the water you'll discover that the weight of the equipment perfectly counteracts your buoyancy, enabling you to easily dive up and down. Your thoughts are amplified by the surrounding silence and the slow motion movement of your companions seems cumbersome compared to the fish that effortlessly dart and glide past.

The Bay of Islands is a brilliant place to learn scuba diving. There are numerous sheltered dive sites from which to view the underwater volcanic landscape that is home to an unbelievable array of marine life. The introductory one day aquatic experience includes two

Scuba Diving in the Bay of Islands   (Bay Guides)

hand-held dives. The five day, island based scuba certification course involves several open water dives and a full grounding in theory and safety procedures. Divers who successfully complete this course receive an internationally recognised certificate.

—**Notes**— The 5-day Professional Association of Diving Instructors (PADI) course, is $325 plus the cost of hiring your equipment. The 1-day introductory course costs $185 all inclusive. Dive shops will not fill tanks or hire equipment to people who are not certified.

6.4 Bay of Islands Sea Kayaking

Paihia

For beginner kayakers (guided), 1 day tours. For the experienced, multi-day trips.

Manoeuvering through the Mangroves, Waitangi Estuary. (Coastal Kayakers)

—**Summary**— The best way to discover the calm waters and intricate coastline of the Bay of Islands is by sea kayak. There are numerous islands to explore, including strange volcanic formations that have created a series of intricate passageways, archways and caves. Dolphins are often seen in the area and can be playful companions.

—**How to Get There**— Contact Coastal Kayakers in Paihia, ☎ (09) 402 8105.

—**Description**— Trips leave from Coastal Kayakers' seafront shed in central Paihia. After some comprehensive instruction, you'll paddle across Waitangi Estuary and into the mangroves. This is a mysterious and peaceful place where you manoeuvre between twisted trunks and low hanging branches; a real contrast to the Haruru Falls, which is your next destination. Rather than just viewing the falls from the outside, you'll paddle through the crashing water until you're on the inside peering out. Then it's an effortless drift out of the estuary with the outgoing tide, towards Motumaire Island. After exploring the island there's time for a swim, before paddling back across the bay to the boatshed.

It is possible for competent paddlers to hire kayaks without a guide. A classic 3-day trip begins by paddling around Tapeka Point to Motuarohia (Roberton) Island. There is great snorkelling in a crystal clear lagoon, and a lookout that gives spectacular views of the Bay of Islands. Paddle past the white sandy beaches of Moturua Island to a camp site on Urupukapuka Island. There is good fishing in the nearby Albert Channel. When the sea is calm it's possible to explore the ocean side of the island, where there are a number of sea caves. One of these is 100 metres long and open at both ends. It requires good timing and steady nerves to paddle through, especially if a swell is running.

On the way back to Paihia, visit the dramatic Black Rocks on the northern side of Moturoa Island. It's definitely worth exploring these hollow volcanic spires.

—Notes— Guided trips are suitable for absolute beginners and cost $60 for 1 day and $40 for half a day. Coastal Kayakers hires out single kayaks and all equipment, including maps, to competent paddlers for $40 per day.

There are several other good sea kayaking companies and sites in Northland. Just pop into a nearby visitors centre to get an up-to-date idea of the range available.

6.5   Poor Knights Islands Diving

50 km northeast of Whangarei

For all certified scuba divers (guide optional), 1 day.

—Summary— The world-renowned Poor Knights Islands Marine Reserve is New Zealand's premier diving location. The Poor Knights rise abruptly from crystal clear waters off the Northland coast. These ancient volcanic remnants are a maze of underwater caves, tunnels and archways, through which countless fish glide and bask in the warm waters.

—How to Get There— Most charter dive boats leave from Tutukaka, a small settlement about 30 km northeast of Whangarei. The islands are 25 km from here.

—Description— During the hour or so it takes to reach the 'Knights', you won't really have any idea where you'll be diving. It's not until the last minute that the dive site is selected. Everything depends on prevailing conditions, and the divemaster's local knowledge is invaluable.

There are over 50 sites to choose from, offering the widest range of diving opportunities within any one area of New Zealand. These surreal islands are very different from the mainland. The sea has pounded huge caverns and archways out of the soft rock, some of them large enough for boats to pass through.

As everyone gears up, the dive master gives a short briefing on things you need to know: What's the depth? Does that cavern lead into a never-ending cave? What's for lunch? Only the essentials are covered—the rest is left for you to discover.

Underwater, the cliffs plunge down to the sea floor, sometimes 100 metres below. Shafts of sunlight filter through large schools of fish, including pink and blue mao mao, who seem oblivious to the presence of divers.

Colourful marine life blankets the island walls and it is sometimes difficult to distinguish between animal and vegetable. The water is warm, often 20°C or more, and visibility is seldom less than 30 metres.

Back on the boat between dives, you fill in logbooks, refill tanks, and talk about your discoveries. The next dive location will offer something completely different, which is one of the reasons why divers keep coming back to the Knights.

—Notes— The Sub Aqua Dive Centre in Whangarei, ☎ (09) 438 1075, hires out all scuba equipment and organises trips to the Knights using its own dive masters.

The Centre charters the 'Pacific Hideaway', skippered by divers Bryan and Eve Bell, ☎ (09) 434 3675. Cost for a full day's diving, including gear, is $130, or only $70 if you have your own gear: and for those who sightsee or snorkel the cost is $55 per day.

6.6 Other Adventures

Three Kings Islands

Situated 53 km northwest of Cape Reinga are the remote and rugged Three Kings Islands. The clear surrounding waters are home to huge schools of fish that glide effortlessly through numerous caves lined with prolific marine growth. There is a nearby shipwreck to explore and some excellent areas to experience the thrill of drift diving. The best visibility and most settled conditions are during March, April and May. A 6-day dive costs $900/$990 per person for group charter/individual booking and is suitable for intermediate to experienced certified scuba divers. For more information contact Far North Sports in Kaitaia, ☎/fax (09) 408 0622.

Kerikeri Kayaking

For a laid back sea kayaking trip, go to the sleepy hollow of Kerikeri (classic small town New Zealand). Northland Sea Kayaking, ☎ (09) 405 0381, run trips along the outer coast just south of Whangaroa Harbour. They also have backpackers accommodation; and a night's stay plus a day's paddling only costs around $60.

Dolphin Swimming in the Bay of Islands

For centuries dolphins have, with their intelligent curiosity and playful acrobatics, fascinated those who come into contact with them. Interacting with such powerful and graceful creatures in their own environment is an exhilarating experience.

Dolphin Discoveries, ☎ (09) 402 8234, run trips twice daily from both Paihia and Russell wharves to the Bay of Islands Maritime Park to view dolphins and whales with an option of swimming with the dolphins.

They use two boats, one with a glass bottom which holds up to 13 passengers. Wetsuits are provided year-round, even though the water is warm in summer. The 4-hour maximum trip costs $75/$45 for adults/children.

Far North Sea Kayaking Expeditions

Over the summer New Zealand Adventures run 6 and 10 day expeditions from the Bay of Islands north to the Cavalli Islands then finish in Whangaroa Harbour. They all have an emphasis on sea kayaking instruction, and all trips involve snorkelling, beachcombing, short hikes and exploring remote Maori Pa (fortified village) sites.

Two tours which are suitable for all paddlers are an exploration of the Bay of Islands, and a paddle through the Cavalli along the Northeast Coast. The guides are able to customise trips anywhere in Northland for the aspiring explorer.

For the adventurer who really wants to learn sea kayaking properly, and at the same time enjoy an amazing adventure in the Far North, contact New Zealand Adventures, PO Box 454, Pahia, Bay of Islands, ☎/fax (09) 402 8596 from December to April, and (03) 782 6777 from May to November.

Trips are run on specific dates and have a maximum group size of 12—book well in advance. 6-day trips cost $750 per person and 10-day trips are $1200. This includes all meals, kayaking equipment and guides.

Waipoua Forest

Fifty km northwest of Dargaville stand the remnants of a once-mighty kauri forest called Waipoua. There is a DOC camping ground, cabins and an information centre 2 km west of Highway 12 at Waipoua Forest, ☎ (09) 439 0605.

From there, a short walk leads to the magnificent, 1000-year-old, 50-metre tall trees. It's about 10 km of easy cycling from Waipoua Settlement (8 km further down the road), through a maze of forestry roads to the coast at Kawarua. Unless you're feeling lucky, Topomap O06 Waipoua is handy.

Cycling the Old Gorge Road

This is an excellent 1-2 hour beginner's trip up the old Waima Gorge Road between Donnellys Crossing and Tutamoe. Part of the road was washed out by Cyclone Bola in 1988 and hasn't been repaired.

From Donnellys Crossing (40 km northwest of Dargaville) head northeast on Kaikohe Road, past the 'Road Closed' sign. After 1 km hop over a gate and continue up Waima Valley on an easy gradient. From the 'Kaikohe Road' signpost at the head of the valley either return the same way (for a fast downhill) or carry on and cycle the Waoku Coach Road (see 6.2). Take Terrainmap 2 Whangarei.

 ### Waru Limestone Bouldering

The Waru Limestone Scenic Reserve is 500 metres north of Hikurangi township (16 km north of Whangarei), beside Highway 1.

Fluted formations of weathered limestone provide good bouldering (see Glossary) for climbers of all experience levels. Chimneys, overhangs and laybacks await the explorers of these castle-like formations.

 ### Whangarei Heads

Although it's not often thought of as a sea kayaking destination, the intricate and stunning coastline east of Whangarei provides great opportunities for all levels of paddlers.

For a fantastic daytrip on a fine day, those with minimal experience can paddle around the awesome Whangarei Heads exploring the numerous bays en route.

Alternatively, experienced kayakers can launch from the small coastal town of Ngunguru (20 km from Whangarei) and paddle south, continuing round the heads and all the way up the Harbour to the centre of Whangarei.

For expert advice about sea kayaking in the area contact Canoe and Camping in Whangarei, ☎ (09) 438 1793 or 025 726 152. They hire out kayaks for $50 per day and can arrange guided trips

 ### Onerahi on Wheels

Some of the best rides in the North Island are a stone's throw from downtown Whangarei. Try exploring the Onerahi forest or choose a specific ride from *Classic NZ Mountain Bike Rides* (see Further Reading).

Here's how to reach the forest. From Whangarei cycle east towards Sherwood Rise on Riverside Drive. After about 4 km turn left onto

Montgomery Ave. At the end of the avenue turn right onto a grassy single track and ride towards the substation in the distance. Turn left when you reach the gravel road and ride past the substation and a 'Waikaraka Walk' sign. This is the start of the forest.

For great views climb to the top of this road then dive off into the centre of the forest and try to get lost.

Take it easy on the downhills—this area is used by walkers and runners as well. Topomap Q07 gives a good overview of the area.

 ### Abbey Cave

Abbey Cave near Whangarei is a good cave system for aspiring cavers. For about two hours, groups squeeze, scramble, and partially swim through various passages and caverns. Spectacular limestone formations are illuminated by numerous glow-worms.

This trip costs $10 per person and a more challenging 3-4 hour excursion costs $18 per person. Trips are run on demand year-round. Contact Bill McClaren, ☎ (09) 437 6174.

 ### Lunatic Laddering

Ladder climbing is an indispensable skill to obtain quick views of the less mountainous parts of Northland.

This technique involves leaning a rung ladder up against absolutely nothing, then climbing as high as possible before it falls over.
Coastal laddering in the surf (for whale watching, of course) is even more interesting.

Laddering   (Adrienne Syme)

7. Auckland

47

7.1   Pakiri Beach Horse Trekking

 70 km north of Auckland

For beginner adventurers (guided), 1-4 nights.

—Summary— The Haddon family run horse treks along the remote and endless east coast beaches of Northland. Trips involve riding in the surf, navigating through native bush and over farmland, and camping amongst the dunes.

—How to Get There— Turn off Highway 1 at Warkworth and head northeast to Leigh. Then drive to Pakiri 10 km away on the Wellsford Leigh Road. Drive down towards the beach until you see the Pakiri Beach Horse Riding house on the left. Book in advance with Pakiri Beach Horse Riding, ☎ (09) 422 6275.

—Description— It's important for you and your horse to get acquainted. Unlike mountain bikes, horses really do have a mind of their own and you'll quickly learn that sometimes left means right and go forward means stand still. The only other riding tip is that when the horse is trotting you need to move up and down with the horse's movements. Alternatively take a neck brace.

There seem to be a never ending supply of horse lovers who know Pakiri Beach and work for the Haddons. They'll take you into the hills behind the beach for awesome views and at a pace which allows you and your steed to become acquainted. Once back on the long open beach you'll be able to either take your horse for a swim in the surf or wander through coastal dunes and forests.

The Haddons will have all your gear at the evening camp for you and after a bar-b-que dinner under the stars and a few cool drinks the aches and pains developed over a day will have subsided.

There is a good chance you will see dolphins just off shore while trekking and very little chance you'll see other people as the beach is almost unending and public access is difficult. On your return journey you'll have a chance to race along the beach or relax and enjoy the pleasures of this semi-tropical coastline.

—Notes— A 2-day trek costs $260, including all food and accommodation. The minimum group size of four can be reduced to two persons if no overnight camping is required. The Haddons also run various other trips ($25/hour all inclusive). Numerous other horse trekking companies operate in the Far North and Auckland regions. Visit the Auckland information centre for more details.

7.2   Goat Island Snorkelling

 Cape Rodney, 70 km northeast of Auckland

For beginner adventurers (guide optional), 1 day.

—Summary— Goat Island is one of New Zealand's most spectacular and easily accessible snorkelling locations. It is only 150 metres off the mainland and the surrounding waters offer you the chance to feed fish amongst an incredible diversity of marine life.

—How to Get There— Turn off Highway 1 at Warkworth and drive northeast to Leigh, then continue north for 4 km on the signposted road to the 'Cape Rodney to Okakari Point Marine Reserve'.

—Description— Since the marine reserve was established several years ago the area has become an underwater Eden. There is good swimming between the beach and the island, and in the shallow water it is possible to hand-feed dozens of varieties of fish. Advice given by a local DOC scientist is to restrict feeding to the main beach only and to feed only fish food, meat or fish bait. Wear some light gloves to avoid becoming fish fodder yourself.

Off the coast you'll encounter large fish such as snapper, cod and mao mao. They, along with the lobsters, seem at ease with the influx of curious snorkellers. You'll often be surrounded and investigated by these normally timid fish.

Goat Island is ideal for the beginner snorkeller as well as the expert. If conditions are calm try spending the day circumnavigating the island. In summer this area may attract 500 people per day, so avoid summer weekends and public holidays if you want some peace and quiet.

—**Notes**— If you lack the experience to explore this area, contact Marco Polo Tours, ☎ (09) 426 8455. For $30 they'll pick you up from Hatfields Beach, and provide all equipment and instruction necessary for two hours' snorkelling. All marine life in this area is protected and rangers are on site to ensure this. Overlooking Goat Island there is a resort-like research complex full of scientists. If you want to know more about the underwater oddities in this area, they'll be happy to help.

7.3   Rangitoto Sea Kayaking

10 km northeast of Auckland

For intermediate paddlers (guided), 1 evening.

—**Summary**— The cone-shaped Rangitoto Island is only an hour's paddling from Auckland's busy shores. After wandering to the top of the volcano to enjoy the sunset, you kayak back across the channel towards the lights of Auckland.

—**How to Get There**— Contact Ian Ferguson's Guided Tours in Auckland, ☎/fax (09) 529 2230.

—**Description**— After meeting at 5.30 pm your guide will introduce you to the Puffin sea kayak and run through the basics of paddling. Your initial tentative strokes will strengthen as you gain balance and trust in yourself and your boat. Don't be surprised if you receive company—blue penguins and dolphins are regular visitors to the harbour and are attracted to these smooth and silent vessels.

An hour or so of paddling takes you to the black basaltic lava flows on the foreshore of Rangitoto Island. Beach your boats above the high-tide line and follow the shingle road built 70 years ago by convict labour. Walking to the summit of Rangitoto (260 m) isn't quite such hard work, and it's worth it for the 360° views of the Hauraki Gulf. At the top you and your group can enjoy supper and the awesome views as the sun sets and Auckland city lights up.

Returning from Rangitoto Island   (Ray Button)

Descend back through the contorted forests of pohutukawa (also known as the New Zealand Christmas tree) by torchlight, then launch into the darkness for the final leg home. Paddling at night is an eerie experience but it's great fun.

—**Notes**— This trip runs every day (weather permitting) and costs $40 per person. You'll need warm clothing, a rain coat, comfortable shoes and a torch.

7.4   The Whatipu Loop

30 km west of Auckland

For beginner trampers, 1 day.

—**Summary**— Just west of Auckland, the steep bush-clad Waitakere Ranges meet the Tasman Sea at the Whatipu Coast. The beach is a large sandy plain, stretching out towards the sea. The Whatipu Loop is a great walk for those who feel like escaping the Auckland sprawl.

—**How to Get There**— Drive or cycle from the city out to Titirangi. Continue south past Huia to the Whatipu road end, where there is a camping ground and car park.

—**Description**— From the car park you'll be able to see the distinctive, young kauri trees sticking up from the regenerating bush like witches' hats. The wide open spaces towards the sea may inspire you to run and leap into the soft spongy grasses. Paratutae Islet, a short distance away, is still stubbornly clinging to the mainland.

Head north along the flats on a 4WD track, staying close to the base of the Waitakeres. There are small sand dunes obscuring caves, caverns and clefts deep within the cliffs. These are worth exploring further—all the better if you've got a torch.

There is a camp site and toilet by one of the larger caves. Pararaha Point is 5 km or so from the car park. A massive sand dune has diverted the Pararaha River, creating a wetland. Walk up the river on the Pararaha Track for 1 km to the Muir Track junction, where there is a small shelter above an obvious camp site.

From here, Muir Track climbs high above the Whatipu coast to meet Gibbons Track. The views on the way make the steep climb worth it. Return to the car park via Gibbons Track.

—**Notes**— Permits required to stay at the camp sites are obtainable from the Arataki Visitors Centre, ☎ (09) 817 7134, near Titirangi. It's also possible to walk all the way to Karehare by taking one of the inland tracks north of the Pararaha River.

Even though the track is well signposted either Topomap Q11 Waitakere or the Auckland Regional Council 'Trackmap Waitakere Ranges' is recommended.

7.5 Black Water 'Rafting' II

Waitomo, 80 km south of Hamilton

For beginner adventurers (guided), 6 hours.

—**Summary**— This fun and exhilarating adventure starts with a morning's training in the art of abseiling, before plunging into the depths of the Ruakuri Cave System. The cave is explored by walking, wading, swimming, and tubing through sculpted subterranean galleries adorned with strange formations and glow-worms.

—How to Get There— Book at the Black Water Cafe, Waitomo, ☎ (07) 878 6219.

—Description— After group introductions, your guides will fit you out and familiarise you with all the technical gear. Then it's off to find a cliff and learn what to do with the equipment you've been given.

When the guides are satisfied that everyone in the group can set up a set or 'rack' of climbing/caving equipment, and abseil down a cliff face, it's time to amble across undulating Waitomo farmland to an insignificant-looking dip in the ground.

This is where you'll begin descending into the Ruakuri Cave, starting with a vertical, 35-metre abseil. The descent into the cave system continues with a flying fox (aerial cableway) ride through pitch black, towards the welcoming lights of your fellow cavers.

From here most of the cave is explored using truck inner tubes. Despite what the name Black Water 'Rafting' might suggest, rafts are too large and heavy to be used in a cave. Instead you must slide, squiggle and swim your way through Ruakuri's rushing underground river using inner tubes which allow you to float down the quiet stretches, navigating solely by the blue-green light of the glow-worms.

Providing all the 'right' turns are taken, you and your seven fellow cavers will eventually emerge back into the light of day, full of a sense of achievement and wonder at all you've experienced during your journey through Waitomo's fascinating nether regions.

—Notes— This trip is called Black Water 'Rafting' II—it costs $125 and leaves daily. Another option is Blackwater Rafting I, a shorter, more mellow trip that costs $65.

Bookings are essential. All equipment, including wetsuit and footwear is provided. All that is required of the adventurer is a towel and swimming togs, a desire for thrills and a sense of humour.

7.6   Lost World

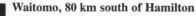

Waitomo, 80 km south of Hamilton

For beginner adventurers (guided), $1^1/_2$ days.

—**Summary**— The Lost World is entered by abseiling down into a gigantic chasm. You then work your way through the vast Mangapu Cave, following a roaring stream for much of the way, and passing magnificent chambers, full of ancient cave formations and glow-worm constellations. It's a safe and exciting opportunity for those with no previous caving experience to enjoy an incredible adventure.

—**How to Get There**— Book through the Museum of Caves in Waitomo, ☎ (07) 878 7788. Details are also available on the Internet, WorldWideWeb site: http:\\www.divelognz.com\waitomo\

—**Description**—Day 1: to enter the Lost World you must abseil down a 100-metre overhanging drop into the Mangapu Cave System. By anyone's standards—climbers, cavers or even bungy jumpers—this is a massive abseil, demanding skill, specialised equipment, and plenty of nerve.

Thorough instruction is given in a series of stages, ranging from 'abseiling' along a flat stretch of paddock to testing your newly acquired skills on a 22-metre vertical cliff. After about 5 hours, when your guides are certain that everyone is confident and competent, you'll head back to Waitomo for the night.

— Day 2: after inspecting the cave through various holes in the ground, you'll be guided in pairs to the edge of the Lost World. Your last contact with the known world is a tenacious tree, from which you can lower yourself over the edge and into the void below. There's no turning back from here. It takes about 20 minutes to reach the bottom of this huge subterranean canyon.

As you recover from the abseil, an eerie mist envelops you, slowly obscuring the entrance above. This is formed by body vapour condensing in the surrounding cold air. After a tasty underworld luncheon, you'll head further into the cave.

Climbing, swimming, walking, and wading up the roaring Mangapu Stream isn't fast, but it's certainly fascinating. In between avoiding drops, whirlpools and waterfalls, you'll see fossilised oysters, huge stalactites and lots of other cave formations for which there aren't even names. This incredible adventure finishes in the early evening—the buzz continues for days.

—**Notes**— This $1^1/_2$-day trip costs \$395 per person and runs on Wednesday/Thursday and Saturday/Sunday each week. All equipment is provided; you just need warm clothes, comfortable boots, a raincoat, and your swimming togs. The 4-hour Lost World Tandem Abseil operates daily.

7.7   Wairoa Rafting

25 km southwest of Tauranga

For all adventurers (guided), 2 hours on the river.

—**Summary**— The hydro-controlled Wairoa is one of New Zealand's most exhilarating rafting rivers. Rapids up to grade V, with steep drops and turbulent water, are enough to satisfy the most ardent rafter and give first-timers the ride of their lives.

—**How to Get There**— From Matamata drive south to Highway 29, then turn left towards Tauranga and cross the Kaimai Range. Just after the Ruahihi Bridge over the Wairoa River, turn right down Ruahihi Road. The entrance to the meeting place is on your right.

—**Description**— This 2-hour trip can only be done on 28 days of the year, when enough water is released from the dam for the Wairoa to become runnable. During these days it becomes the most heavily rafted and canoed river in the country.

A short drive from the meeting place takes you to the put-in point just below a power station. A beautiful stretch of still water just below the dam is a great place to sharpen up your rafting skills (or at least try to learn some), before the roar of big water heralds the point of no return. Mother's Nightmare, Double Trouble and The Devil's Elbow (don't let the names put you off) lead to a grade V waterfall. Rafts that mess up this one get grilled in The Toaster. The Rollercoaster is the hardest and last major rapid before the river eases off. If you're still keen, try body surfing in the final rapids to cool off after all the adrenalin-pumping action.

—**Notes**— Almost every rafting company in the world rafts the Wairoa. Two of them are River Rats, Auckland, ☎ (09) 309 2211; and Rafting Fantastic, Rotorua, ☎ (07) 348 0233. Trips cost about $79.

7.8   Other Adventures

New Zealand Nature Safaris

NZ Nature Safaris run several 9-10 day eco-adventure tours that connect with each other through the North and South Islands. Their tours involve hiking, caving, kayaking, camping, and swimming, around many of the remote and beautiful areas mentioned in this book. They also have a few 'secret spots' up their sleeve and visit some of the best wildlife locations around the country en route.

Although a moderate level of fitness is required, no special skills are needed and all camping equipment is provided. You just need a backpack, sleeping-bag, boots and a raincoat. On average the tours cost $65 per day and around $15 per day extra is spent on food and accommodation costs, such as camp/cabin fees.

A maximum group size of nine travel together in one of the safari minibuses. With no hidden costs these prices compare favourably to independent travel in New Zealand.

If you want to experience the nature and wilderness highlights around the country and your time is limited, then these enjoyable and convenient tours solve a lot of hassles. For more information about each individual trip read the relevant mentions in the Auckland,

Nelson and Southern Lakes chapters and/or contact NZ Nature Safaris at 52 Holborn Drive, Stokes Valley, Wellington, ☎/fax (04) 563 7360; e-mail: nzns@globe.co.nz

North Island Safari On this 9-day tour from Auckland to Wellington, NZ Nature Safaris zigzags through the highlights of the North Island

Tunnel Beach, Coromandel Peninsula   (New Zealand Nature Safaris)

combining adventure action, wildlife, cultural interpretation, and relaxation.

Head south to the volcanic landscapes of Rotorua. There will be opportunities to swim into an underground beach, soak in a secret hot pool in the bush and learn about Maori legend. Next it's time for some hiking; first in the world-renowned Jurassic rainforests of Whirinaki and then amongst the live volcanoes of Tongariro National Park—a surreal moonscape of scarlet mountain slopes and emerald crater lakes.

The final days are spent exploring the limestone caves of Waitomo before journeying down the remote western coast to Mt Egmont National Park where the last night is spent in a cosy hut high on this alpine volcano. You'll also visit the DOC National Wildlife Centre before continuing to Wellington. This tour leaves fortnightly from

Auckland and costs $585 per person. For more information and bookings contact the ACB Travel Centre in Auckland, ☎ (09) 358 4874.

Riverhead Forest

Riverhead is a large pine forest 15 km west of Browns Bay (North Auckland), which has some of the best mountain biking close to Auckland. It's criss-crossed by gravel roads, 4WD tracks and single track through rolling hills, up to 180 metres high.

Most riders cycle up the roads to a high point and then make their way down on the single tracks. Watch out for forestry trucks, motorbikes and war game soldiers. Riverhead Forest is large enough to get lost in for a few hours so get into the exploring spirit of things.

For more information and maps contact the Recreation Tourism section of Carter Holt Harvey at Woodhill Information Centre, ☎ (09) 420 8660, or Adventure Cycles, Fort St, toll-free ☎ 0800 33 55 66. They also have maps of Whitford Forest, 10 km southeast of Auckland, and hire out bikes from $20-$35 per day (including full suspension bikes). They're open from 7am to 7pm, 7 days a week.

Mt Eden Quarry

Smack bang in the heart of Auckland, amidst factories, a prison, and a motorway, is one of New Zealand's best rock climbing areas. The Quarry is a series of jointed volcanic columns towering 20 metres above the footie (football) field of Auckland Grammar (school).

These climbs are a real test of rock climbing technique and rely mainly on natural protection; however, bolted climbs are becoming more common. Around the corner, to the right of the main cliff (the Long Wall), are a series of smaller cliffs (the Short Wall).

To get there from the city, go over Grafton Bridge towards Auckland Hospital. Continue along Park Road into Mountain Road, until you reach Auckland Grammar on your right. The cliffs are within the school grounds. For more information read *Quarry Climbs* (see Further Reading).

Great Barrier Island (Aotea)

Only 80 km northeast of Auckland lies a Pacific island ripe for adventure. Great Barrier Island offers premium mountain biking, bush walking, horse trekking, snorkelling and sea kayaking amongst a relaxed setting of subtropical forest, secluded beaches, hot pools and historical relics. The forests are particularly lush because there are no possums on the island to eat them. There is also abundant bird and marine life in the coastal nooks and crannies.

It's easy to plan your own trip, just buy the 259 Great Barrier Island map and drop into the DOC visitors centre at Port Fitzroy. For accommodation, horse treks and sea kayak hire contact Fitzroy House Outdoor Centre, ☎ (09) 429 0091. Ross Adventures, ☎ (09) 357 0550, run guided sea kayaking trips here and around Waiheke Island. The main transport to the island from Auckland is Fullers Ferry, ☎ (09) 377 1771, costing $89 per person and $20 per bike return. The ferry trip takes 3 hours. If you're strapped for cash, consider the 6-hour barge option.

Exploring Great Barrier Island
(Guy Stephens)

Stony Bay

At the tip of the Coromandel Peninsula, a newly marked 4WD track connects Stony Bay and Fletchers Bay providing a great cycle touring route around Coromandel. This 7 km gap in the road around the peninsula takes 1-2 hours to ride. There are DOC camping areas at both of the beautiful bays, great swimming and pleasant bush walks.

Hahei Marine Reserve

This recently established marine reserve is on the eastern side of the Coromandel Peninsula near Hahei. There is a carpark and information board at the end of Grange Road near Cathedral Cove. The reserve stretches from the western end of Hahei Beach to Cooks Bluff, and includes several small islands and the northern tip of Mahurangi Island. Plans are afoot to set up an underwater trail for snorkellers and divers. Already a great spot for swimming and diving, this lovely spot can only get better as the marine life recovers.

Hot Water Beach

If you are on the east side of the Coromandel Peninsula, look out for Hot Water Beach (just south of Hahei Marine Reserve). At low tide you can scoop out a hole in the sand and intercept thermally heated water on its way to the sea. Plonk yourself in the hole and enjoy a natural hot water bath. Hot Water Beach is signposted off Highway 25, about 30 km southeast of Whitianga.

Waiwawa River

This is a short, scenic trip with about six playful rapids (grade II maximum). Coroglen is on Highway 25, on the eastern side of the Coromandel Peninsula, 20 km south of Whitianga.

From here take the Tapu Coroglen Road that follows the Waiwawa River west. On your left, 3 km from Coroglen, there is a 4WD track leading through a few metres of bush to an old concrete-bottomed ford. This is the get-out point and is used as a river-level gauge.

If the river is flowing 10 cm or more over the ford, then you can comfortably tube the short section up river. If the water is brown then it's too high.

Start 3 km upriver where the road crosses Taranoho Stream. Immediately on the left after the stream is a gate leading into a grassy area. The put-in point is at the river, 60 metres away.

Pauanui Trig

This excellent 2-4 hour ride in the Coromandel is great for all levels of mountain biker although route finding can prove to be interesting.

Whangamata Cycles on the main street in Whangamata hire bikes and equipment for only $30 per day.

From Whangamata (eastern side of the Coromandel Ranges) head north on Highway 25 for 11 km, then turn right at the Opoutere turn-off and ride down Opoutere Road for 7 km. Some 50 metres past a gate on your left, stop at a fork with two gates and a forest sign. Jump the gates and cycle up the gravel road for a few minutes, stopping at a second fork that splits three ways—Phoenix Road is the small gravel route to the left. After cycling up it for 10 minutes, you'll drop down to a fork in a grassy clearing, where you turn right.

Another 10 minutes and you'll reach another intersection where you carry on straight up to Ohui Road. Turn left down Ohui Road for a few hundred metres then turn right onto Trig Road.

Carry on up Trig Road to the top of a hill, with 'Gumdiggers Road' on the left, opposite the unobvious Peter Rabbit's Cotton Trail on the right. Head straight through and take the first left turn; it's a small gravel road.

Stay on the main track until you reach a T-intersection at the top of a 100-metre long steep section. Turn right onto a dirt single track which leads up to the trig a couple of minutes away. The 360^0 views from Pauanui Trig are awesome—you can spot White Island on a clear day.

From the trig, backtrack to Gumdiggers Road and turn left onto Peter Rabbit's Cotton Trail—single track is usually only this good in your dreams. Just keep on veering left and you'll eventually reach a gravel road where you should turn right, then left, then left again.

From here the quickest way back to Opoutere is straight ahead on the main gravel road, but it's much more fun to turn right, back onto the narrow track you started on. Don't forget to turn left this time at the grassy clearing.

Haggis Honking

Haggis Honking Holes is one of the more 'sporty' caving

trips run by Waitomo Adventures, Museum of Caves, ☎ (07) 878 7788. A 4-hour workout involving squeezes, waterfalls, ladder climbs, abseils, and caverns adorned with various formations and glow worms manages to satisfy most adventure aficionados. Cost is $120 per person and all you need is a towel and socks—local King Country ethnic costume we believe!

 ## Waitomo River Kayaking

Waitomo Wilderness Tours run a number of kayaking daytrips from the Museum of Caves, ☎ (07) 878 7640, in Waitomo. Their popular 4-5 hour guided tour involves paddling through an intimate limestone gorge in their 'frenzy' sit-on-rather-than-in kayaks. Stillness, punctuated by plinking dripping water, the occasional river rapid, and a side trip to a glow-worm cave (which you can paddle into in good conditions) make this a memorable trip. Cost is $85, minimum of 2 persons. All kayaking gear, wetsuit, flashlight, and hot soup provided.

 ## The World's Worst Tramp

The 'Kauaeranga Valley-Table Top' tramp involves hard physical toil in unrelenting mud. This trip has no highlights, no rewards and no views. Your most poignant memory will be of returning to your car after about 8 hours of grovelling. This track is so unpleasant and environmentally unsound that it hasn't even been acknowledged on the new Topomaps.

Walk up Kauaeranga Valley until you hit the track to Table Top and Mt Rowe. A long grovelly climb takes you to a mud-filled canal known as the Mt Rowe-Table Top Track. A possible diversion is to slime your way up Mt Rowe (795 m). Otherwise wade for 2 km through a trench filled with mud and submerged logs. Eventually a track takes you back to the road via Wairoa Stream. If you want a view, take a ladder.

8. East Cape & Hawke's Bay

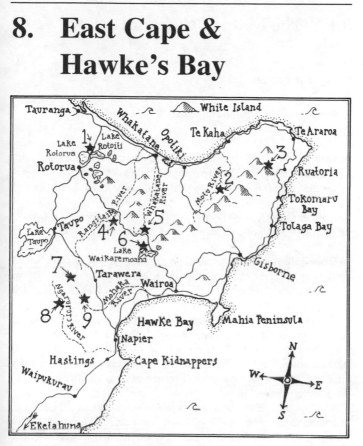

8.1 The Kaituna Cascades

 Rotorua

For all adventurers (guided), $2^1/_2$ hours return from Rotorua.

—**Summary**— Try this for a short, sharp and memorable rafting trip. The Kaituna River is a scenic rollercoaster and the highlight (or object of greatest dread) is a 6-metre waterfall about halfway down.

—**How to Get There**— Book through Rotorua Information Centre, ☎ (07) 348 5179, or contact Kaituna Cascades, ☎ (07) 357 5032.

—**Description**— The Kaituna River is a narrow bush-lined channel containing a series of pools and drops as it cuts through old lava flows. Because there isn't much that's dull on the Kaituna River, the rafting safety routine needs to be performed high and dry in a gravel pit beside the highway. Soon after you've become accustomed to the sport of gravel-pit rafting, you'll launch onto the river and swirl your way downstream. After 10 minutes the first 'air time' occurs as you plummet over the 3-metre weir at the site of one of New Zealand's first state hydropower stations—a swan was once followed over this drop.

The highlight of this bouncing trip is a 6-metre waterfall, known as Hinemoa Step, about halfway down the river. As the two guides anchor the raft, you're able to gaze downstream and watch the glassy water disappear over the edge. Far below there is a cauldron of thrashing whitewater. A last minute briefing to stress the importance of holding on and fusing with the raft seems unnecessary—there is nothing you'll want to do more.

After erupting through this narrow slot into the void, the next 30 seconds will be a little confusing. Following a brief foray into the world of submarine rafting, you're fairly likely to emerge upright. The water now has a chance to pour out through the designer gaps of your self-bailing raft which self-bails even faster when it's upside down. It's with a euphoric feeling of relief that you raft down the remaining grade III and IV rapids to the take-out point. Here there is yet another chance to plummet metres into the river—this time by jumping off a high cliff. In total you experience about 40 minutes in, over and under the Kaituna River.

—Notes— Kaituna Cascades charge $49 and run several trips a day year-round. Six other companies now raft this river. Contact the Rotorua Information Centre for more information.

A Raft Guide Unloads the Raft on the Kaituna River (Adventure Photography)

8.2   The Mysterious Motu River

Raukumara Range, southeast of the Bay of Plenty

For all rafters (guided), or experienced kayakers, 3-5 days.

—Summary— Forging its way through the vast Raukumara wilderness, the Motu (meaning severed) is the most isolated and untouched of all the North Island rivers. It was the last area of New Zealand to be mapped and still remains much of a mystery. Without a doubt, this is one of the country's finest river adventures.

—How to Get There— From either Gisborne or Opotiki drive to Matawai on Highway 2. From here follow Motu Road to Motu township, 15 km away. The put-in site is a few kilometres downstream of Waitangirua Station (7 km east of Motu) on a rough 4WD track.

—Description— The Motu River ranges from grade III to V depending on the flow, and reaches a fearsome grade VI when in flood. From the put-in site it takes 3-5 days to reach the Bay of Plenty, 90 km away. The three main gorges are the Upper, Te Paku and the Lower. Within the Upper Gorge there are tight steep rapids that are impassable in flood. Te Paku Gorge is a deep and narrow stretch with no major rapids. The Lower Gorge, however, contains some of the most difficult rapids on the river. Log jams can sometimes be a problem in the Upper and Lower Gorges.

The first two groups to venture down the Motu River (in 1919 and 1935) both took 10 days before emerging at the Bay of Plenty coast. At the other extreme, a kayaker is reputed to have paddled it in 7 hours, when it was in very high flow and the rapids were grade VI!

Motu River Expeditions run a 4 day rafting trip down the Motu River. This involves driving from Hassall's farm (on Bell Road, 30 km southeast of Whakatane on Highway 2) to the put-in site at Waitangirua Station and paddling down to the first camp site just above the Upper Gorge.

During the next 2 days you manoeuvre your way through the infamous gorges, and raft down legendary rapids such as Bullivant's Cascade, The Motu Slot and Double Staircase. The sheer power and beauty of this river are unforgettable.

On the 4th and last day you'll only paddle for a couple of hours before being picked up by a jet boat, which takes you down the last, slow flowing, 18 km to the Motu highway bridge beside the coast.

—Notes— To raft the Motu contact Motu River Expeditions in Whakatane, ☎ (07) 308 7760 or (07) 312 3179. Trips cost $565. Experienced kayakers and tube rafters should read Graham Egarr's *North Island Rivers* (see Further Reading). Walking down the river is impossible and tramping out over the surrounding ranges would take days, so go well prepared with extra clothes, food and repair equipment. To bike into and raft the lower half of the Motu, see Motu Bike 'n' Raft in section 8.10 of this chapter.

Topomaps X15 Omaio and X16 Motu are essential. Also take the Motu River descent guide map—it is waterproof and has good descriptions of the river and rapids. It can be purchased for $1 from DOC in Opotiki, ☎ (07) 315 6103.

This beautiful river has been earmarked for hydro development since the 1950s, but it is currently protected by an Act of Parliament.

8.3   Mt Hikurangi Bike 'n' Hike

East Cape, 130 km north of Gisborne

For intermediate adventurers in summer, 1-2 days.

—**Summary**— High above the East Cape, Hikurangi is a peak entwined in both ancient and modern legend. Maori tradition tells of the peak being the resting place of the demigod Maui and his canoe after he hauled up the North Island on his fishing line. More recently it has become renowned for being the first place on the mainland to see the light of the new day.

Climbing Hikurangi involves winding up through farmland, before entering the bush and continuing up onto the crescent-shaped summit.

It's worth riding a mountain bike as far up as possible; it's howling good fun on the way back down.

—**Landowners**— Hikurangi belongs to the Ngati Porou tribe. Permission to cross Pakihiroa Station must be obtained from the Station Manager, ☎ (06) 864 0962.

—**How to Get There**— From Gisborne, travel 130 km north on Highway 35 before turning left (near Ruatoria) onto a gravel road signposted 'Pakihiroa Station'. After 20 km you'll pass a turn-off to the DOC Raparapariri Homestead. About a hundred metres further

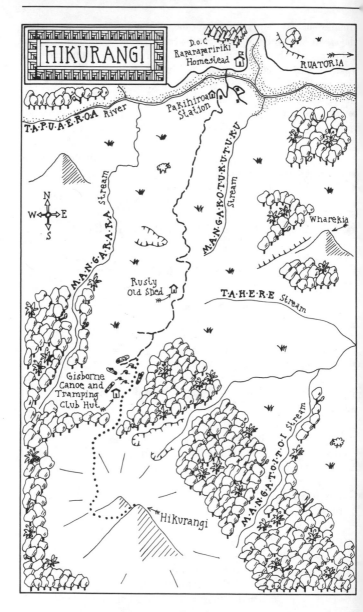

down the road, turn left and cross the Tapuaeroa River to Pakihiroa Station. Park near the sheds at the bottom of the hill.

—**Description**— Pakihiroa Station is one of the many East Cape farms losing its land, roads and buildings under rapidly rising riverbeds. This is because the mountains on the East Cape are eroding faster than the rivers can carry away the debris.

From Tapuaeroa River bridge take the road heading straight up the hill past the houses. The 4WD track leading up Hikurangi veers off to the left (through a gate), just before the road ends at the top house.

It's not possible to see the mountain from the valley, only the sheer cliffs of Wharekia to the south and Whanokao to the west. You have to climb steeply up to 423 metres where the ridge flattens out before you get your first glimpse of Hikurangi.

Ignore the turn-off to the left after the fifth gate and continue climbing steeply. Two more gates and a rusty old shed down to the right are passed before you reach a fork in the track. Veer left and continue for another 300 metres until, after a slight downhill, an indistinct foot track branches off to the left.

This track is marked by an almost invisible cairn accompanied by an equally indistinguishable reflector far off in the distance. You can either leave your bikes here, or carry them up through a landscape of old tree stumps to the Gisborne Canoe and Tramping Club Hut (16 bunks), about 30 minutes away. Carrying bikes up to the hut is a grind, but it's worth it if you enjoy face-planting on extreme downhills.

Whether you're biking or walking, the hut should take 3-5 hours to reach from Pakihiroa Station. It has good views and the only water on the trip, so is a logical place to stay the night. The summit is 1-2 hours' walking and scrambling from here.

Follow a track that climbs steeply up the hill directly behind the hut, into the bush. Once in the alpine scrub, follow the snow poles around the west side of Hikurangi. When the snow poles end, sidle across scree slopes to an obvious chute which takes you, wheezing and panting, to a saddle just below the summit.

The highest point is marked by a trig on your right, about five minutes away. If your party moves up this chute keeping close together there is less chance that someone will be hit by a dislodged rock. In winter, snow and ice make this a serious alpine climb from the chute onwards.

At 1752 metres, this is the highest mountain for hundreds of miles around: on a fine day the panorama from the top is fantastic. To the west is the vast and mostly untracked Raukumara State Forest Park and to the east the Pacific Ocean.

Return the same way, being careful not to dislodge rocks upon others and following the snow poles around the mountain. If you've left bikes at the hut, watch out for the gates as you ride down—they can appear suddenly. Always leave them as you found them: open, shut or stuck to your front forks.

—**Notes**— There are two fords between the highway and Pakihiroa Station which are often too rough for two-wheel-drive cars. Accommodation is available at Raparapaririki Homestead (contact DOC in Gisborne for the keys, ☎ (06) 867 8531).

The Gisborne Tramping and Canoe Club hut costs $2 per night; book with Chris Sharp, ☎ (06) 862 5677. Take plenty of water—this area can be hot and dry. Be prepared for rapid and extreme weather changes. Topomap Y15 Hikurangi is recommended.

8.4   Rangitaiki Whitewater Sledging

 Based at Rotorua

For all adventurers (guided), 1/2 day return from Rotorua.

—**Summary**— This exciting sport involves swimming, with the aid of your sledge and flippers, through whitewater that would take years to master in a canoe.

Although the rapids seem magnified because you're actually in the river, not on it, it soon becomes apparent that the sledges are actually very stable. Nevertheless, accelerating down cascades into a deafening white froth won't easily be forgotten.

Rolling a Whitewater Sledge on the Rangitaiki River (Adventure Photography)

—How to Get There— Book at the Rotorua Information Centre, ☎ (07) 348 5179, or contact Whitewater Sledging in Rotorua, ☎ (07) 349 6100.

—Description— The Rangitaiki River runs past Murupara township, 40 km southeast of Rotorua on Highway 38. A short drive from Murupara takes you to the put-in site, where a sedate stretch of river disappears around a bush-clad bend. This tranquil scene helps calm the nerves as you don your wetsuit, life jacket, helmet, and flippers. After a brief safety talk, you're ready to jump in and learn how to control your large kitchenware craft.

The first big rapid, Red Knight Corner, teaches you the importance of picking a good line early on. In high flows it also provides good surfing. Despite the extra padding on the wetsuits, anyone (including the guides) can get a bit bruised from hitting rocks. Otherwise it's a relatively safe sport.

Another 20 rapids with names like Alligator, Short Sharp Shock, The Helicopter, and The Gap are waiting down river. These range from grade II to III+ and are evenly spread out along the next 10 km. The guides give instruction before the more difficult rapids and always lead the way.

If you're still keen when you reach the take-out site then consider doing the 'Upper Rangitaiki Trip'. It involves sledging nine gnarly rapids upstream from the normal put-in site and you can then continue with the standard trip described above. Jeff's Joy (grade IV), with its difficult grade III approach rapids and extremely powerful water, is the scariest of them all. The aptly named Popout is also very powerful but not quite as terrifying.

—**Notes**— The standard Rangitaiki River trip costs $90; the longer trip for experienced sledgers is $95. You may be able to arrange to do both trips in one day for a reduced cost. The company, Whitewater Sledging, has been set up in New Zealand by the planet's most experienced sledger, a Frenchman called Moustache.

Take your togs, towel and some warm mittens if you suffer from cold hands. The season lasts from October 1 to May 15, subject to weather conditions. This section of river is also commercially rafted and is very popular amongst canoeists.

8.5   Te Urewera Horse Trekking

Ruatahuna, Urewera National Park

For all adventurers (guided), 1-5 days.

—**Summary**— Te Urewera is more than just a land of mountains and dense bush; it is the land of the Tuhoe people, 'children of the mist'.

Te Urewera Adventures is run by local people and offers horse treks into this wild and rugged area. In this uniquely Maori adventure you are likely to learn more from your hosts about Maori culture than some Pakeha New Zealanders will ever know.

—**How to Get There**—
Ruatahuna is on Highway 38, about 100 km drive southeast of Rotorua (on the way to Lake Waikaremoana). Book well in advance with Margaret or Whare Biddle of Te Urewera Adventures of New Zealand, Ruatahuna, Private Bag 3001, Rotorua, ☎ (07) 366 3969,

—**Description**— On a 3-day trek the area explored on horseback is within the largest tract of native forest remaining in the North Island. Following the Whakatane River from Ruatahuna, you are guided through steep regenerating bush country to a clearing at Tawhiwhi. The first night is often spent here before entering the National Park. Only Tuhoe people and their guests are allowed within the National Park on horseback.

The next day you'll enter thick bush as the track follows the river down to Hanamahihi flats. The kit bag sitting in front of the saddle provides a solid hand hold as the track twists and dives through the forest.

Urewera Horse Trekking   (S.Burton)

Finally, after snaking through several kilometres of grasslands, you'll reach the permanent camp at Hanamahihi. On longer treks riders have a rest day either here or further down the river. Even on the 3-day trek there is plenty of time to explore these quiet places. It is possible to do a large rugged loop via Waikare River and Waikare-whenua. Otherwise you will ride back up the Whakatane River to Ruatahuna. The length of your trip depends on your riding ability and dedication; you can be taken on anything from a sedate plod to an epic journey.

—Notes— Treks cost anywhere between $108 for a day to $720 for five days. We recommend going for at least two days. Absolutely everything is supplied—you just need the clothes on your back. Te Urewera Adventures also run walking, fishing and hunting trips.

8.6   Waiau to Waikaremoana Tramp

Urewera National Park, 100 km southeast of Rotorua

For intermediate/experienced trampers, 4-6 days.

—Summary— The Urewera is the North Island's largest and least known National Park. Many of its peaks and streams still remain unnamed. This area of magnificent forest, rivers and lakes is steeped in fascinating Maori history.

This tramp takes you down the Waiau River and over a 1000-metre high ridge to Lake Waikaremoana. Although the distances covered each day aren't huge, tramping experience is required to negotiate the many river crossings.

—How to Get There— The track leaves Highway 38 at Mimiha Bridge (signposted), 40 km southeast of Murupara and 6 km west of Ruatahuna. Waikaremoana motor camp is a further 50 km to the southeast on a winding and unsealed road.

—Description—
Mimiha Bridge to Parahaki Hut; 4-6 hours

From Mimiha Bridge follow an old 4WD track south through regenerating farmland. After 1-2 hours you'll reach the national park boundary at the bush edge. From there drop down to Parahaki Stream, 10 minutes away. Head downstream to Te Totara Stream about an hour away. If the stream is up, take the longer and less scenic all-weather track.

Te Totara Hut (8 bunks) is about 15 minutes upstream from where Te Totara Stream flows into Parahaki Stream. This historic hut was built 30 years ago from split totara. If you got an early start, continue down Parahaki Stream to a swingbridge at the Waiau River, about 2 hours away. 500 metres past the swing bridge is Parahaki Hut (9 bunks). Once again, there is an all-weather alternative if the river is up.

Parahaki Hut to Te Waiotukapiti Hut; 4-6 hours

From Parahaki Hut it's about $1^1/_2$ hours down river to Central Waiau Hut (8 bunks). There are many major river crossings on this section so if the river is high use the all-weather track on the true right bank.

Continue downstream to Te Waiotukapiti Hut (6 bunks), 3-4 hours away. Follow the white markers down the true right bank. At Blue Slip the track climbs away from the river for 30 minutes to avoid a gorge. After this section you'll cross the Maungangarara Stream, which is uncrossable in flood. If the river level is high, stay an extra day or two at Central Waiau Hut.

Te Waiotukapiti Hut to Pukekohu Range Campsite; 6-8 hours

The next day head up Te Waiotukapiti Stream (30 minutes down from the hut) for 4 km to where a signposted track climbs onto the Pukekohu Range. There is an alternative all-weather track that you can take instead of travelling up Te Waiotukapiti Stream. It crosses the Waiau River on the cableway to follow a well marked ridge-track, north of Te Waiotukapiti Hut and emerges at the upper Te Waiotukapiti Stream (20 minutes downstream from the track that leads up onto Pukekohu Ridge). Both the stream and the ridge-track alternative take about 3 hours.

Once on Pukekohu Range follow the track north along the ridge to Pukekohu Helipad (just by a fork in the track). A tent and water are needed for camping at the helipad, and a camping stove is recommended. Really keen people may wish to continue on to Lake Waikaremoana 2-4 hours away.

Pukekohu Range to Te Puna Hut; 4-7 hours
From the helipad take the right-hand track that leads down to Manganuiohou River. Then climb out of this valley, over a smaller ridge, before dropping down to Maraunui Bay on the shores of the lake. Marauiti Hut (18 bunks) is 2 km away, perched on the edge of the secluded Marauiti Bay. Aim to spend the night at Te Puna Hut (18 bunks), a further 2-3 hours away.

Te Puna Hut to the Highway; 3-5 hours
This is the shortest day of the trip and the track is in excellent condition. After a good sleep-in wander around to Whanganui Hut (18 bunks) and then on to Highway 38.

—**Notes**— Contact DOC in Murupara, ☎ (07) 366 5641, the night before heading off to ask how high the rivers are. If they're dangerously high then consider doing the Lake Waikaremoana Track instead. It's worth learning a bit about this fascinating area beforehand—just pop into the DOC visitor centre.

The Lake Waikaremoana huts are often full in summer. On Mondays, Wednesdays and Fridays a City Connection bus drives from Wairoa to Rotorua in the morning and back again in the afternoon. It can be booked through any Intercity Office. Topomaps V18 Whirinaki and W18 Waikaremoana are essential.

8.7   Kaimanawa Loop

 Kaimanawa Forest Park, 40 km east of Mt Ruapehu

For intermediate trampers, 4 days.

—**Summary**— The Kaimanawa Mountains, with their wide open valleys, lush beech forest and tussocky tops, provide excellent tramping. There are long fine periods in summer, contrasting with bitterly cold winters that bring snow down to the valley floors. For those who really want to get away from it all, this is one of the best four-day tramps in the North Island.

—How to Get There— From Taupo, drive east on Highway 5 for 26 km before turning right onto Taharua Road. After another 9 km turn right onto Clements Road. The tramp starts at Te Iringa car park and picnic area, 7 km down Clements Road. It finishes at the Clements road end a further 12 km away.

—Description—

Te Iringa to Oamaru Hut; 4-5 hours

From the Te Iringa car park follow the well-marked track through beech forest to Te Iringa Hut, 1-2 hours away. Continue south along the ridge, down to and across the Kaipo River (2-3 hours from the road end). Oamaru Hut (12 bunks) is situated in a wide open valley about 2 hours away. The hut is often full in summer but there are heaps of excellent camp sites close by.

Oamaru Hut to Boyd Hut

The next morning walk up the true left of the Oamaru River across grassy river flats, then follow the track into the bush. It continues in bush for 2-3 hours before crossing over Waitawhero Saddle and descending into the wide tussocky Ngaruroro Valley. Ford the Ngaruroro River before heading south for 600 metres to the head of the airstrip. From here, a track leads up to Boyd Lodge (16 bunks), 500 metres away. This is where the Ngaruroro River tubing expedition starts (see section 8.8).

Boyd Hut to Cascade Hut; 6-7 hours

From the airstrip, walk up the wide open flats of the Ngaruroro Valley. After about an hour cross the Ngaruroro River and head up to the river terraces above Te Waiotupuritia Stream. There is a track of sorts, but it's often easier to pick your own route up the valley (stay on the true left).

Eventually the red tussock flats end and a well-marked track leads you through mountain beech forest to Waiotupuritia Saddle. Descend to the Kaipo Saddle Track and continue for half an hour to Cascade Hut (6 bunks).

Cascade Hut to Te Iringa

On the last day the track follows the true right of the Tauranga Taupo River downstream for about half an hour, before climbing steeply to traverse an unnamed ridge.

Every now and again you can see Lake Taupo and the central plateau volcanoes through gaps in the bush. From the end of the ridge, the track generally follows Hinemaiaia Stream to the Clements road end.

Hopefully you've either got a keen runner in your group or you've arranged for someone to pick you up. It's 12 km to the Te Iringa car park—a pleasant road bash (walk) as road bashes go.

—Landowners— Much of this tramp is on Maori land. Permission to cross it should be obtained from Air Charter Taupo, ☎ (07) 378 5467.

—Notes— Vehicle theft and vandalism at the road ends in this region are chronic. For peace of mind, leave your car at Sika Lodge, ☎ (07) 378 4728, near the start of Clements Road. Apart from a vehicle security service, they also offer accommodation and guided tramping trips. Topomap U19 Kaimanawa is essential.

8.8 Ngaruroro River Tubing Expedition

Kaweka State Forest Park, between Taupo and Hawke's Bay

For experienced kayakers or tubers, 4-6 days.

—Summary— The grade II to III Ngaruroro River is a great wilderness journey for rafters, tubers and kayakers. The technical difficulty of the rapids and the remote location make this both a serious undertaking and a wildly rewarding trip. There are long spells of settled weather in this region during summer.

—How to Get There— Kayakers and rafters must fly (or at least have their crafts flown in) to Boyd Lodge from Taupo Airport, whereas tubers can trek in (see details below).

Flights cost $75 per person, and are organised through De Bretts Aviation, Taupo, ☎ (07) 378 8559 or Air Charter Taupo, ☎ (07) 378 5467. The trip ends at the Kuripapango bridge on the Napier-Taihape Road.

—Description— If you choose to tramp in, it will take 1-2 days (see 8.7 Kaimanawa Loop). Aeroplanes land on a small airstrip in the middle of the Kaimanawa Mountains. Here the upper Ngaruroro River meanders through an open alpine valley. Tubers should take time to construct a solid raft—doing repairs on the move can be a hassle. Either spend the first night at Boyd Lodge (16 bunks) above the airstrip, or get a few hours' rafting under your belt.

After 6 km the river closes in to provide exciting tubing, and is big enough to warrant using a four-tube raft. Camp before you enter this fast gorgey section. The rapids through the gorge to Ngaawaparua Hut (6 bunks) are up to grade III, so be careful.

From Ngaawaparua Hut, there are chutes, tumbling rapids, and quiet pools in shady canyons. There are five well-spaced huts and bivouacs before the take-out at the Napier-Taihape Road, 2-3 days away.

Even though there are plenty of beautiful camping spots, try to aim for a hut each day as travel is deceptively slow and it is easy to overestimate distance travelled, especially if tubing or rafting. The first sign of civilisation is the water gauge 4 km upstream of the Kuripapango bridge on the Napier-Taihape Road.

—Notes— As this is such a remote trip all parties must be experienced and well prepared. Topomaps U19 Kaimanawa and U20 Kaweka are essential.

8.9   The Mohaka Tramp 'n' Tube

Kaweka State Forest Park, 50 km northwest of Napier

For beginner adventurers, 2 days.

—Summary— The Mohaka is a large clear river flowing

through beautiful native forest. After walking to the Mangatainoka hot pool, you can then float and swim back down the Mohaka River. It's a relaxing trip for adventurers in need of a holiday.

—How to Get There— From Napier drive 51 km northwest on a minor road to Puketitiri. A few kilometres from this small township, turn right onto Hot Springs Road. Continue for 10 km before turning left onto Makahu Road. Drive as far up this road as possible towards the Mangatutu Thermal Springs Reserve picnic area. There are a couple of fords that are uncrossable in flood.

—Description— There are some small hot springs at the road end, but they don't compare to the Mangatainoka Hot Pool 3-4 hours' walk up the valley. On your way in you'll have to sidle high to avoid a couple of bluffs, but otherwise it's easy tramping.

Half an hour up the valley from Te Puia Lodge there are plenty of camp sites around Mangatainoka Hot Pool. Pump up your truck tube and test it by floating in the hot pool for a couple of hours. If you have time left in the day, walk up the river and have a practice run down the easy rapids back to the hot pool.

The next day as you pack your gear, ask yourself, 'How dry do I want it to be at the end of the day?' Put on your bash hat and buoyancy vest, and get set for a hard day's fun. The rapids from the hot pool to the car park reach grade II and are generally long, stopper-filled fun traps. Keep the group together. The Mohaka is a large river requiring your full attention.

Keep an eye out for landmarks such as Te Puia Lodge, so you can measure your progress. There is a tricky rapid 2 km down river from Te Puia Lodge which sometimes needs portaging; check it out before tubing down it. It takes 3-6 hours' tubing to reach the get-out point at the Mangatutu Reserve picnic area. There is a steep track leading up the bank on the true right.

—Notes— This is an excellent beginner's trip, but water safety skills are essential. The get-out point can be hard to see from the river so wander down and have a look at it on your way in. Take Parkmap 12 Kaweka.

8.10 Other Adventures

Lake Kayaking in the Rotorua Area

If you feel like escaping the tourist-hum of Rotorua city try kayaking around one of the nearby ancient volcanic crater lakes. Hidden in the forest on their shores are several short walks and secluded campsites, which combined with kayaking provide the perfect way to explore this scenic and tranquil area.

Adventure Kayaking in Rotorua, ☎ (07) 348 9451, can help you with everything you need. They run one and two day guided trips ($75 and $210 respectively) with everything including food provided, or, for those with kayaking experience, hire out boats for $35 per day.

Whakarewarewa Forest

Whakarewarewa is an area of exotic and native forest, approximately 8 km square in area, on the southeast outskirts of Rotorua. It is covered with a labyrinth of forest roads and walking tracks, and has two purpose built mountain bike tracks. Visit the information centre on Long Mile Road, Rotorua, to buy a map and plan your excursion. After trying the signposted mountain bike tracks, we recommend you ride, via the route of your choice, to lakes Tikitapu (Blue Lake) and Rotokakahi (Green Lake). Bikes can be hired from bike shops in Rotorua.

Note: Green Lake is Tapu (sacred/forbidden)—no swimming or boating is allowed.

Motu Bike 'n' Raft

This 'adventure combo' is one of the most exciting wilderness trips in the country. The first day involves mountain biking into the Motu River via the Otipi Road. This is a premium mountain bike ride and those who find the uphills a bit tough have the option of waiting for a lift from the 4WD vehicle bringing the rafts in.

After camping for a night beside the Motu you'll raft down Te Paku

Gorge and the lower Motu gorge (see 8.2 Mysterious Motu River). A jet boat will ferry you down the last long flat section of the river out to the coast at the Bay of Plenty.

This 2-day adventure costs $325 per person and includes all equipment, meals, transport and guides. For more information and bookings contact Dreamers and East-Capers in Opotiki, ☎ (07) 315 6304.

Urutawa Single Track

This 3-4 hour mountain bike ride follows a challenging single track through native bush not far from Opotiki (Bay of Plenty). An average level of fitness and bike handling skill are essential. At the end of the ride you can clean the mud off by swimming in a warm, crystal clear river. The trip costs $40 per person for groups of three or more and includes transport, bikes, and a guide. It's less if you've got your own bike. Phone Dreamers and East-Capers, ☎ (07) 315 6304, in Opotiki for more information.

Hicks Bay Diving

There is superb skin diving at both Hicks Bay and Lottin Point. Hicks Bay is 186 km north of Gisborne on Highway 35; Lottin Point is another 25 km on from Hicks Bay, and 4 km north from Highway 35. For diving gear, a place to stay and more information about diving in the area, contact Don or Diane Oates at the Hicks Bay Backpackers Lodge, ☎ (06) 864 4731. They also run trips out to the nearby East Cape lighthouse, a spot famous for its sunrises.

Whirinaki Forest

Hidden between Taupo and Lake Waikaremoana, the fantastic podocarp forests of Whirinaki were saved from the axe in the 1980s after a prominent conservation battle. Many people, including eminent British botanist, David Bellamy, disrupted logging by camping in the tree tops. Several tramps start from the end of River Road, just out of the ex-logging town of Minginui (about 30 km south of Murupara). A popular 2-day loop heads up the Whirinaki River to Central Whirinaki Hut and then back the next day via Mangamate

Hut. Also, an excellent 5-day tramp heads right up the Whirinaki Valley before making its way back via Central Te Hoe, Te Wairoa, and Moerangi huts. We predict this will be one of New Zealand's next 'Great Walks'. For more information contact DOC at the Murupara information centre, ☎ (07) 366 5641, and buy Topomap V18 Whirinaki. Whirinaki Lodge, ☎ (07) 366 3235, offer a car shuttle service to and from the road end. In high flows the Whirinaki River provides fine tubing.

Lake Waikaremoana Hike 'n' Paddle

Perhaps the best way to enjoy the Lake Waikaremoana 'Great Walk' is to add a bit (or a lot) of kayaking for variety. If you are keen to do the whole 3-4 day tramp then start by catching the water taxi ($10 per person) from the motorcamp at Waikaremoana to Onepoto. Spend the next few days walking around the scenic Lake Waikaremoana to Whanganui Hut. From the hut, hop into a sea kayak and paddle back across the lake to the motorcamp.

Your tramping gear can be taken by the boat that transports the kayaks. Kayak hire and delivery is $65 per person, contact Bay Kayaks at Lake Waikaremoana, ☎ (06) 837 3737. They run several guided trips around the lake and are flexible towards any trip plans you may have. The lake is huge and destination points many, so the choices are unlimited. Get hold of Parkmap 273 Urewera and start planning.

Te Mata Peak

During the summer, paragliding courses and one-off tandem jumps are run at Te Mata Peak (The Sleeping Giant), 10 km southeast of Hastings. This peak dominates the Hawke's Bay landscape and a flight from the top is the perfect way to get a feel for the lie of the land. Tandem jumps provide the safest introduction to paragliding and cost $90. Contact Shaun Gilbert, ☎ 025 441 572. If you would rather learn how to control a paraglider yourself then have a go at one of the courses held in the foothills. A 1-day introductory course costs $140 and a four-morning PG1 course, which includes at least one tandem jump off Te Mata Peak, costs $280. Contact flight instructor Tim Whittaker on ☎ 025 480 480.

Maraetotara Dam

This is an excellent place to spend the day undertaking a variety of lunatic activities. Jumping from the weir, or tubing the approach and exit rapids, should fill your adrenalin requirements. The water around the weir is very still and usually free of obstacles (check it anyway, just in case).

Head east out of Havelock North on Te Mata Road, which turns into Waimarama Road at the edge of town. Follow Waimarama Road for 11 km before turning onto Ocean Beach Road. Follow Ocean Beach Road for 2 km and turn left down the Maraetotara Valley. You'll see an old powerhouse and, 2 km beyond that, a carpark from where a small track leads to the dam.

The Cauldrons—Cape Kidnappers

The Maraetotara River has carved a series of deep bowls in soft mudstone, which are great for sliding down. In summer the water is warm and material abounds for the inevitable slime fights. The Maraetotara River flows out to the coast near Cape Kidnappers, 20 km southeast of Napier. The river crosses the road to Cape Kidnappers 300 metres past Te Awanga township. Park 800 metres past the river, next to a gravel road on the right. Wear old togs and walk 4 km up the river from the road to this natural playground. This is private property, so ask the Neilson family of Summerlea Station in Clifton for permission; ☎ (06) 875 0350.

9. Taranaki & Tongariro

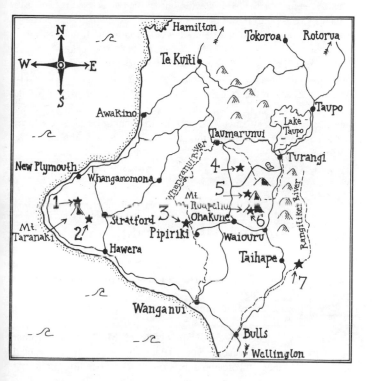

Volcanic Update

Since September 1995 Mt Ruapehu, one of the two active volcanoes in Tongariro National Park, has experienced an increase in activity. Towering clouds of ash and steam, the odd lahar (mud flow) as well as the chance of a rock landing on your head has resulted in the Department of Conservation occasionally restricting access to within 1 or 2 km from the summit. Generally, this sporadic activity is unlikely to affect access to the remaining 99% of the park although ash falls may have an effect on the quality of the drinking water in hut water tanks and streams at times. The activity may continue for some time, but is unlikely to pose major threat to life in or around the Park. For up-to-date information contact the Department of Conservation in Turangi ☎ (07) 386 8607 or at their Internet site on the World Wide Web: http://www.cybercorp.co.nz.

9.1   Climbing Mt Taranaki

 Egmont National Park, 25 km south of New Plymouth

For experienced climbers, 1 day.

—**Summary**— The huge volcanic cone of Mt Taranaki/Egmont (2518 m) dominates western North Island. In the past it has erupted millions of tonnes of volcanic debris onto the surrounding plains. At present it dramatically influences the weather and is a magnet to trampers, climbers and skiers.

The most popular and shortest route to the summit is from North Egmont road end. In summer Mt Taranaki is usually a straightforward climb, however, it is a serious alpine trip in winter.

—**How to Get There**— Drive 15 km southeast of New Plymouth on Highway 3 before turning off onto Egmont Road. After another 15 km you'll reach the DOC North Egmont Visitor Centre at the end of the road, where you can get a weather forecast and leave your intentions.

—Description— As Mt Taranaki is an extremely exposed peak the summit climb shouldn't be attempted in bad weather or poor visibility. The weather is difficult to predict and changes quickly—always take an ice axe and clothing suitable for bad weather conditions.

From the Camphouse (up the hill from the visitor centre) climb the steep translator road through contorted kamahi and totara forest to Tahurangi Lodge (private).

The summit route continues climbing from the track junction just above the lodge. Wooden staircases stop people trampling on the fragile volcanic slopes. The steps lead onto North Ridge, where you follow the snow poles up to Lizard Ridge (2200 m). From here make your way up the rocky crest following snow poles along the worn track. As you ascend, extraordinary views unfold, providing a welcome distraction from the strenuous climbing.

Outstanding Views from the Summit of Mt Taranaki   (Chris Prudden)

Tongues of snow remaining from winter often extend down from the summit crater. If you haven't got an ice axe and can't avoid these, turn back—they may be easy to kick steps in during the middle of the day, but later on they'll probably freeze into solid icy slopes.

Without an ice axe you'll be unable to stop yourself if you start sliding.

Lizard Ridge eventually leads you to what's known as the Summer Entrance Ledge. Again, watch out for ice, even in mid-summer. Climb through into the flattish crater beneath the summit mound on your right. Cross the permanently snow-filled crater and climb up opposite Sharks Tooth to the summit a short distance away.

Route finding on the descent can be extremely tricky in bad visibility. Always go down the same way you came up.

—**Notes**— *This route description does not apply to the mountain in winter.* When covered in ice and snow, Mt Taranaki is no place for the inexperienced. More people have died on this mountain than on any other in New Zealand—most by sliding to their deaths on icy slopes, or when hit by rock fall.

In summer the heat radiating from the dark scoria rock is intense, so take sunglasses, sunblock and plenty of water. If the winds start to pick up prepare to descend—bad weather is imminent. Take an ice axe and know how to use it.

If you are keen to climb to the summit but don't have the skills to do it independently, hire a guide. For around $220, a mountain guide will lead up to four people to the summit in summer. Contact Mountain Guides Mt Egmont, Chris Prudden, ☎ 025 474 510 or ☎ (06) 758 8261.

Skiing from Mt Taranaki's summit is another challenging adventure, but for expert skiers only. Topomap P20 Egmont or Parkmap 09 Egmont is essential.

9.2   Around Mt Taranaki Tramp

Egmont National Park

For intermediate trampers, 3 or 4 days.

—**Summary**— There are several excellent tramping trips around the volcanic cone of Mt Taranaki. Circumnavigate the mountain on low level tracks through totara and kamahi forests or follow shorter high level ones through 'goblin' forest and alpine vegetation.

—How to Get There— The Plateau road end, above East Egmont (Stratford Mountain House), and Dawson Falls road end can both be reached by turning off Highway 3 at Stratford.

—Description—
There are two ways of doing this tramp: the 3-day high level option from Dawson Falls or the 4-day low level option from East Egmont.

Dawson Falls to Waiaua Gorge Hut; 1 day
The 3-day high level route from Dawson Falls follows the summit track until just after the Kapuni Lodge turn-off, before sidling to the west (past the Lake Dive turn-off) beneath Fanthams Peak and Bob's Knob. It then descends to Waiaua Gorge Hut (16 bunks). This section takes 5-6 hours.

The track can be treacherous when snow-covered, as it passes through a bluffy section. If the weather is bad you can still tramp around the mountain in 3 days by walking for 7-9 hours on the low level track (via Lake Dive).

East Egmont to Waiaua Gorge Hut; 2 days
If you want to do a 4-day trip, or conditions are grim, leave from East Egmont and take the low level track (this spaces the huts out well). From East Egmont tramp via Dawson Falls to Lake Dive Hut (16 bunks) on the first day (4-5 hours).

On the second day, descend 740 metres before sidling up on an endless boggy track to Waiaua Gorge Hut (5-6 hours). There are great views from the hut.

Waiaua Gorge Hut to Holly Hut; 5-6 hours
From here the track sidles around the mountain to Kahui Track on the right, which climbs up to Kahui Hut (6 bunks). It then climbs up to a short section of alpine vegetation before descending to Holly Hut (40 bunks).

To avoid the alpine section, drop down Puniho Track and follow the Stony River Track up to Holly Hut. From the hut it's worth visiting Bell Falls and the sphagnum moss swamp—they are both about an hour away.

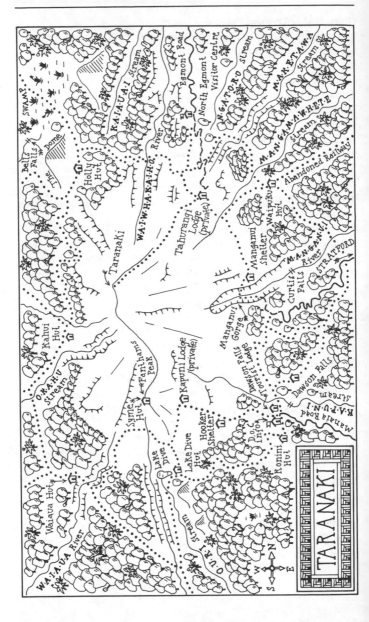

Holly Hut to Dawson Falls; 5-7 hours

From Holly Hut, the Round-the-Mountain track weaves its way upwards, passing a couple of unstable slips before joining the track that climbs up from North Egmont past Dieffenbach Cliffs. After climbing a little further, you meet the Puffer Track junction at Tahurangi Lodge (private). From here you sidle down past Manganui Ski-field (where there is a public shelter) to The Plateau road end. A 1-hour descent through subalpine scrub and goblin forest takes you back to Dawson Falls. You can avoid much of the alpine section on the last day by following either The Puffer or preferably The North Egmont track, down to a lower level track system. These take you to Dawson Falls by way of Maketawa Hut (16 bunks) and Stratford Mountain House.

—Notes— By starting at Dawson Falls you can check the weather forecast and leave your intentions at the DOC visitor centre. The high level track sections are very exposed to bad weather and can be treacherous in snowy conditions. Take a stove as firewood is scarce. Mangahume Hut, marked on some maps under the west side of Fanthams Peak, has been removed.

This trip can be done from the North Egmont road end, which also has a DOC visitor centre. Cars often get broken into at The Plateau road end. Topomap P20 Egmont or Parkmap 09 Egmont National Park is essential.

9.3 Whanganui River Canoeing

Whanganui National Park

For beginner paddlers (guide optional), 4 days.

—Summary— This is one of New Zealand's best Canadian canoeing trips, through an area rich in Maori and European history. There are many unforgettable sights and sounds on this old river route from the central North Island to the coast.

The Whanganui is a large river with dozens of grade I to II rapids, carving its way through rugged bushclad hill country.

Tramping Around Mt Taranaki   (New Zealand Nature Safaris)

Athough it's a canoeing trip, DOC promotes it as one of the 'Great Walks' (see 'Submarine Walking', at the end of this chapter). The increasing involvement of local Maori in the management of this National Park makes the trip even more culturally and historically interesting.

—How to Get There— The trip begins at either Taumarunui or Whakahoro. Taumarunui is 65 km west of Turangi via Highway 41; Whakahoro is 43 km west of Owhango, which is on Highway 4. The trip finishes at Pipiriki, 27 km west of Raetihi (and 80 km up river from Wanganui).

—Description— Absolute beginners should start this trip from Whakahoro to avoid the longest and most difficult day on the river. The trip timetable we suggest here can easily be modified as there are two or three designated camp sites scattered between each of the huts. There are 197 rapids from Taumarunui to Pipiriki.

Taumarunui to Whakahoro
From Cherry Grove in Taumarunui your first day is spent learning how to paddle, finding out you can't have two captains in one boat and exploring a river that once had 30,000 people living on its banks. Shooting the grade I rapids is straightforward but watch out for the occasional log jam.

At Whakahoro there is a 20 bunk hut and camp site. It is a good place to stay for the first night. Tie your boats well clear of the river, as it can rise extremely quickly.

Whakahoro to John Coull Hut
On the second day, to John Coull Hut (24 bunks) at Puketapu Landing, the river valley closes in, with 50 metre mudstone cliffs rising straight from the water. Be ready to stop at the Kirikiriroa Lookout and Tamatea Cave on the way.

John Coull Hut to Tieke Hut
On your third day you'll paddle past Mangapurua Landing. You can land here and follow the well-marked track for 40 minutes to the Bridge to Nowhere. This impressive concrete bridge, 44 metres above the Mangapurua Stream, was built back in the depression days (the 1930s not the 1980s). The settlers were no match for the harsh climate

and tough terrain, and the settlement was abandoned in the 1940s. Continue paddling to Tieke Hut (20 bunks), 11 km down river from Mangapurua Landing.

Tieke Hut to Pipiriki
On the last day you'll pass through a steep gorge before reaching a couple of fun rapids. The trip ends about an hour beyond the gorge at the small village of Pipiriki.

—Notes— Information on transport services, canoe rental, commercial operators, and the park itself can be obtained from DOC, who have offices in Wanganui, ☎ (06) 345 2402; Taumarunui, ☎ (07) 895 8201; and Pipiriki, ☎ (06) 385 4631. Prices vary, as does the quality of the boats hired, but a single kayak is $20-$30 per day and a two-person Canadian canoe is about $35 per day. You'll also need a 'hut and campsite pass' which is $25 if bought before starting your trip and $35 if bought on the river.

Do not drink the river water because it is polluted by Taumarunui's sewage. The huts and campsites have water supply and toilets. For more information get hold of the NZ Canoe Association's *Guide to the Whanganui River* (see Further Reading) and/or the DOC brochure on the Whanganui Journey. Also take map NZMS 258 Whanganui River.

The conservation future of this region looks good. A large part of the Whanganui River catchment became a National Park in 1986. Added to this, Electricorp then lost a ten year legal battle; as a result they are not allowed to draw as much water for hydro-electricity production. Recreational kayakers first raised the debate in the early 1980s. Now future generations will be able to enjoy this restored landscape.

9.4 Tongariro Forest Crossing (42 Traverse)

Tongariro Forest, 20 km northwest of Mt Ruapehu

For intermediate riders, 3-6 hours; 40 km.

—Summary— This is one of the best mountain bike adventures on the North Island. From the main highway beside Mt Ruapehu you ride on old disused logging roads through Tongariro Forest to Owhango, 40 km away. The trip involves brilliant biking and an overall descent of 570 metres.

—How to Get There— From National Park township, drive northeast on Highway 47. After 16 km you'll reach Kapoors Road (signposted) on your left. It's too rough for most cars but a good downhill on your bike, so park here and start pedalling.

—Description— After riding down Kapoors Road for 7 km, you'll reach a turn-off on your right. Head north on this 4WD track and follow the main ridge past high points 831 and 793 (marked on the map). It's an undulating track with two or three major turn-offs, so have the map handy.

From point 793 there is an absolutely superb downhill all the way to Waione Stream. The bush encroaching on the track has been slashed, leaving some wicked spears just waiting to skewer a speeding biker. Safety glasses are a good idea; they also keep mud out of your eyes.

When you reach Waione Stream, turn right and follow the track downstream for a few hundred metres. The track then hangs another sharp right and climbs steeply away from the river for 100 metres before turning left and sidling downstream again, at a higher elevation. Before long you'll hit the main ford across the Waione Stream. Just stick to the main 4WD track from here on and you shouldn't go wrong.

The way to Owhango is via Te Kaha and the marked pumice quarry. It's nice to finish on a downhill, so arrange to be picked up at the Whakapapa River bridge. There's a picnic area, swimming hole and walking track at the bridge, and a camping ground just up the road.

—Track Conditions— 35% gravel road, 65% 4WD track.

—Notes— Although the track is 99% rideable, the area is isolated and the long descents make crashing fairly likely. Take extra clothes, food and first aid, and make sure someone responsible knows what you're up to. The ride can be done as a round trip: it's 30 km (1-2 hours) from

Owhango back to Kapoors Road via National Park township. Bikes can be hired from Turangi Leisure Rentals, ☎ (07) 386 8658 for $35 per day. DOC signposted this trip in 1994 but the *Tongariro Forest Adventure Map* and a compass are still recommended for navigation.

9.5   Around Ngauruhoe

 Tongariro National Park

For beginner/intermediate trampers, 2-4 days.

—Summary— This tramp passes through the unique and varied landscape of Tongariro National Park. Relatively young volcanoes have formed fascinating craters, cliffs, lakes, and rock formations, making this the North Island's most popular tramping area. There are numerous interesting sidetrips along the way. This is one of the Great Walks promoted by the Department of Conservation. In the peak period of summer (January/February) nearly 12,000 people use this track system, so either plan to miss this period or enjoy the company.

—How to Get There— This return trip leaves from The Chateau in Whakapapa Village, on the northwest side of Mt Ruapehu.

—Description—
The Chateau to Mangatepopo Hut; 2-3 hours.
From the Chateau, follow the Mangatepopo Track northeast for about $2^1/_2$ hours to Mangatepopo Hut (24 bunks). The hut is 15 minutes from the Mangatepopo road end.

In this area there is an ecological struggle occurring between the introduced heather and many of the native alpine plants.

Mangatepopo Hut to South Crater; about 2 hours.
From Mangatepopo Hut, the track follows the Mangatepopo Stream to the head of the valley, where it climbs steeply for 300 metres to South Crater. This incredibly flat volcanic moonscape lies between Mt Tongariro and Mt Ngauruhoe.

If you have time you can either ascend the scree slopes to the steaming crater of Mt Ngauruhoe (from South Crater, 4 hours), or climb the poled route up Mt Tongariro (from Red Crater, 2 hours). On a clear day you'll get great views from the top of these active volcanoes. Take some food, water and wind-proof clothes, as the weather can change rapidly.

Tongariro National Park in Winter
(Malcolm O'Neill)

South Crater to Oturere Hut; 2-3 hours.

On the way to Oturere Hut visit the Emerald Lakes, which stand out in striking contrast to the scarlet volcanic landscape. (This is where the track to Blue Lake and Ketetahi Hot Springs branches off—see Tongariro Crossing, section 9.8 of this chapter.)

The track descends through contorted lava formations and crosses a volcanic desert on the way to Oturere Hut (24 bunks). The rocks in this area are great for scrambly bouldering.

Oturere Hut to New Waihohonu Hut; 2-3 hours.

From Oturere Hut it's a pleasant stroll over rolling country and through beech forest to New Waihohonu Hut (22 bunks). This hut is $1^1/_2$ hours' walk from the Desert Road (Highway 1).

New Waihohonu Hut to Whakapapa; 5-6 hours.

From New Waihohonu Hut there is a gentle 3 hour walk up to Tama Saddle between Mt Ruapehu and Mt Ngauruhoe. On hot days you can cool off in the clear waters of the Lower Tama Lake. If you have time, the Upper Lake is also well worth a look. Its steep sides and depth are an indication of the volcanic powers that created this landscape. From the saddle continue west to Taranaki Falls, which tumble 25 metres into a deep pool. It's easy to climb in behind the falls and get an inside-out view. From here take the lower track back to Whakapapa Village.

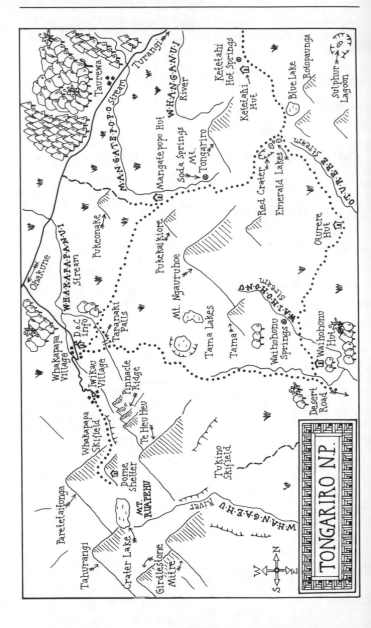

—Notes— In the summer holidays, Tongariro National Park is a nightmare for people wanting peace and quiet. Mangatepopo and Ketetahi road ends are notorious for car theft. The area is hot and dry during summer—carry plenty of water. In winter this trip should only be attempted by experienced alpine trampers, as the area is covered in snow and is subject to extremely bad weather. Parkmap 04 Tongariro National Park is essential.

9.6   Skwalking on Mt Ruapehu

Tongariro National Park

For intermediate skiers with alpine experience.

—Summary— Skwalking is a combination of skiing and walking. Only a few minutes from the edge of many skifields you'll find a wild alpine environment. Wander even further up these slopes and you're likely to enjoy an excellent off-piste (off the skifield) ski run back down. During good snow and weather conditions you will probably see tracks left by other sensible people who are escaping the clutter and aggravation that a skifield creates.

—How to Get There— From National Park township head east on Highway 47 for 11 km before turning right onto Highway 48. Drive to Iwikau Village (Whakapapa Skifield) at the road end.

—Description— The traditional route to the Crater Lake of Mt Ruapehu starts from the top of the Knoll Ridge T-bar on Whakapapa Skifield. There is a new T-bar that goes higher on the west of the field, but none of us have skwalked from there because in the past it's been buried in too much snow to operate. Have a chat to the skifield staff at the top of the lift; they will have a good idea about what sort of snow conditions you can expect. Take some food, drink and windproof clothes. The weather on Mt Ruapehu can change suddenly, making things cold and confusing.

Leave the top of the Knoll Ridge T-bar (2230 m) and continue up the valley on foot. Once the banging lifts, hissing pulley wheels and babbling people are left behind, only your breathing and the crunching of boots in the snow will break the silence. By 2500 metres, the valley becomes little more than a small depression on a broad steep slope. Trundle up this slope and climb onto the foot of a small ridge to the right of The Notch (to the right of high point 2642). Head south along this ridge and either pop over Dome (2672 m) to Dome Shelter, or skirt around it to the right and ski down via The Col into the crater. The steaming Crater Lake is an extraordinary sight.

Don't wait too late in the day before returning. If it has been warm, a wickedly hard crust will form on the snow as it freezes in the late afternoon, making skiing down virtually impossible. It's always a good idea to take an ice axe and crampons.

The ridges radiating down from Mt Ruapehu are very similar, which can make route finding tricky on the way down. Make sure you return by the same route you came up.

—**Notes**— If the weather packs in, turn back following your tracks. This is no place to be when you can't see what you're doing. Find out about the avalanche conditions from the ski patrol before heading up. Some maps show Dome Shelter as being next to The Notch—this is incorrect, it is just below the top of Dome on the southern side. Ski gear can be hired from the Powder Horn Ski Shop in Ohakune, ☎ (06) 385 8888. Take a compass and know what to do with it. Parkmap 04 Tongariro National Park (with its excellent large scale map) is essential.

9.7   Rangitikei River Rafting

Rangitikei River, east of Taihape

For all adventurers (guided), 1 day.

—**Summary**— The beautiful and remote Rangitikei River has a sustained section of grade V water making this the most exciting rafting trip in the lower North Island.

—How to Get There— Contact either Rangitikei River Adventures in Mangaweka (at the DC3 aeroplane), ☎ (06) 382 5747.

—Description— After entering the river, serious rafting begins almost immediately. There are a few grade III to IV rapids that provide good practise for the even more turbulent water ahead.

At one place the river flows slowly for over 100 metres through The Narrows, a deep 4-metre wide slot. It's amazing to see how the river has cut and shaped different forms. This is the last chance to relax before you reach The Gates rapid, soon followed by Max's Drop—a raft-eating waterfall. In quick succession Fulcrum, Foaming Rapid (a raft wrapper) and See Thru are run, requiring spot-on navigation and powerful ferry gliding. Eventually the river opens out and there are plenty of chances to storm other rafts and jump off cliffs.

—Notes— The trip costs $95, including wetsuits, food and transport.

9.8 Other Adventures

The Whangamomona Loop

Here's a fantastic 52 km day trip suitable for intermediate and experienced riders. From Whangamomona Township (60 km east of Mt Taranaki), cycle down Whangamomona Road (now mostly 4WD track) to the 'Bridge to Somewhere', about 20 km away. This road was built in the 1920s to allow returned servicemen to settle the land. After battling for 10 years the government gave up fixing the road and the settlers walked off the land.

Ride over the bridge to Aotuhia Station, passing the farmhouse and the barking dogs. Just before the second farm gate turn left over the grass and ford Kuri Stream twice before picking up the remains of Okara Road. This is tricky to navigate, so double check with your Topomaps and compass (especially if you start following a single track for more than 50 metres).

After a few kilometres the 4WD track improves and farmland starts to replace native bush. Follow your nose out to Highway 43, via Canoe Flat and Tangarakau River. At the Highway turn left and ride 7 km back to Whangamomona.

—**Notes**— You must contact Patrick at Aotuhia Station, ☎ (06) 762 5868, and Rob at Okara Station, ☎ (06) 762 3892 for permission to ride through their farms.

Remember to leave gates as you find them. The Whangamomona camping ground is $5 per night. Take a compass and Topomaps R19 Whangamomona and R20 Matemateaonga.

 ## Huka Falls Run

This popular track follows the Waikato River from Taupo to the spectacular Huka Falls, roughly an hour away depending whether you're running or walking. Jog out of Taupo township on Spa Road and turn left at County Ave. At the end of the avenue go across the grass to the river where a narrow track leads downstream to Huka Falls. After visiting the falls you can either continue to Aratiatia Dam or return the same way.

 ## Lake Taupo Kayaking

Taupo Micro Adventures run several trips on and around this huge volcanic lake. From a 3-hour trip to the nearby Maori rock carvings right through to a week-long exploration around the lake's coast, Taupo Micro Adventures have the experience and local knowledge necessary for a safe yet unforgettable journey. They also offer unusual trips into the seldom visited Pureora Forest Park. For more information contact them in Taupo, ☎ (07) 378 3413.

  ## Craters of the Moon

This thermally active area is covered with a maze of tracks that are fun to explore by bike or on foot. Most of the steam and mud holes are concentrated in one spot and there is little danger of running into them. Be careful though because if you did the results would be horrific. Vehicle theft and vandalism at road ends in this region are chronic so you may want to leave your car in town. Bikes can be hired from Rapid Sensations, ☎ (07) 378 7902 or 025 928 366 or 0800-22-RAFT.

Head north from Taupo township on Highway 1 for almost 5 km before turning left onto Karapiti Road. From here just head in and explore—the area is not large, so you won't get lost for long. Riding on the farmland next to the forest is allowed if you leave the gates as you find them and don't chase the stock. It takes 1-4 hours to become familiar with the area.

The Waikato River Rapids

Both of the following areas are excellent spots for paddling. The Reids Farm Reserve in Wairaki Park is signposted 4 km from Taupo on the true left of the Waikato River. There is good camping beside the river. A slalom course has been set up in this Grade I water, which provides beginners with perfect training opportunities. *Warning:* Huka Falls (grade VI) is only 1 km down river. *Do not* attempt these falls.

The Ngaawaparua Rapids (Fulljames, grade III) is the North Island's most popular kayaking play spot. Turn off the Taupo-Rotorua Road 12 km north of Taupo. Follow the signs for 5 km to the National Equestrian Centre. After 100 metres turn into Aratiatia Rapids Scenic Reserve, drive 4$^{1}/_{2}$ km and park next to the toilet.

When water is released at variable times daily from the Aratiatia Dam 6 km upriver, the rapid is one large standing wave that can be kayaked, surfed, tubed, or swum. There is a slow deep pool at the bottom in which to recover; the recirculating eddy makes multiple runs a breeze. The land you cross to reach the Ngaawaparua Reserve is privately owned so please treat the area with respect. The rapids are marked on Topomap V17 Wairakei, as Fulljames.

Volcanic Rock Climbing

Whanganui Bay provides the best rock climbing in the North Island. Set in beautiful surroundings on the western shores of Lake Taupo, it has huge cliffs of volcanic rock with many classic climbs. Access is not easy and the best way to get there is to go with a club. Determined individuals should look for a copy of *Whanganui Bay Rock* (see Further Reading)—it's out of print now so try the library. Also, the crag is on Maori land. You will be asked for about $10 per day as Koha (a small gift) for climbing there. For information on many other crags in the area, read Pete Manning's *Central North Island Rock* (see Further Reading).

Okupata Caves

These caves make an excellent trip for those who enjoy dark dank places full of insects with two-inch long legs and bodies that look like something out of 'Aliens'.

Travel 14 km east from National Park township on Highway 47 until you see John McDonald Road on your left. Follow the signposted rough gravel road for 11 km to the cave carpark. The cave system is perfect for the beginning explorer. Incredible constellations are created within the cave by glow worms and the rock formations suggest giants have been at play with their building blocks.

Make sure you remember the route you took into the cave and take a reliable torch (helmets are recommended). For those who want to practice caving without a torch, put masking tape over your eyes, spin around several times and carry on as normal. For more information phone DOC on ☎ (07) 386 8607.

Tongariro Crossing

This is the most popular 'Great Walk' in the North Island. Taking only 1 or 2 days, you cross an amazing volcanic landscape, climb to 2000 m, and pass the Ketetahi natural hot springs.

From Mangatepopo road end follow the track past Mangatepopo Hut (24 bunks) and up the valley to the South Crater (2 hours). For details on climbing Mt Ngauruhoe, read section 9.5 (Around Mt Ngauruhoe). Otherwise follow the track across the crater and on to the photogenic Emerald Lakes, 2 hours away. This is a good area for a long lunch break. From the lakes continue to Ketetahi Hut (1 hour) and the nearby hot springs for a long soak. The road end is only another 2 hours down hill.

Go well prepared. Extreme weather can occur at any time of year. In winter, alpine skills, crampons and an ice axe are needed. Take plenty of water. Mangatepopo and Ketetahi huts are often overcrowded in the summer. Do not leave any valuables in your car at the road ends around this area—theft and vandalism are common. Alpine Scenic Tours, ☎ (07) 386 8918, can drive you into both road ends. Parkmap 04 Tongariro National Park is an excellent and essential source of information.

Whakapapa River Rafting

Plateau Guides run a couple of excellent trips on the Whakapapa River and its tributaries. One of them runs down the Whakapapanui River, northeast of Mt Ruapehu. As the captain of your own two-person raft, you're bound to learn a lot from the interesting mishaps you have along the way. Starting below the Matariki Falls, you run grade II to III rapids for $2^1/_2$ hours to the Whakapapa Intake where the river is run dry by diversion into the Waikato catchment for electricity generation. The environmental costs associated with this intake may cause you to think twice every time you switch on a light.

The other rafting trip is a run on the Whakapapa River between the Whakapapa Intake and Ohinitonga Bridge. It takes in numerous grade III to IV rapids amongst stunning scenery. For 5 hours you are at the mercy of the water god Electricorp, because the flow level needs to be high to raft this section. In low flows this section can only be run by experienced rafters in small two-person rafts.

Trips cost $75 and include transport from Raurimu (7 km north of National Park on Highway 4). Contact Plateau Guides, ☎ (07) 892 2740.

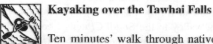 **Kayaking over the Tawhai Falls**

Ten minutes' walk through native bush from Highway 48 (the Whakapapa road) takes you to Tawhai Falls on the Whakapapanui Stream. This 6-metre drop is safe (at the right flows) and no paddling experience is needed to kayak over it. After a short training session in an inflatable kayak you're ready to head for the edge.

Most people who brace correctly when they hit the water at the bottom stay upright. Those who tip out are helped to the bank by a guide. Contact Plateau Guides in Raurimu, ☎ (07) 892 2740. They charge $50 per person for two plunges.

 Tongariro Bike 'n' Raft

This unique adventure combination has all the elements of a true classic; great scenery, exploration, adrenalin, and physical effort followed by relaxation. The trip starts with an excellent mountain ride through lovely beech forest all the way to the rafts on the banks of the Tongariro River.

The river is a fun grade III+ and again the scenery is superb. On the way you'll stop for lunch and explore the hidden Puketarata Falls and at the end of the trip you can enjoy a long soak in one of the local hot pools.

If this sounds like your idea of fun then contact Rock'n'River Adventures in Tokaanu, ☎ (07) 386 0352 or ☎ 025 721 640. This trip costs $110 per person and they supply all the rafting and biking equipment needed.

Other companies also run a variety of trips on the Tongariro River and can be contacted through the Turangi Information Centre, ☎ (07) 386 8999. For example, Tongariro River Rafting, ☎ (07) 386 6409, are willing to cater for any white water fantasy you may have. Prices are dependent on trip requirements.

Bungy Jump

Leaping off an excessively high place with a stout rubber band tied to your feet almost passes as a normal activity these days. Reaching terminal velocity as you hurtle towards the river far below is an unforgettable death-cheating mega buzz.

The central volcanic plateau has a few bungy sites that are just as thrilling as the more famous southern ones. One of the less touristy ones has its base beneath Mangaweka's DC3 aeroplane, 54 km south of Waiouru on Highway 1. They do a 43-metre jump over the Rangitikei River. Sometimes things are a bit quiet around here so give them a ring first to check they are there. If there are four or more people, they will set up the bungy specially for you.

Contact Rangitikei River Adventures, ☎ (06) 382 5747 or, after hours, ☎ (06) 322 8362. The cost is $90 and includes a T-shirt. Taupo, 2 hours drive north, has a 45-metre bungy—contact Taupo Bungy, ☎ (07) 377 1135.

Submarine Walking

Step one: find a medium to large sized, slow-flowing, preferably warm river.

Step two: invent a reason to need to cross it.

Step three: select an aesthetically pleasing rock about one quarter of your (desired!) body weight. Place your mask and snorkel in the usual places.

Step four: carry the rock into the river. Initially it requires a reasonable amount of strength to carry the boulder, but once you're in the river it's all up to balance.

Although we have yet to try it, we believe it would be an interesting way to do the Department of Conservation's Whanganui River 'Great Walk' (see section 9.3). Wear steel capped boots and watch out for jet boats.

10. Wellington

10.1 Otaki River Canoeing

 Otaki Forks, 80 km north of Wellington

For beginner/intermediate paddlers (guide optional), 2-4 hours on the river.

—**Summary**— The easily accessible and scenic Otaki River is a great paddle, in normal flows, for grade II kayakers. There are plenty of playful rapids that spill into deep swimming holes. None of them are too gnarly and they can all be portaged if need be.

—**How to Get There**— Turn southeast off Highway 1, 2 km south of Otaki. Follow the signposted road for 16 km to Otaki Forks, where there is a car park, camping area and DOC caretaker.

—**Description**— In the middle of the Waiotauru River, opposite the car park, there is a large rock. If water is flowing over or near the top of it then the section of river upstream has enough water to be runnable. To paddle the upper section drive another 2 km to the road end, where there is a car park on a large river terrace above the Waiotauru River. Get in here and ferry glide across to the true right. Paddle a few hundred metres upstream to the first major bend where there is a good rapid. Between here, and the footbridge beside the main car park, there are some excellent rapids bordering on grade III. The river then becomes very rocky until it joins the Otaki River. In low flows it is best to portage parts of this section.

The usual put-in site for the Otaki River is at a signposted canoe track on the true left of Roaring Meg Stream (800 metres downstream from the main car park). If you are new to kayaking then launch from here. After a kilometre or so of rolling rapids and calm stretches, the river narrows and turns sharply to the left as it hits a bluff on the right. This is known as Pinnacle Rapid and paddlers should be careful to avoid the rock in midstream (keep hard left). This is a popular paddlers' playground.

The first take-out point is a further kilometre down on the true left beneath the footbridge. A steep 4WD track leads up to the road. Downstream from the footbridge, the river becomes more gentle as it flows through the lower gorge. It takes a further hour or so to reach a vehicle bridge, which is the lower take-out point (on the true left). About halfway down the lower gorge there is a track on the true left, which can also be used as a take-out point.

—**Notes**— The Otaki River can be paddled year-round although it's a bit rocky in low flows. The Tararua Outdoor Centre, ☎ (06) 364 3110, is passed on the drive in to Otaki Forks. They run guided trips and hire out kayaks, rafts and equipment and run a drop-off and pick-up service. Their hire rates are about the lowest in the country and are listed in their pamphlet available from the Wellington Information Centre. Topomap S26 Carterton is useful.

10.2   Tubing the Upper Otaki

Tararua Forest Park, 30 km south of Levin

For experienced tubers, 2-3 days.

—**Summary**— This trip involves a half-day tramp into the Tararua Ranges to reach the launch site, followed by 10-14 hours of remote tubing. The Upper Otaki is generally a beautifully calm river interspersed with easy rapids every few hundred metres. The exception to this is the gnarly gorge section about a third of the way down. Steep rocky sides enclose you in this fast narrow section with tight turns, log jams and two waterfalls—the larger of which is portaged by most sensible tubers.

—**How to Get There**— Turn southeast off Highway 1, a couple of kilometres south of Otaki. Follow the signposted road for 16 km to Otaki Forks. There is a car park, camping area, DOC caretaker, and, on the other side of the river, a hut to stay in.

—**Description**—
Otaki Forks to Bivvy Camp; 10-12 hours
From Otaki Forks cross the suspension bridge over the Waiotauru River and take the signposted track, initially across farmland, to

Waitewaewae Hut (30 bunks). The track takes you to another swingbridge, which crosses the Otaki River then sidles up an old bush tramway beside Waitatapia Stream to Plateau. After a flat section of bush, the track leads down to an intersection in Arapito Creek. Branching off to the left there is an all weather track to the new Waitewaewae Hut; stay in or beside Arapito Creek and within ten minutes you'll reach a perfect raft construction and launching area on the banks of the Otaki River. If you haven't got at least six hours of daylight left then stay the night at Waitewaewae Hut, 500 metres upriver, rather than risk being benighted in the gorge.

After constructing a suitable craft, don your wetsuit and helmet and launch away. After a couple of hours, begin asking yourselves the following questions:

Has a sudden eclipse-like atmosphere befallen the river? Can a powerful rumbling be heard in the not so distant distance? Indeed, has the river become...a GORGE?!

If so, tighten your helmets and life jackets, group closely together, and position your paddles for action. As soon as the river twists to the right, jump to the left and scramble up the rock to safety. But if you don't move fast enough and your worst fears are realized, whatever you do, don't let go of your raft.

The froth immediately below the waterfall will rob you of your buoyancy and power of projection. Be especially wary of log jams and make sure all rapids are safe before entering them. You may wish to portage a few more tricky sections, but they are easy to spot and avoid.

After about another hour, the river will open out and slow down. Halfway down the river, on the true left, at the first large clearing, is a small bivvy hut hidden amongst the toetoe (flax-like shrub). Although it's a derelict scunge hole, there is a good area for camping nearby and it's the first reasonable flat spot after the gorge.

Bivvy Camp to Otaki Forks; 4-8 hours

From here the second day is relatively easy, because it is shorter and calmer. After 4-8 hours exit the river at Otaki Forks, 600 metres downriver from the swing bridge, and walk 300 metres further up the Waiotauru River to the car park. Alternatively, if you have time and can arrange to be picked up further downriver, the tubing for the next several kilometres is easy and enjoyable (see section, 10.1 Otaki River Canoeing). A notable exception about 2 km down from the

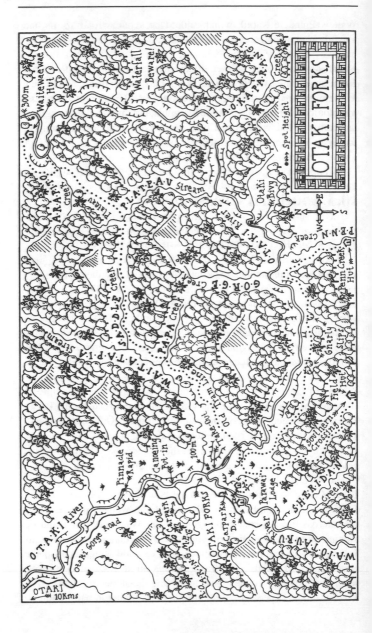

forks is Pinnacle Rapid, which should be scouted for hazards and possibly portaged.

—Notes— A wetsuit, helmet, life jacket, and swimming skills are essential. During winter it is too cold to tube. Tragically, a few drownings have occurred on this river and not all of them in the places you would expect. Portage the risky rapids and always stay in sight of each other. If the river is in flood, don't even think about tubing it. Topomap S26 Carterton is essential.

10.3 Southern Crossing

 Southern Tararuas, 50 km north of Wellington

For intermediate/experienced trampers, 2-3 days.

—Summary— This is a classic Tararua tramp. Four hours' walking takes you from Otaki River up onto the southern Tararua Range. As you climb above the bushline, views open up from Mt Ruapehu in the north to the Kaikoura Mountains in the south. The final section is a long descent along Marchant Ridge to the Kaitoke road end.

—How to Get There— Turn southeast off Highway 1, a couple of kilometres south of Otaki. Follow the signposted road for 16 km to Otaki Forks. There is a car park, camping area, DOC caretaker, and, on the other side of the river, a hut to stay in.

—Description—
Otaki Forks to Field Hut; 2-3 hours
Usually a weekend tramp, the trip starts at Otaki Forks on a Friday evening. After complaining loudly about the weight of your pack, head across the suspension bridge over the Waiotauru River and up the first short hill onto Plateau Paddock. Walk diagonally across this flat, following marker poles to the foot of Judd Ridge and up the Fields Track 'footpath'. The track zigzags up at first and then levels out before entering the bush and following the ridge up to Field Hut. The hut holds 25 people and quadruple that number in bad weather.

Field Hut to Alpha Hut; 5-7 hours

The next day climb steeply up to Table Top, where you enter a boggy section of alpine tussock. A gentle climb up Dennan and over the barren, wind-blasted Hut Mound takes you to the fridge-like Kime Hut (25 bunks, 2-3 hours from Field Hut). If the weather is fine, it's worth walking the extra hour to have your lunch on Mt Hector, which is marked with a war memorial cross.

From there you'll see Wellington to the south and the plains of the Wairarapa to the east. If the weather is bad you'll be lucky to see the tips of your fingers.

Walking from Mt Hector to Alpha Hut takes 2-3 hours along the main range of the Tararuas. After crossing the Beehives traverse the Dress Circle around to Mt Alpha, and drop steeply to Alpha Hut (14 bunks).

Navigation along the Dress Circle is difficult in bad weather—be careful not to go down the wrong ridge.

Alpha Hut to Kaitoke road end; 6-9 hours

The next day, climb gently from Alpha Hut for half an hour before descending straight to Hells Gate saddle between the Tauherenikau and Hutt River catchments. Marchant Ridge runs south from Omega on the other side of Hells Gate. The Devil tendered successfully to build this ridge—it is long and tiring.

Soon after reaching The Burn, an area of forest that was accidentally burnt down in 1938, you re-enter the bush and sidle down to the dilapidated Dobsons Hut.

From Dobsons Hut (5-7 hours from Alpha Hut) the track gradually turns into a two-lane highway where regenerating bush competes with gorse. About an hour later you'll reach the Kaitoke road end car park. Highway 2 is only 3 km away and the hitch-hiking from there into Wellington is usually quite good.

—Notes— This trip can be done in both directions. There is no water on Marchant Ridge. Snow can fall at any time of the year and visibility can often be reduced to a few metres, making compass navigation skills essential. In winter the tops are covered in snow and ice, making this a serious alpine trip. This route is often done by local tramping clubs who welcome visitors. Topomap S26 Carterton is essential.

The fine line between fun and hysteria on the Kaituna River

Adventure Photography

Descending the anchor line, Bay of Islands

Mike White, Inset: Akira Yamada

Cross country skiing on the Pisa Range

From the summit of Mt Cook

Meeting the locals, Abel Tasman National Park

The golden beaches of Abel Tasman National Park

Riding into Skippers Canyon on the old pack track

Mount Ruapehu, Tongariro National Park

A telemark descent of Mt Taranaki

A quick descent of the Wairoa River

Mist Rolling over the Tararua Ranges   (Allan Corry)

10.4 Waiohine Gorge

 Tararua Forest Park, 20 km west of Masterton

For experienced trampers and tubers, 2-3 days.

—Summary— The Waiohine is one of the most scenic rivers in the North Island. It is also the longest, most isolated river in the Tararua Ranges and contains a difficult gorge section that offers challenging tubing for the experienced.

—How to Get There— Turn west off Highway 2, onto Norfolk Road, 4 km south of Masterton. At the end of this road, 16 km away, is the Holdsworth car park where there is a DOC caretaker, public telephone, camping ground, and a lodge available for public use.

—Description—
Holdsworth road end to Mid Waiohine Hut; 5-7 hours
Access to the Waiohine Gorge from Holdsworth road end involves climbing Mt Holdsworth (1470 m) then heading west over Isabelle before dropping steeply to Mid Waiohine Hut (6 bunks). There are two huts on the way up Holdsworth: Mountain House (20 bunks) about halfway and Powell Hut (24 bunks) on the bushline. It takes most parties another 3 hours to climb over Mt Holdsworth and descend to Mid Waiohine Hut.

Mid Waiohine Hut to Totara Flats; 6-9 hours
The gorge itself starts a kilometre downstream from the hut, past the swing bridge. In places it becomes quite narrow and dark, and has an eerie feel about it. There are usually some good chutes, although it varies depending on the river level. At least four of them need to be carefully scouted before deciding whether to tube or portage them. Always err on the side of caution.

A couple of hours further on, the 'bad gorge' (as described on older maps) begins. In one particularly impressive section, two large trees on either side meet 30 metres above. Other sections are not so narrow and involve picking your way amongst gnarly rock gardens.

After 4-6 hours you'll reach the Neil Creek confluence, which is known as Hector Forks. Continue floating down the gorge, over the occasional tight drop, passing some large erosion slips on the way. After 2-3 hours of sometimes 'bony' tubing you'll reach Totara Flats, which is just around the corner from a large swing bridge.

Totara Flats was farmed early this century. There are three huts in the vicinity: the old and new Totara Flats huts on the true right and Sayers Hut on the opposite bank.

Totara Flats to Holdsworth road end; 3 hours
The walk from the flats back to Holdsworth road end via Totara Creek takes about 3 hours. Alternatively you can continue tubing down to Walls Whare road end about 4 hours away (see section 10.8, Lower Waiohine Gorge).

—Notes— Attempting this trip in high flows would be very dangerous. The only shelter between the Mid Waiohine Hut and Totara Flats is Neil Forks Hut, about 2 hours' tramp up the creek from

Hector Forks. Log jams are a danger in this river. Holdsworth road end has a resident DOC ranger. Topomap S26 Carterton is essential.

10.5 Hutt Gorge

 Kaitoke Regional Park, 15 km north of Upper Hutt

For experienced tubers (guide optional), 4-8 hours.

—Summary— The Hutt Gorge provides the best tubing (grade II to III) close to Wellington. However, it is potentially dangerous and has seen numerous accidents in the past. For the experienced it is a classic day trip, passing through some beautiful native forest.

—How to Get There— From Upper Hutt head 15 km north along Highway 2. Turn left into Kaitoke Waterworks Road and after 1 km turn right over a bridge. After a couple more kilometres turn left to reach Pakuratahi Forks car park 100 metres away.

—Description— The main dangers in the gorge are submerged log jams, which can easily snag and trap the unwary. These hazards change from flood to flood.

Start tubing at the Pakuratahi Forks car park. The first 1 km section to a large concrete bridge (known as the 'bridge of no return') provides a good warm-up. From here down there is only one other recognised exit point and you are pretty much committed to going the whole way. The other exit point is via the spur on the true left opposite Putaputa Stream and is often used by Search and Rescue. It leads up to a track on a ridge to the southeast, which runs from the put-in to the take-out sites. The most potentially dangerous rapids start soon after the 'bridge of no return' and end about 5 minutes past Putaputa Stream. These must be scouted to check for hazards before entering them. The gorge between Putaputa Stream and Kororipo Stream (2/3 the way down) contains the hardest rapids of up to grade III+. Their names—Corkscrew, Pinball, Rocky Horror Picture Show—say it all. Not all of these can be portaged in higher flows.

Tubing in the Tararua Ranges   (Hugh Barr)

Near the end of this section, the water becomes deep and slow moving. Above, there are some high rocks that are excellent for jumping off. It's always a challenge to see if you can land on your tube as it floats by.

As the gorge opens out, the river flows over several small shingle rapids. In low flows this can be a long bumpy haul. The exit point is at the landing on your true left, 200 metres past some power lines.

To reach the take-out point from Upper Hutt, head north on Highway 2 for about 6 km. Turn left about 50 metres past the Te Marua Golf Club, where there is a signposted road to the Te Marua Water Treatment Plant. Continue on 1.5 km of sealed road past a gate (locked between dusk and 8am) to the pump station building. Take the left fork over a small rise to the landing. Most people leave a vehicle here so they can get back to the put-in site. Beside the river bank there is a river gauge, which should always be checked.

—**Notes**— People constantly underestimate the length and difficulty of the Hutt Gorge—leave before 10am. An automatic river level reading can be obtained by ringing ☎ (04) 526 7264, but it is not as accurate as the visual gauge at the take-out point. From 0.6 to 1.0 m is okay for tubers, but anything higher is too dangerous. The gorge becomes runnable for canoeists at 1.0 m with grade III-IV rapids. For more information contact the Regional Park Ranger, ☎ (04) 526 7322. Top Adventures, ☎ (04) 477 1420, raft the gorge every weekend during the winter months. Trips cost $75.

10.6 The Big Coast

Rimutaka Range and Palliser Bay

For beginner riders of medium fitness, 2 days; 110 km.

—**Summary**— This ride is suitable for beginner and expert alike. Fantastic views of the Kaikoura mountains, the Turakirae seal colony and a ride over the Rimutaka Ranges along an old incline railway make this an interesting and varied trip.

—**How to Get There**— Start by catching the commuter train from Wellington to Upper Hutt, and finish with a ferry trip from Days Bay across the harbour to Wellington. Phone the Railways Intercity line, ☎ (04) 472 5409, and the East West Ferry Service, ☎ (04) 499 1273, for their respective timetables.

—**Description**—
Upper Hutt to Mukamuka Stream; 5-7 hours
From the Upper Hutt Railway Station, follow the main road (Highway 2) north for 10 km before turning right onto a gravel road, signposted 'Rimutaka Incline Walk'. A gentle hill climb on a gravel road leads up to the Rimutaka Summit, where you'll find a picnic area and the longest of the four incline tunnels. If you haven't got a torch just concentrate on the speck of light at the end of the tunnel almost 600 metres away.

One km after the tunnel you'll encounter Siberia Gully; it is famous for its gale force winds—last century a ten tonne locomotive was blown off the tracks here! From the other side you can relax and coast down for 5 km to Cross Creek Station, where you cross a footbridge on your right and cycle through manuka forest to a little shelter on the edge of the farmland. From here take the gravel road for 1 km before turning right at a sealed road. This leads you past Lake Wairarapa and Lake Onoke to the coast at Palliser Bay, 35 km away. By this stage the road will have improved to 4WD quality. From here cycle past a group of beaches at Ocean Beach to Mukamuka Stream about an hour away. Between Mukamuka Stream and Mukamukaiti Stream, there are plenty of good camp sites. There is also a derelict shelter at Mukamukaiti Stream.

Mukamukaiti Stream to Days Bay; 5-6 hours
The next day continue to Turakirae Head. The terraced beaches around here were created by a series of earthquakes, lifting land above sea level each time (the lowest beach was lifted in 1855). The seal colony is a few hundred metres from the main track—for a closer look try to pick up one of the smaller tracks that leads down to Turakirae Head.

A few kilometres on you'll cross the Orongorongo River and soon meet up with a sealed road again. It leads past a gravel pit car park beside the Wainuiomata River. Leave the road and drop down beside the gravel pit to cross the river about 100 metres upstream from the lagoon. This is normally a knee-deep crossing. However, should the water reach parts unmentioned, try at the river mouth—it's sometimes blocked off with shingle. Be very cautious about crossing at the river mouth if it isn't blocked off.

On the other side an unrideable sandy 4WD track traverses below the hills and leads to the large rocks at Baring Head that can be seen in the distance. Baring Head is a popular rock climbing area (see section 10.8, Baring Head). Wipe the sand off your feet and have a go.

About 150 metres around from the rocks the 4WD track becomes rideable again and develops into a gravel road as it follows the coast to Eastbourne and Days Bay, 1-2 hours away. Having spent all but your ferry fare (around $7) on takeaways, head down to the Days Bay Wharf for the twenty minute trip to Wellington.

—Track Conditions— 35% tarseal, 25% gravel, 40% 4WD track.

—Notes— Water is scarce on this ride and not drinkable unless boiled or treated. The coastline is very exposed to bad weather so go prepared with suitable clothing. Don't forget to take a repair kit as well. Take Terrainmap 8 Wellington.

10.7 Haurangi Crossing

Southern Wairarapa

For experienced riders, 1-2 days; 104 km loop.

—Summary— Most of this ride involves cycle touring through picturesque Wairarapa countryside. Crossing Haurangi Forest Park, however, provides challenging mountain biking and a 1-hour bike-push up a steep hill. The views and long downhill to the coast make it well worthwhile.

Fit riders may also wish to ride around Cape Palliser, the southern tip of the North Island.

—How to Get There— From Wellington, either drive or take the train to Featherston and then travel southeast along Highway 53 to Martinborough 17 km away. Another alternative is to catch the train to Upper Hutt and cycle via the Rimutaka Incline (see section 10.6, The Big Coast)

—Description— Head southwest from Martinborough on Jellicoe Street. Turn left after 2 km, then right after another 10 km; both intersections are signposted 'Haurangi Forest Park'.

After 17 gravelly kilometres, you'll pass through a gate and climb the last 4 km to the top of the hill where there is a small car parking area and a Haurangi Forest Park boundary sign.

From there, descend on a fast 4WD track to the first of five stream crossings. After 1½ km in the valley, you'll come to a left-hand fork at the base of a humungous hill. A further 200 metres down the valley is Sutherlands Hut (10 bunks), which is the best place to camp overnight.

The next morning starts with the main obstacle of the ride, a steep 500 m climb up to the ridge. It's at least an hour to the top, mostly walking up a steep 4WD track. From the top (just above the large slip), the track follows the ridge west towards the sea. It's mostly downhill for about 9 km before dropping steeply down to Hurupi Stream. It then climbs straight up on the other side to a gate beside a park boundary sign.

From here take the 1 km diversion to the Putangirua Pinnacles and back. These gigantic alluvial towers, some of which are capped with castaway islands of bush, are well worth seeing.

Return to the gate beside the park boundary sign and descend through farmland on the obvious 4WD track to the Palliser Bay coast. From the coast you can ride back to Wellington via The Big Coast ride (see section 10.6) or return to Martinborough on the country back roads.

Alternatively, our pick of the bunch is to head south and ride round Cape Palliser (see section 10.8, Cape Palliser).

—Track Conditions— 60% tarseal, 20% gravel, 20% 4WD track.

—Notes— The trip is best done north to south. There is a pub and motorcamp at Lake Ferry. This is a hunting area so wear all your neon gear. Topomap S28 Palliser or Terrainmap 8 Wellington is essential.

10.8 Other Adventures

 ### Caving Indecision?

Those who enjoy a physical and psychological challenge and don't mind getting wet and muddy should try Indecision (PT17) in the northern Wairarapa. It's a good introduction to the sporty side of caving and involves climbing, abseiling, crawling, wading and even squeezing if you're keen.

All beginners will need a guide and equipment for this 2-day underground exploration that costs $110 per person. Phone Top Adventures, ☎ (04) 477 1420, for more information and bookings.

 ### Northern Crossing

For experienced trampers this Tararua crossing, northwest of Masterton, takes 2-3$\frac{1}{2}$ days. It's a less developed and wilder version of the Southern Crossing. The ability to follow rough tracks and use a map and compass is essential.

If doing this trip in a weekend, start at the end of Upper Waingawa Road (14 km northwest of Masterton) and head into Mitre Flats Hut on Friday night (3 hours). On Saturday, climb up to Mitre and along the tussocky tops to Tarn Ridge Hut. This hut was built in 1994 and has great views of the Waingawa catchment. It is positioned 30-40 minutes walk south of the old hut and is 100 metres off the crest of the ridge. The next day continue north along the ridge, over the rugged Waiohine Pinnacles and Arete, to Te Matawai Hut. Arete Bivvy, 200 metres off the main route, is a small emergency shelter. In fine weather the easiest and most scenic way out from Te Matawai Hut is via South Ohau Stream. If the stream is up, the Gable End track is best. Both routes lead to the Ohau road end, a few kilometres east of Levin. Alpine experience is required in winter, and Topomaps S25 Levin and S26 Carterton are essential.

 ## Karapoti Classic

The Akatarawa Forest is a large hilly area about 10 km northwest of Upper Hutt that has gravel roads and 4WD tracks running through it. It is Wellington's best mountain biking region, and amongst other excellent rides boasts the renowned Karapoti Classic. For an adventure in this forest, buy Topomap R26 Paraparaumu, plan a trip (make sure someone at home knows all about it), and then go for it. For specific information about the Karapoti Classic, refer to *Classic New Zealand Mountain Bike Rides* (see Further Reading).

 ## Lower Waiohine Gorge

The Waiohine River flows out of the Tararua Ranges onto the Wairarapa plains 10 km west of Carterton. To get there drive 4 km north of Greytown on Highway 2 before turning left and following the 'Waiohine Gorge' signposts to the Walls Whare car park at the end of the road. On the way in you will pass the take-out point, which is 3.5 km past the end of the tarseal, where the road drops down to the river level.

Launching from Walls Whare gives you about 5 km of scenic grade I and II tubing or kayaking—the perfect beginner's trip (in normal flow). However, the usual safety precautions should be observed, in particular steer well clear of the big log jam just below the car park.

Another good trip for intermediate tubers is the Waiohine River, from Totara Flats down to Walls Whare. This involves a tramp in, followed by 2-3 hours floating down through a series of grade II rapids. If you require transport, kayaks or guides for this trip contact ORCA in Carterton, Wairarapa, ☎ (06) 379 8692.

Mountain Biking in the Capital

From casual one-hour jaunts to day-long epics (or more), if you've got cycling legs then don't pass through Wellington without finding out why locals claim it's the 'mountain biking capital of the world'.

If you're interested in a guided trip or would prefer to hire bikes and explore on your own, contact Wellington Mountain Bike Adventures, ☎ (04) 3846 886 or Ocean Earth, ☎ (04) 5773 733. Most bike shops in Wellington sell a compact regional mountain biking guide for about $9.

Sea Kayaking to the Islands

There are several interesting sea kayaking trips that can be done to DOC nature reserve islands close to Wellington. Beginners can try a relaxing paddle out to Somes Island in the harbour, and possibly plant some native trees while they're out there. Those who already have some paddling experience could aim for an exploration of Kapiti or Mana Islands by kayak.

Orca Sea Kayaking in Lower Hutt run a variety of guided trips to cater for all abilities. A three hour trip costs $45 per person, all equipment included. For more information phone ☎ (04) 5773 733.

Baring Head

Wellington's most popular rock climbing area is on the Wainuiomata coast, east of the harbour entrance. Half a dozen solid greywacke outcrops sit on the beach like huge sunbathing armadillos. Baring Head provides good bouldering for both beginners and rock climbing gymnasts, and is the scene of annual climbing competitions. Ropes are seldom used as the sand at the bottom of most climbs is soft to land on. It takes nearly an hour to drive through Petone, over the hill and down the Wainuiomata Valley. As soon as you reach the coast, park in the gravel pit next to the Wainuiomata River. From here it's a 20 minute walk west to the rocks that can be seen in the distance. Which route you take depends on the state of the river. A good rule of thumb is to cross at the car park if you can, otherwise walk along to the mouth. Be careful crossing here—it's a long cold swim to Antarctica. An enjoyable alternative to driving is to catch the Days Bay ferry from Wellington and cycle around the coast to Baring Head. This pleasant ride along a gravel road takes about an hour.

 Cape Palliser

This 130 km ride takes 2 days and circumnavigates the southeast tip of the North Island.

From Martinborough ride south via Pirinoa (which has a shop) to the coast. Five hundred metres after reaching the coast you'll pass the Haurangi Forest Park entrance and a camping area. If you have a spare hour or two, visit the Putangirua Pinnacles, a miniature Grand Canyon. Continue round the coast to the tearooms at Ngawihi which have a good view of this little fishing village. We suspect that Ngawihi has more bulldozers per head of population than anywhere else on the planet. It's only a few kilometres from here to Cape Palliser lighthouse. From here a 4WD track continues along the coast, passing a large seal colony en route.

About 8 km from the lighthouse you'll have to walk a 1 km sandy stretch that ends with a short downhill to the DOC hut at Te Rakauwhakamataku Point. There are several good camping spots between the lighthouse and White Rock, but the hut is the only spot with a reliable water supply. From White Rock, follow the main road to Martinborough, 55 km away.

A Lunatic Cycles off Days Bay Wharf   (Mathew Nicol)

Wharf Jumping

Next time you're bored on a summer afternoon, try wharf jumping. It's quite a simple activity really. First pick a good wharf—not too high, not too low and with no safety rails on the end. Days Bay in Wellington has a wharf that's just right. Calmly cycle down to it and accelerate along its full length - don't stop. If you're still bored by the time you hit the water, see a psychiatrist.

Don't put your feet in the toe-clips (swimming with a bike isn't easy) and clean your bike thoroughly afterwards or it'll fall to bits.

11. Nelson & Marlborough

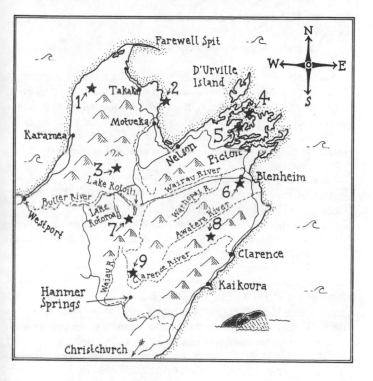

11.1 The Heaphy Track

Kahurangi National Park

For fit beginner trampers, 4-5 days.

—Summary— The Heaphy is the most popular tramp in Kahurangi National Park. For 78 km this magnificent track leads you through a huge variety of scenic delights, from subtropical coastal forest in the west to wind-swept, subalpine tussock expanses in the east.

The sheer diversity, plus the high standard of the track and huts, makes the Heaphy a classic, loved by generations of trampers.

—How to Get There— Karamea Taxis, ☎ (03) 782 6757, operate a service to the West Coast track end, 16 km north of Karamea. Collingwood Bus Services, ☎ (03) 524 8188, and NWN Trampers Service, ☎ (03) 528 6332, provide transport to and from the eastern side, 35 km up the Aorere Valley from Collingwood. There are phones at both track ends.

—Description—
Road end to Perry Saddle Hut; 5-6 hours
From Brown Hut (20 bunks), 500 metres past the car park, cross the Brown River and make your way across a paddock, through a bit of scrubby vegetation, until you join an old packhorse track.

This is a remainder from last century, when the Heaphy provided a link between the Nelson and West Coast gold fields. Ever since those days of gold-crazed pioneers, there have been proposals to turn the Heaphy into a road.

Opposition to this reached a crescendo in the 1970s, and ironically the controversy has made the Heaphy one of New Zealand's best known walking tracks.

The pack track gently winds its way up through mature beech and podocarp forest. Continue past Aorere Shelter to Flanagan's Corner (915 m), the highest point on the track. Perry Saddle Hut (40 bunks, gas stove) is about 2 km away.

Perry Saddle Hut to Saxon Hut; 4-5 hours

Perry Saddle Hut at Perry Saddle marks the eastern boundary of the Gouland Downs Scenic Reserve. The Gouland Downs are a sea of subalpine tussock, flaring red and gold, floating upon a bog of acidic soil. Scattered islands of limestone support woodier vegetation, predominantly silver beech. The Downs were grazed in 1915 before James Drummond, a far-sighted naturalist, proposed turning the area into a wildlife refuge for native birds. To this day, screeching great spotted kiwi and 'moreporking' ruru (native owl) can be heard disturbing the peace at night.

Walk across the Gouland Downs, over Cave Brook to the historic Gouland Downs Hut (14 bunks). There are some neat limestone caves to be explored behind the hut. The track then contours around the Slate Range, at the very edge of the tussock expanse, to Saxon Hut (20 bunks, gas stove). Saxon Shelter, possibly marked on your map, has been removed.

Saxon Hut to James Mackay Hut; 3-4 hours

As the track gently undulates through the diverse Mackay Downs, an old county boundary signpost appears hopelessly out of place. Fingers of scrub, reminiscent of unkempt suburban hedges, intertwine through open tussock clearings. Stonehenge-like rock outcrops complete this mysterious scene.

James Mackay Hut (40 bunks, gas stove) overlooks the Heaphy River and is a great place from which to watch fiery West Coast sunsets.

James Mackay Hut to Heaphy Hut; 5-6 hours

Gradually descend through West Coast rain forest to Lewis Hut (40 bunks, gas stove). From here follow the track beside the sluggish Heaphy River, through impressive bush dotted with giant rata trees. Nikau palms become more numerous and the smell of the ocean drifts up the valley. Local *te namu* (sandflies) will be out to greet you. Heaphy Hut (40 bunks, gas stove) is on a river flat, not far from the coast.

Heaphy Hut to Kohaihai Shelter at the road end; 4-5 hours

After four days of bush and tussock, a day by the seaside walking through lush groves of nikau palms is a pleasant change. Don't let

Classic New Zealand Swingbridge
(Malcolm O'Neill)

the tropical image entice you too far into the rip-infested Tasman Sea—people have been swept away by freak waves in the past.

There are a few small shelters along the way, presumably used by people in the past who were stopped by flooded sidestreams, all of which are now bridged. The Kohaihai River and shelter at the road end are just on the other side of a short, sharp saddle.

—Notes— This is one of the DOC 'Great Walks'. The track surface is hard, so watch out for blisters. At the time of writing DOC were investigating having the track open to mountain bikers at certain times of the year. If you're interested check with DOC in Nelson—it's a great ride.

The Whangapeka Track (see chapter 12, section 12.11) is a good way to return to the Nelson area and some people believe it's an even better tramp. Trackmap 245 Heaphy is essential.

11.2 Abel Tasman Sea Kayaking

40 km northwest of Nelson

For beginner paddlers (guide optional), 1 or more days.

—Summary— Sea kayaking is a great way to explore Abel Tasman National Park's islands, lagoons and hidden coves. As well as being a bit quicker than walking, kayaks can comfortably carry some of the

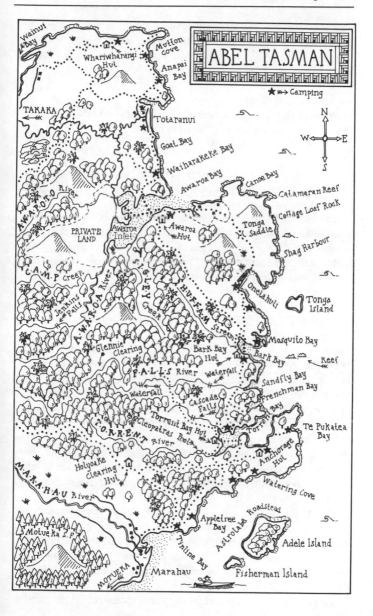

ABEL TASMAN

★ ⇢ Camping

luxuries that you would normally leave behind on a tramping trip. Sea kayaking gives you the freedom to explore off the beaten track and meet the locals—seals, dolphins and wekas. Try this guided tour, or hire a kayak and do your own exploring.

—**How to Get There**— From Nelson it's 60 km to Motueka. Marahau is on the coast, a further 18 km north of Motueka. Contact Ocean River Adventure Co., Marahau, ☎ (03) 527 8266; or Abel Tasman Kayaks, Marahau, ☎ (03) 527 8022.

—**Description**— Below we have described a two-day guided tour. There are several other guided trips available as well and, if you're experienced, you can plan your own unguided trip.

The morning starts by cramming the hatches of the kayaks with tents, billies, food, wine, sleeping gear, and more food. In the cool of the morning it's a struggle to load the heavy, double kayaks onto the trailer (will they really float?). The much lighter single kayaks flump easily on top of the groaning pile.

As you paddle out of Marahau your guide will take you through the safety procedures, paddling instructions and rudder operations, before setting course for Coquille Bay. Continue at a leisurely pace along the coastline, passing golden beaches, rocky headlands, and small caves along the way to Watering Cove. This is where explorer Captain D'Urville replenished his water supplies in 1827. Lunch is munched at Te Pukatea Bay, before cruising to Mosquito Bay where the tents are set up under a mature canopy of manuka and kanuka. With plenty of daylight left there is time to go exploring and collect firewood, or try fishing or snorkelling.

Evening entertainment is provided by wekas and possums. The flightless weka is a tireless vagabond attracted by food and shiny objects. It is capable of performing lightning speed right-angle turns while escaping with the booty. The noxious possum enjoys absolutely anything to do with food.

The next morning, at the crack of dawn, slice through the mirror-like brackish water and explore the lagoon behind Mosquito Bay. Speed back to sea and head for Tonga Island, the site of a local seal colony, about an hour away. You'll find the young seal pups here very inquisitive; almost as curious as some of the people visiting them.

There are plenty of opportunities to take photos before you need to turn for Onetahuti Beach, where the launch picks you up for the trip back to Marahau. As master of your own silent craft, there is something magical about exploring the lagoons and golden beaches of Abel Tasman National Park.

—Notes— This two-day tour costs $225 per person and includes camping and kayaking gear. Those with previous kayaking experience, can hire boats and gear for around $40 a day. Maps with additional kayaking features marked on them are supplied.

11.3 Mt Owen Caving

STOP PRESS — Just as this guide went to press, we received news that this trip was no longer being offered.

11.4 Nydia Bay Track

Marlborough Sounds

For intermediate/experienced riders, 5–8 hours; 28 tricky km.

—How to Get There— Ride or drive 26 km northeast from Rai Valley to the top of Opouri Saddle (488 m).

—Description— From Opouri Saddle experienced single track riders can head down the gnarly bridle track to the right, while intermediate riders descend Tennyson Inlet Road. At the bottom turn right and cruise 3 km to Tennyson Inlet township. Carry on round the bay to the start of the Nydia Bay Track. This rock and root riddled track will lead you over Nydia Saddle (370 m), round Nydia Bay and over a second saddle, Kaiuma (387 m), before spitting you out at Kaiuma Valley. It's very technical—and rewarding. If you can average 7 km per hour you'll be doing well. Part of the track follows the route of a 1910 timber railway line.

In Kaiuma Valley follow the walkway markers across two sections of farmland to the Kaiuma Bay Road. If you're not being picked up from the road end then follow this 23 km gravel road to Highway 6, about 3 km west of Canvastown.

—Notes— This is best done without panniers. In dry weather it's 90% rideable north-to-south or 60% rideable south-to-north. In wet weather it's mostly unrideable either way. There's a backpackers' hostel and DOC lodge at Nydia Bay, but no shops.

To avoid carrying extra gear, which would make the technical riding difficult, we recommend you base yourself from Pelorus Bridge (camping and cabins available) and do the 100 km loop in one day. This involves a lot of gravel road riding, so you'll need to be fit and get an early start.

Take Topomap P27 Picton or Infomap 336 Marlborough Sounds.

11.5 Marlborough Sounds Sea Kayaking

Marlborough Sounds Maritime Park

For all paddlers (guide optional), 5-7 days.

—Summary— This trip takes you from the remote Tennyson Inlet to Picton, across all three of the Marlborough Sounds. There are beautiful camp sites, fish to be caught and cooked over hot embers, and dolphins and rare birds to be seen. The whole area is steeped in fascinating history and, as the Maori discovered long ago, the best way to explore it is by waka (canoe or sea kayak).

—How to Get There— Hire kayaks (and a guide if necessary) from Marlborough Sounds Adventure Company, Picton, ☎ (03) 573 6078. For $170 they will drive you and your kayaks from Picton to Tennyson Inlet.

—Description— After a safety and skills briefing, you'll launch at Duncan Bay and paddle down Tennyson Inlet, bound for your first camp site at Tawa Bay. Beginners may prefer to paddle in double kayaks as they're faster, more stable and carry more gear (for example, a gourmet spread).

On the way you can take time out to pick mussels and oysters. At Tawa Bay the bush grows to the water's edge and the wekas sneak around like curious camp wardens.

On the second day the predominant northwesterly wind usually helps push kayakers along the Tawhitinui Reach towards Clova Bay. Just before Waimaru Bay, you'll pass the gannet (takupu) colony, a rare nesting place of these large yellow-headed birds. Watching takupu dive for fish from 50 metres above the water is awesome. A flock of feeding gannets often indicates there are dolphins nearby. The camp site is in Otatara Bay, just north of Clova Bay.

The next day paddle west around Opaniaputa Point, and then up Pelorus Sound to Nydia Bay. In Pelorus Sound the wind should once again be behind you, and if you're paddling with the tide as well, you'll fly along.

The great Maori chief Te Rauparaha also came this way when he raided the local Ngati Kuia tribe around 1828. The camp site is in the northern part of the bay, near where the Nydia Track starts climbing away from the coast. If you feel like a break from kayaking, go for a bush walk. There are good views from Nydia Saddle, about an hour away.

From Nydia Bay head further up Pelorus Sound and into Kenepuru Sound for a brief taste of civilisation, and a long overdue shower at St Omer House (at St Omer Bay). This lodge has a restaurant and self-contained cabins ($15 per person per night). There are also two brilliant little camp sites a kilometre south of here at Weka Point and Ferndale. Look for the fascinating Amakoura shipwreck, marked on the map. It has been sitting there, waiting to be salvaged, since 1951.

The next day, paddle across to Portage. At the shop you can stock up on provisions and organise to have your kayaks transported to Torea Bay in Queen Charlotte Sound. For three or four kayaks transport costs $20. For hundreds of years, various Maori tribes also transported their canoes across this narrow neck of land. From Torea Bay it takes 3-6 hours to cross Queen Charlotte Sound to Picton.

Kayak Sailing in Pelorus Sound   (Simon Kennett)

—**Notes**— Paddlers are fully briefed and fitted out when they hire a sea kayak. If you are an absolute beginner you may be advised to hire a guide for part or all of your trip.

Apart from the Marlborough Sounds Adventure Company, sea kayaks can also be hired from Lowe Tourist Promotion Co, at Sunnyvale Motels in Waikawa Bay, ☎ (03) 573 6800. Book ahead during summer. Rental rates are around $40 per day. The price drops after a few days' use and off-peak discounts are available. Schedules should be flexible because the weather is hard to predict. Topomaps are supplied with the kayaks.

11.6 Nelson Lakes Back-Country Skiing

 Nelson Lakes National Park, 80km southwest of Nelson

For competent skiers with alpine experience, 2-7 days

—Summary— The Lake Angelus basin is an awesome area, perched high within the mountains of Nelson Lakes National Park. It is a superb place from which to explore the surrounding alpine world—a world with less prestige than the Mt Cook or Mt Aspiring regions, but of equal splendour and offering many similar challenges. This back-country skiing adventure is an excellent way to discover these quiet mountains during the dramatic winter months.

—How to Get There— First, phone the DOC information centre at St Arnaud, ☎ (03) 521 1806, to find out what the snow conditions are like. If the conditions and weather forecast are good then drive to St Arnaud (80 km southwest of Nelson). Turn off Highway 63, 2 km west of St Arnaud and drive to the Mt Robert road end 5 km away.

—Description— From the car park tramp for 1-2 hours up the appropriately named Pinchgut Track onto Mt Robert (1411 m). The treeless slopes passed along the way are the result of burning and grazing since the end of last century. Higher up, a miniature forest of lichen hangs tangled within another forest of stunted mountain beech. Two small shelters are passed before reaching the Mt Robert Ski Field. This club field first opened in the late 1940s and is continuing the tradition of 'climbing to ski'—you have just walked up its access track.

By now you should have reached snow, unless warm frontal rain has washed it away (or did none fall in the first place?). The snow conditions on Robert Ridge can be extremely variable. Hard snow, powder drifts, ice-glazed rocks, and blue ice, as well as wet surface slides, can make travel hazardous.

From the skifield, climb steadily along the main ridge for 3 km. Then sidle to the left of point 1777 to a small saddle on the northwest side of Julius Summit. You can either drop the 80 metres into the basin on your west and skin out the other side or traverse Julius Summit. From the other side of the basin continue along Robert Ridge for a straight 2 km to where it splits. The route leads down the western spur and across a small saddle, to the top of a slope 100 metres above Lake Angelus. Most of the route from Mt Robert to Lake Angelus is marked by snow poles.

The final descent to the small tarn in Angelus Basin should convince anyone that skiing with packs is hard work. If the tarn is frozen (test it carefully), then you can skin straight across to the hut on the far side. It takes 5-7 hours to reach Angelus Hut (35 bunks) from the road end. However, gear failures often slow a group down, so make sure you get an early start. Although it's a fine spot to relax, the surrounding area is crying out to be explored. In the evening light, cruise up to Bristol Pass above the lake, for a peek at the setting sun over the distant West Coast. The ski back in fading light has its own urgency, as you try to cheat the darkness and end up clattering back across the frozen Lake Angelus to the hut.

The next day can be devoted to exploring the fresh white world to the south. Hinapouri Tarn, Sunset Saddle and even the steeper slopes of Mt Angelus (2075 m) have been known to fall prey to sets of parallel ski tracks.

The trip home along the Robert Ridge is also something to look forward to. An overall loss of more than 300 metres over the 10 km run gives this a convincing downhill feel. If you run out of snow at the end of the ridge it doesn't actually matter that much; the carpet grass does almost as good a job.

—**Notes**— Avalanches kill people in this area. If you don't have an understanding of avalanches, make sure you're with someone who does. Be prepared for rapid weather changes any time of year.

This trip requires an ice axe and crampons, cross-country skis or downhill skis with ski-mountaineering bindings, and ski skins. Even on a fairly direct route such as this, there are plenty of nasty spots that you'd be crazy to try to ski. If you're unsure, swap your skis for crampons before it gets too dangerous. Lake Angelus is not frozen all year round, so be careful. Topomaps M29 Murchison and N29 St Arnaud are essential.

11.7 The Molesworth Rainbow Ride

 From Blenheim to St Arnaud, via Hanmer

For intermediate riders, 3-7 days; about 305 km.

—**Summary**— This is New Zealand's longest mountain bike touring trip. It passes through the country's largest farm, Molesworth Station, then follows the Clarence River up into Rainbow Station. The whole area is flanked by the massive Kaikoura Range to the east, and Nelson Lakes National Park to the west. There are no shops, no towns and very few cars; plenty of rivers, lots of tussock and endless mountains.

—How to Get There— If heading down from the North Island on the ferry, just cycle from Picton to Blenheim. Cyclists from south of Kaikoura should do this round trip from Hanmer.

—Description—
Blenheim to Hanmer, 2-4 days
From Blenheim, ride south on Maxwell Road and head over Taylor Pass on a gravel road. This takes you to the main sealed road heading southwest up the Awatere Valley. After about an hour the seal ends and the road climbs high above the Awatere River before dropping down to Jordon. There are many hills on this sluggish gravel road, and those with zero fitness and plenty of equipment may start to lose enthusiasm at this point.

At the Hodder River bridge there is a public toilet and some good trees to rest under on hot days. Soon, however, you must tackle the formidable Upcot saddle—a steep granny gear climb which is probably easier to walk.

From the Taylor Pass turn-off it takes 6-10 hours of riding to reach the old Molesworth Homestead where there is a pleasant DOC campsite (but no safe water supply). During the public season (see notes), visit the DOC caravan and part with $7. Camping is not permitted between here and the historic Acheron Accommodation House a good 5 hours away.

From Molesworth Homestead there is a steep climb to the top of Ward Pass, from where it's downhill all the way to the Acheron River which is safe for drinking. From Isolated Saddle it's undulating all the way to the Accommodation House, at the confluence of the Acheron and Clarence rivers, where there is more good camping and a drinkable water supply.

From Acheron Accommodation House it's about an hour's cycling, beside the Clarence River, to the Hanmer Springs turn-off (via Jollies Pass).

Those who've had enough of wide open spaces, fresh air and magnificent scenery should turn off here and cycle 10 km on a long fast downhill to civilisation: hot pools, ice creams and a campground.

Hanmer Springs to St Arnaud, 1-2 days.

This 100 km pylon road follows the route originally used to drive stock from Marlborough down to Canterbury. Head out of Hanmer on Jacks Pass Road. Cycle over Jacks Pass and down to the Clarence Valley, then turn left. From here it is 35 km to the turn-off to Lake Tennyson (a 3 km detour). Lake Tennyson is very exposed to bad weather so you may want to camp near the Clarence River bridge or head over Island Saddle (8 km away) to Coldwater Creek where there are more pleasant camping areas. The last few kilometres up to Island Saddle (1372 m) are steep and unrelenting, but even if you have to walk, the rewards of a great downhill and excellent views make it worthwhile.

From the saddle it is another 50 km through tussock, then beech forest, to Highway 63. There are several fords en route which may be impassable after heavy rain. About half an hour after crossing Rough Creek, veer left at the 'Rainbow Forest Park' sign, and climb the last few kilometres to the highway.

Once you reach Highway 63 it's an easy 10 km west to St Arnaud where you will find the tranquil Lake Rotoiti, a general store, motorcamp and backpackers hostel.

From St Arnaud it's 100 km on Highway 63 back to Blenheim. It's practically all downhill on a sealed road and there's usually a tailwind, so pump your tyres up hard for what could be the easiest 100 km you've ever cycled.

—Track Conditions— 25% sealed road, 75% gravel, several fords.

—Landowners— Molesworth Station is open to the public for six weeks in January and February. Outside of this period, permission is required from Don Reid, Molesworth Station, Private Bag, Blenheim, ☎ (03) 575 7045.

For the Hanmer to St Arnaud section of the ride, permission to cross Rainbow Station must be obtained from Mr or Mrs Graham, ☎ (03) 521 1838. Both stations are closed for mustering in November and March, and in winter because of deep snow. Leave all gates as you find them.

—**Notes**— Take a gas cooker because fires are not allowed on Molesworth Station or in the precious remnants of native bush north of Coldwater Creek. Go well equipped, and be prepared for snow at any time of year. Carry extra water in summer as temperatures often rise above the 30s and river water is not always drinkable. Further information can be obtained from DOC in Blenheim, ☎ (03) 572 9100. Take Terrainmap 11 Kaikoura.

11.8 Mt Tapuae-O-Uenuku

Inland Kaikoura Range, 100 km south of Picton.

For experienced alpine climbers, 3 days minimum.

—**Summary**— Mt Tapuae-O-Uenuku, the highest mountain outside the Southern Alps, sits at the head of the Hodder Valley, overlooking endless mountain ranges to the west and the Kaikoura coast to the east. In both winter and summer, this remote peak offers an inspiring introduction to serious climbing.

—**How to Get There**— Drive 20 km south of Blenheim on Highway 1 before turning right up the Awatere Valley. After 55 km of mostly gravel road you'll cross the Hodder River on an old wooden truss bridge. Park on the grassy flat by the hay barn.

—**Landowners**— Permission *must be* obtained from A S and B H Pitts to park cars near their hay barn and tramp up the Hodder Valley. Their address is Gladstone Downs, Private Bag, Blenheim; ☎ (03) 575 7471.

—**Description**—
Hodder River Bridge to Hodder Huts; 6-9 hours
After asking the farmer's permission, head through the gate opposite the hay barn and tramp up the Hodder Valley on a farm track high above the river. Stay on the main track and after an hour you'll reach

Winter Traverse of Mount Tapuae-O-Uenuku　　　　　(Mike Sheridan)

a small cairn on your left. From here a steep and indistinct track leads down to the river, 80 metres below (just upstream from the Hodder-Shin confluence).

Now psych yourself up for a 4-8 hour tramp up the Hodder River. Don't bother trying to keep your boots dry—you have to cross the river about sixty times. It is usually knee deep, but it rises fast during heavy rain and can be dangerous.

About halfway to Hodder Hut, just past two large shingle flats, there is an impressive waterfall on the true left. It's not far from here to the Trail Stream confluence within one of the gorges. One hour upstream from the confluence the track climbs 150 metres, on the true right, to avoid a series of waterfalls. After traversing through a small patch of beech forest, you break out into an alpine basin. By this stage you will have become well acquainted with the needle-like fronds of the wild Spaniard plant (with fronds like these who needs enemies).

The track then crosses the Hodder River and continues up on the true left to the hut. There are actually two comfortable huts, only 10 metres apart, situated on a lovely little knoll overlooking the valley. They are a welcome sight, especially after clambering up the last scree slope.

Hodder Huts to the top and back; 8-12 hours

Early the next morning, follow the track behind the hut, which sidles for 200 metres then descends gently to the river. A cairned track leads up the true right of Staircase Stream to a high alpine basin. Head south across the basin, below the prominent bluffs, gradually climbing towards an unnamed peak (2711 m). Climb up the gully to the north of this peak. There is a steep section near the top. Once on the summit ridge, continue up on straightforward slopes to the summit of Tapuae-O-Uenuku. There is an attractive rusty pipe on the very top. The Clarence River snakes far below while mountain peaks disappear into the distance.

From the summit descend the snow slopes to the saddle just below Pinnacle. This involves picking your way through a small bluffy section. Drop off the saddle veering south, above the bluffs that you walked under in the morning, and rejoin your earlier route back to the hut. Remember, if the weather packs in or your party is having difficulties, abandon the traverse and go back the way you came up.

—**Notes**— The Hodder Huts cost $4 per night per person, which should be sent to the Marlborough Tramping Club, PO Box 787, Blenheim.

Take full alpine tramping gear at all times of the year. Experience with ice axe and crampons is essential for a safe trip. In winter watch out for avalanche-prone slopes, especially late in the afternoon on hot days. A rope may be necessary for less experienced members of a party. Topomap O30 Awatere is essential.

11.9 Clarence Canoeing Expedition

 Inland from Kaikoura

For grade III paddlers (guide optional), 3-5 days.

—Summary— The Clarence River is nestled between the inland and seaward Kaikoura mountain ranges. It twists and weaves its way for over 200 km, from subalpine tussock lands, through shadowy gorges, to the South Pacific Ocean.

This is spectacular country; a barren and harsh landscape scorched by blazing suns. The Clarence gives adventurous paddlers a unique opportunity to experience a remote, large scale river expedition without having to face any particularly nasty rapids.

—How to Get There— From Hanmer Springs, drive north over Jacks Pass to the Molesworth-Rainbow road. Turn right and follow the Clarence River down towards Molesworth Station. After 15 km the road crosses the river at the put-in point, just upstream of the Acheron River confluence.

—Description— Single kayaks provide the quickest means of travel down the Clarence, as long as they are not laden down with too much gear. Larger open boats, such as Canadian canoes, or inflatable kayaks, are excellent but require higher water flows to keep them afloat.

One possibility is to go down in single kayaks with a back-up support raft (see Notes). This also allows your non-kayaking friends to join the trip.

There are plenty of camp sites outside the three main gorges. Avoid getting stuck in the gorges at dusk unless you like sleeping in your boat. Long hours on the water are required to cover the large distances and winds can hamper progress.

At first, the river is wide and braided. If you've never paddled braided rivers before, this will provide a learning experience. Many channels end with a 'shingle scraping', making it necessary to hop out and find deeper water. After a couple of hours you'll reach the entrance to the first gorge, where the Dillon River joins on the true left. Amidst the sharp, shattered rocks and bluff-buffering waves, there is a grade III drop known as The Chute.

After this there are no difficult rapids and the river gradually opens out at Quail Flat on the true right. There is an obvious camp site here, identified by huge poplar trees visible from the river.

Between Quail Flat and the start of the lower gorge, 50 km away, there are numerous tight, grade II to III rapids which are dotted with tombstone-like rocks. Ravine Hut is on the true left, 3 km upriver from the gorge, and is not obvious from the river.

Below here, there are dozens more grade II to III rapids, the most notable being Jawbreaker and Nosebasher. These lead to a great roller coaster, white water finish just before the Highway 1 bridge at Clarence. It's just as well that you've spent the last couple of days sharpening up your kayaking skills!

—**Notes**— Don't even consider doing this trip in winter. The area is very remote and isolated and it can be a serious trip in high flows. Parties must be fully equipped and self sufficient. It's worth taking a mountain radio (see Clubs & Contacts). The river can be too low to paddle from mid-January.

The Clarence River is commercially rafted from September through to January. A 5-day trip costs about $575 all inclusive. Support rafts and guides can also be provided for canoeists.

Contact Action in Marlborough, ☎ (03) 578 4531, or Ultimate Descents, ☎ (03) 528 6363, fax (03) 528 6792. Topomaps N31 Archeron, O31 Kaikoura, O30 Awatere, and P30 Clarence are recommended.

11.10 Other Adventures

Paynes Ford

Paynes Ford Scenic Reserve is 4 km south of Takaka in Golden Bay, where Highway 60 crosses the Takaka River. From here, towering limestone cliffs lead up the river. There are many popular, bolted climbing routes on them.

If you don't have the gear or the inclination for serious climbing but still feel in the mood for a wee adventure, try your hand (and feet) at the traverse problem 100 metres downstream from the bridge.

Here the river has cut into the cliffs, leaving a deep pool framed by a grooved, pocked and pitted overhanging cliff face. The traverse to the recessed, stage-like platform is a doddle, but getting beyond there requires consummate skill and a committing right-hand lunge. If you master this move, you'll find it gets progressively more difficult the further you go.

Numerous channels and pocks (some big enough to grovel into and rest) provide entertaining climbing until you finally pump out and peel off, dropping into the cool, reviving river.

Abel Tasman National Park Coastal Walk

This famous coastal track between Marahau and Wainui Bay attracts tens of thousands of walkers each year. Golden beaches and lush native forest, accessible only by boat or foot, make this a trekkers paradise.

However, if you're keen to explore the coast without crashing into other trekkers at every hut and campsite, avoid it during summer. Spreading the load of visitors throughout the year helps enhance the wilderness experience for everyone.

We expect that a booking system will soon be introduced for this 'Great Walk'.

Nelson Paragliding and Rockclimbing

For an exciting tandem flight or one day introductory course, contact Airborn Paragliding and Rockclimbing School in Nelson, ☎ (03) 543 2669. They also take people rock climbing and abseiling, and you can attain the PG1 and PG2 (pilots licence) paragliding qualifications.

Take hard-wearing outdoor clothing and ankle-supporting footwear.

Dun Mountain

From Brook Street in Nelson, ride or walk up either end of the Dun Mountain Walkway to the intersection signposted 'Fringed

Hill 1 hr' and 'Dun Mtn 4 hrs'. Continue along the Dun Mountain Track (4WD), through native bush to Third House Hut. From there to Windy Point and Coppermine Saddle the track narrows, and some parts are too rough to ride. Continue on foot if you prefer.

On a fine day it's worth climbing Dun Mountain (1129 m), definitely on foot (about 1 hour), for the awesome views.

For obvious reasons mountain bikers need to go slow on the downhills—this is a very popular area for walking.

Mountain bikes can be hired in Nelson from Bridge Street Cycles, ☎ (03) 548 3877, and Stewarts Cycle City, ☎ (03) 548 4344. For this trip, and others in the area, take Topomap O27 Nelson.

West Coast Wilderness Safari

Departing weekly from Nelson, this adventurous nature tour takes 10 days to travel to Queenstown via many of the natural wonders of the West Coast. Kahurangi, Paparoa and Westland National Parks are all visited en route.

Lots of overnight hikes mean sleeping in huts and cabins, under rock overhangs and on beaches.

You explore canyons, caves, and coastline and even kayak across a lagoon surrounded by rain forest. We rate it as the perfect trip for the eco-adventurer with limited time or expertise.

This NZ Nature Safaris tour costs $650 per person and can be booked by phoning or faxing (04) 563 7360, Wellington. For more general information on NZ Nature Safaris see chapter 7, section 7.8.

Quinney's Bush

New Zealand's most eccentric camping ground is nestled amongst tall trees at Motupiko, about halfway between Nelson and Murchison. Relaxed and ramshackle, Quinney's Bush is strewn with flying foxes (aerial cableways) and other dilapidated pieces of industrial-sized playground equipment.

A remnant of the 1960s, we rate it as the country's most adventurous camping ground.

Pelorus Bridge to Nelson

The seldom visited Mt Richmond Forest Park is a large bush-clad range, south of Nelson. The most popular tramp in the park starts from Maungatapu road end, 12 km west of Pelorus Bridge on the Blenheim-Nelson Road. If you're travelling by bus then you'll have to start from Pelorus Bridge and walk down the quiet Maungatapu Road.

On the first day follow an easy track beside the Pelorus River, passing Captain Creek Hut to Middy Hut (6 bunks), 5-6 hours from the road end. The next day take the track that climbs to Rocks Hut on the Bryant Range, about 3 hours away. Then climb round Dun Saddle and Windy Point, down past Third House shelter and on to Brook Valley Road just near the Brook Valley Motorcamp (3-5 hours from Rocks Hut).

The centre of Nelson is only 5 km down valley. Topomap O27 Nelson or Parkmap 274 Mt Richmond is essential.

 Maungatapu Track

This popular 35 km cycle touring 'shortcut' from Pelorus Bridge to Nelson, crosses the Bryant Range on a rough 4WD track. From Pelorus Bridge follow Maungatapu Road for 12 km to a 'Club Mud' sign, then veer right and start climbing.

From Murderers Rock it becomes very steep, but the saddle is only 3 km away and the views from the top are great. Then it's mostly downhill all the way to Nelson.

For more information refer to *Classic New Zealand Mountain Bike Rides* (see Further Reading), or ask at the local DOC office. Cross country runners really enjoy this trip as well and take about the same length of time as mountain bikers (4-6 hours).

 Wakamarina River

The Wakamarina River flows under Highway 6 (the Nelson-Blenheim road) at Canvastown, 10 km west of Havelock. Whakamarina Road takes you 15 km upstream to a DOC camping ground at the road end.

From here there are many tight grade III rapids, including some difficult drops and chutes. The hardest one, Tinopener, is about halfway down from the road end, under a footbridge. Keep an eye out for gold claims as you spin and swirl along. This is a great trip for experienced tubers.

 ## Queen Charlotte Walkway

Considered by some as an alternative to the Abel Tasman Track, the Queen Charlotte Walkway, just north of Picton, is actually quite different. It has more hills, spends less time right beside the coast, crosses a couple of roads en route and is not quite as scenic as the Abel Tasman. However, it is less crowded and cyclists are allowed on the track. You can sea kayak to or from several parts of the walkway (see below).

To walk the whole 58 km track from Ship Cove to Anakiwa takes 3-4 days, but there are numerous entry/exit points to the track so it is easy to do a shorter trip if you wish . There are several campsites en route as well as a few hotels/hostels.

The section of track from Kenepuru Saddle north is closed to mountain bikers in December and February. Only experienced bikers should attempt the whole track because it presents difficult riding between Kenepuru saddle and Te Mahia (there is a pleasant road riding alternative to this section though). Beginner riders should just do the section from Te Mahia to Anakiwa. Much of this clay based track is unrideable when wet.

All the information you need is contained in a DOC pamphlet about the track which is available at local information centres.

Nelson Lakes Tramping

Nelson Lakes National Park is a marvellous place for trampers of all abilities. An excellent 5-6 day trip for intermediate trampers leads up the Travers Valley, over Travers Saddle and down the Sabine Valley, to Sabine Hut at the head of Lake Rotoroa (4 days).

From Sabine Hut, continue to St Arnaud via the new Sabine to Speargrass Track out to the Mt Robert road end (1-2 days). Alternatively, if your party is fit, and the weather looks fine, you can

Nelson Lakes in Winter   (Grant Harpo)

climb over Mt Cedric to Angelus Hut and out via Robert Ridge, or Travers Valley, the next day.

In winter, crampons, ice axes, and a wary eye for avalanches are essential for a safe trip. During autumn, wasps can be a serious problem so you should carry medication for stings, such as antihistamine pills.

There are plenty of shorter trips to do as well—for more information ask at the DOC visitors centre in St Arnaud, ☎ (03) 521 1806.

 ## Kayaking from Picton to Ship Cove

From Picton paddle across Queen Charlotte Sound to a lovely campsite hidden in the bush at Kumutoto Bay. By the end of the day you should be quite proficient at cutting through, or surfing with, the bow waves of fishing boats and ferries. Blumine Island, further along Queen Charlotte Sound, is your next destination.

It's a deserted island that only kayakers seem to know about and has an excellent camp site in the large, unnamed western-facing bay. There are some well hidden WWII gun emplacements on the north side of the island that were manned by American soldiers over 50 years ago.

The next day head over to Ship Cove via Motuara Island. The whole of Motuara Island is a bird sanctuary. The wide variety of inhabitants is incredibly tame. Little blue penguins keep an eye on you as you pass only a metre or two away.

It's only a short paddle across to Ship Cove, from where the water taxi can take you and your trusty kayak back to Picton.

This trip can be done in either direction depending on the predominant wind direction and also combines with the Queen Charlotte Walkway (walking or cycling—see earlier section of this chapter). For kayak hire information, see the Notes for section 12.5, Marlborough Sounds Sea Kayaking.

 ## Dolphin & Seal Swimming

This is an exciting way to discover the grace and beauty of seals or dolphins in their natural environment. After being taken out in a small boat, and decked out in a wetsuit, mask and snorkel, jump in the sea and have an exhilarating encounter with these intelligent marine mammals. Book through the Kaikoura Information Centre on the beach front; ☎ (03) 319 5641. Prices per person are $40 for seal swimming, and $75 for dolphin swimming.

Pillocking

Pillocking originated in 1991 near Havelock and, surprisingly, at the time of writing hadn't managed to spread beyond this tranquil little town.

It involves taking a rubbish-bin lid down to the harbour's mud flats during low tide. While holding the lid (preferably a large plastic one) on the mud in front of you, run as fast as possible and attempt to skim across the muddy flats.

Obviously it can only be done during low tide; becoming incredibly muddy is an unavoidable bonus. The national title is held by a Havelockonian, for 'pillocking' an incredible 2.6 km to a local shipwreck and back.

12. The Wild West Coast

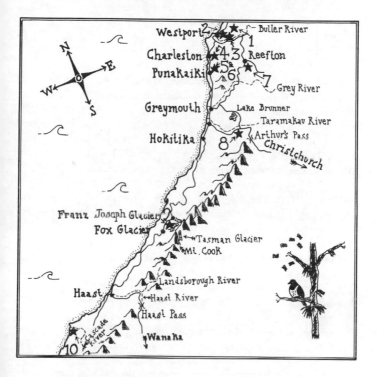

12.1 Denniston Shortcut

 Northeast of Westport

For intermediate riders, 4-8 hrs; 33 km.

—Summary— Originally pioneered by a group of hardcore cycle tourers living in the ghost town of Denniston, this ride is an excellent shortcut for those cycling east towards Murchison. A maze of rough gravel roads and 4WD tracks take you through Orikaka State Forest to Iron Bridge on the Buller River, 3 km northwest of Lyell.

Landowner Bernard Menzies, ☎ (03) 789 0223, *must* be contacted for permission to ride through his land at New Creek.

—How to Get There— Ride 20 km northeast of Westport on Highway 67, before turning inland at Waimangaroa to tackle the character building 8 km (sealed road) hillclimb to Denniston.

—Description— From Denniston, ride inland on the main sealed road towards Burnetts Face. Do not turn right towards Sullivans Mine. The seal soon ends and you descend to Burnett Stream. At the bottom, keep left on the main road and take the bridge across Burnett Stream.

The gravel road will lead you past a burning coal mine (marked on the map), across a surreal 'Dr Who' type landscape, and into the forest.

The mine has been burning underground since it was accidentally lit in 1953. About five minutes past the burning mine you'll cross Cedar Stream (signposted). Take the next turn on the right, about 200 metres away, leading into a 4WD track that takes you up a short steep hill.

When you're almost at the top, turn left at the four-way intersection. At the next fork, by the pylons, turn right, then right again after 50 metres. Now just stay on the main gravel road and enjoy the steep downhill to a hut at Stevenson Stream. This hut may be a rusty old corrugated-iron dump, but it's a nice place for a rest stop.

Many of the road cuttings around here have uncovered rich coal seams buried just below the surface. Just after reaching the top of the next steep hill, turn right.

A gnarly gravel road then takes you down to Mt William Stream. Cross it, climb steeply for another 15 minutes then cruise along a short flat section to a T-intersection. Turn left over a gate and down to Orikaka (Mackley) River.

The Orikaka River is uncrossable in flood so take care. On the other side, the last 20 minute uphill awaits. At the top, navigation becomes a bit dicey—there are pylons and roads heading off all over the place, and the map is way out of date. Two sets of pylons lead south to the Buller River, while the other set (the one you should follow) points east to New Creek along a route described as follows.

At the first intersection after the hill climb, veer right (south) away from a tin hut. Cruise straight along on the main gravel road, past any turn-offs, for about 500 m, till you drop down to a major T-intersection. Turn sharp left (back towards your pylons) and within 50 m you'll start descending quite fast. Stay on the main road, and in 5-10 minutes you'll reach an intersection with a 'Blue Duck' sign pointing back uphill. Veer left and meander up to a saddle where you should veer left again.

From there it's mostly downhill or flat on gravel road to Iron Bridge on Highway 6.

—Track Conditions— 80% gravel road, 20% 4WD track.

—Notes— For 90 years Denniston was the site of a huge coal mine and 'the eighth wonder of the world', the Denniston Incline. This steep railway, used for transporting coal down the hill, was powered by using the descending loaded wagons to pull the empty ones back up. It's well worth a look.

In wet weather, West Coast rivers rise to flood levels very quickly and this trip is not possible. In winter, temperatures can drop well below freezing. If any new roads have been added to the maze since this was written, or any old roads washed away, don't panic—just follow the pylons. Many roads and two sets of pylons have been built since the first edition of Topomap L29 Inangahua was printed, but its topographical information is still essential.

12.2 Adventure Cave Rafting

Based at Greymouth

For beginner cavers (guided), 4-5 hours.

—Summary— This trip is an excellent introduction to the sometimes demanding world of caving. Streams and rivers flow through the dense bush-covered limestone landscape of the Paparoa region, disappearing every so often only to re-emerge at unexpected points further on. This very same water has sculpted a secret world below, a subterranean labyrinth of passageways and caverns.

—How to Get There— Contact The Wild West Adventure Company in Greymouth, ☎ (03) 768 6649 or freephone ☎ 0800 22 3456.

—Description— Taniwha Cave is 10 minutes' drive north of Greymouth within an area of native bush. It takes half an hour of squelching along in your wetsuit to reach the cave entrance. It's not exactly welcoming; a small hole worn through the limestone opens into a large chamber below. These holes, or *tomo*, are scattered throughout the area and are always ready to swallow unsuspecting cavers who venture off the track.

Once underground, the cave follows a tumbling stream through various glow-worm lined chambers. These patient hunters are waiting for insects, attracted by their phosphorescence, to fly into their silken traps. According to Maori mythology, glow-worms preserved the world's first glimmer of light before Tane gave the Sun and the Moon to Rangi.

Underfoot, the mudstone, siltstone and limestone provides an ideal boulder hopping surface, similar to emery paper. No slippery, malicious mosses survive down here and the ever-present water has carved out jug-like handholds. At times it is worthwhile travelling with headlamps turned off—that large squishy thing moving next to you is less likely to be a killer cave eel than a fellow caver.

Up above, at a point resembling the high tide mark, limestone tentacles of varying colours ooze forth like octopuses and spiders. Fortunately, they move too slowly to catch you. The regular flooding prevents them growing below a certain level, and also stops sensible cavers from going underground when it's raining.

Eventually the stream levels off and gets deeper. Some forward-thinking soul has left a bundle of inflated truck tubes here. What an effortless way to travel. In places the roof comes down through the utter darkness to within inches of the water.

Between a Rock and a Wet Place   (Greg Carlyon)

The exit back to the world of light is through a tunnel system aptly named The Toilet Bowl. Plumbers will really like this bit. A series of S-bends provide you with the perfect opportunity to 'flush away' the cavers below. Eventually you'll emerge from this other world, blinking at the sunlit sights of the forest.

—Notes— This trip costs $85 and contains many different options. You can take the easier route and float the main glow-worm chambers or try some more challenging variations like the waterfall plunge or the 100-feet hydroslide. A hot spa, showers and drinks are provided at the end of the trip.

12.3 Buller Rafting

 40 km east of Westport

For all adventurers (guided), 5 hours.

—Summary— Fed from Lakes Rotoiti and Rotoroa, high within Nelson Lakes National Park, the Buller River is the gateway to the West Coast of the South Island. This trip, down one of New Zealand's largest rivers, combines white water rafting with a tour of the spectacular Buller Gorge.

—How to Get There— Buller Adventure Tours (BAT) is located 9 km inland from Westport on Highway 6.

—Description— From BAT base, it's a 40 minute drive in the BAT-mobile to the earthquake section on the Upper Buller Gorge, where the trip begins. A massive slip triggered by the Inangahua earthquake in 1968 has created a huge lake, followed by a long series of bouldery rapids. Since then, silt has slowly built up in the lake making this section faster.

Once the rafting begins, listen carefully to your guides—they know what they're doing. The reason for this becomes obvious as soon as Whopper Stopper approaches. After howling through this rapid there is a brief reprieve before entering the Gun Slinger.

Leaping off the river cliffs further down is a good break from rafting. It's an interesting exercise in group psychology to see if you can get everyone to jump at once. Another unusual challenge (for those keen enough) is to swim a grade III rapid. This is a hands-on lesson in river dynamics.

After several more rapids, the river enters a picturesque gorge leading to the Pop-Up Toaster, a real meanie, and Keith's Cauldron, which boils against a cliff. This marks the junction with Lyell Creek and the site of a once thriving, but now completely dead, gold-mining town—boom, lust, bust, then dust.

The BAT-mobile will pick you up at the exit point just below Iron Bridge, and return you to BAT-base after a brief stop at Berlin's Hotel.

—Notes— In high flows the Buller becomes a grade IV river. There are several rafting companies who raft the Buller: three of them are Buller Adventure Tours, ☎ (03) 789 7286; Rapid River Rafting Co. in Nelson, ☎ (03) 542 3110; and Action In Marlborough in Blenheim, ☎ (03) 578 4531. The trip costs from $75.

12.4 Underworld Rafting

Charleston, 30 km south of Westport

For all adventurers (guided), half day return from Westport.

—Summary— This popular trip involves a short walk through beautiful native forest in the Paparoa National Park, exploring amazing cave formations in one of New Zealand's largest caves, tubing through glow-worm lit grottos and rafting in the Nile River. Points of interest are explained in a series of interpretive talks.

—How to Get There— Contact Norwest Adventures, Westport, ☎ (03) 789 6686. They provide transport from Westport to the road end in Paparoa National Park near Charleston.

—Description— A 30 minute walk leads through the lush native forest, for which the West Coast is famous, and under towering limestone cliffs to the banks of the Nile River. Now it's time to don wetsuit and helmet, collect a tractor tyre tube and climb up to the entrance of the enormous Metro cave system.

At this point your guide will give a talk, providing an insight into the life of the cave, its formations and inhabitants. This is also where the adventure begins, and to say much more would be giving it away. Suffice to say you'll clamber, cower and coerce your way through this underworld for about half an hour before tubing out the very last stretch.

A little more tubing down the Nile, in broad daylight, and you'll be back where you forded the river just over an hour earlier.

—**Notes**— Norwest Adventures, ☎ (03) 789 6686, charge $70 for this half-day trip, available in wet or fine weather, and supply all equipment needed. You just need your togs and a towel.

If you're keen for something a bit more gung-ho, the same company offers longer, more demanding caving trips in the same area. They are not recommended if you fear confined spaces, the dark, fast-flowing rivers, open spaces, slow-flowing rivers, or West Coast sandflies.

12.5 The Inland Pack Track

Punakaiki, Paparoa National Park

For beginner trampers, 2-3 days.

—**Summary**— Lush West Coast rainforest and flowing limestone rock formations make the Paparoa National Park a photographer's dreamland. The historic Inland Pack Track was built in 1867 to avoid the harsh coastline between the Fox and Punakaiki Rivers. There are no big climbs, nothing to be conquered or overcome. This is an intimate and ancient environment that fuels the imagination and invites exploration.

Much of the track has been upgraded and provides easy walking. Parts of it, however, are still very boggy, and an untracked section down Fossil Creek and through Dilemma Gorge involves many river crossings.

—**How to Get There**— Drive or catch the daily Intercity or one of the backpacker buses to Punakaiki on the West Coast (Highway 6).

—**Description**— The trip starts at Punakaiki and ends 16 km to the north, where Highway 6 crosses the Fox River.

Punakaiki to Bullock Creek; 3 hours

From Punakaiki walk up the true left of the Pororari River, on a well-maintained track. It leads through a grove of nikau palms and

into a magnificent limestone gorge. A few kilometres up the gorge
you'll reach the Inland Pack Track proper (signposted). Turn left
down to and across the Pororari River. This crossing is not normally
a problem, but should not be attempted in flood.

Once on the other side, the track climbs gently through a
sinkhole-riddled beech forest to a cleared area near Bullock Creek.
This is a popular area to camp, but don't pitch your tent too close to
the dry streambed—it floods quickly. Head northeast on an old farm
track to a ford across Bullock Creek. The track resumes on the other
side and is well signposted.

Bullock Creek to Ballroom Overhang; 4 hours

After crossing another section of forest pockmarked with sinkholes
you drop down to Fossil Creek. Within half an hour's walk down this
creek bed, you'll reach Dilemma Creek and soon enter its narrow
limestone canyon. Layers of limestone, mudstone and gravel have
been worked on over the centuries, leaving striking sculptures
throughout the area. The Dilemma is whether or not to travel down its
flood-prone course while it's raining.

When you reach the Fox River (signposted), walk downstream
(left) for 100 metres to a safe crossing point next to a campsite. If the
river is too high to cross then you'll have to camp here, otherwise
cross the river and walk upstream for 1 km to the Ballroom Overhang
on the true right. Over time, the river has carved out a massive area of
limestone, leaving behind a brilliant sheltered camping area. Twenty
tents can easily fit under the huge curved roof. Carefully store your
food away from rats at night; many packs have served as tasty entrées
as they chew through to the main course inside.

There are several adventurous side trips in this area. The Fox River
Caves provide an excellent introduction to caving in this area. To go
any further than a few hundred metres, however, requires specialist
caving equipment and expertise. After crossing the Fox River about
half way between the Ballroom Overhang and the Highway, head
back upriver to the caves following a track on the true right.

Ballroom Overhang to Highway 6; 3 hours

From Dilemma Creek, there is a well-developed track down the Fox
River to Highway 6. About halfway down, it crosses from true left to

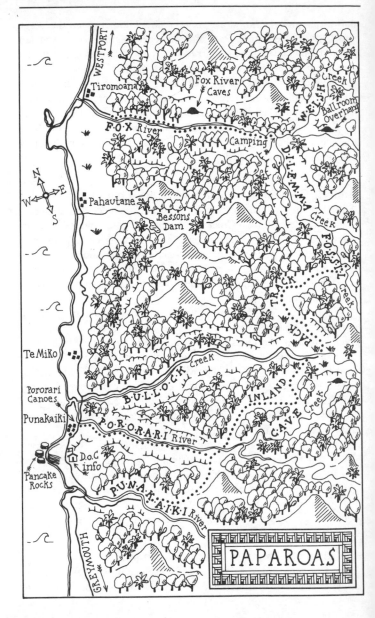

true right. This crossing is quite straightforward unless the river is in flood, in which case you should just set up camp and wait it out.

—Notes— There are no huts on this track. Rainfall is measured by the metre on the West Coast, and will test anyone's camping equipment and experience to the limit. If the rivers rise suddenly, as they are apt to do, you may be stuck for a day or two. Don't worry, it happens all the time, they fall just as quickly as they rise. For more information contact DOC at Punakaiki, ☎ (03) 731 1895. Topomap K30 Punakaiki or Parkmap 12 Paparoa National Park is essential.

12.6 Pororari Canoeing

 Punakaiki, Paparoa National Park

For beginner paddlers, 1 day.

—Summary— Intimate yet stunning, the Pororari River typifies Paparoa National Park. Guarded on both sides by beautiful native forest and huge limestone cliffs, this emerald river is best explored from the seat of a canoe with paddle in hand.

—How to Get There— Head for the pancake rocks of Punakaiki, 50 km north of Greymouth. To hire canoes contact Punakaiki Canoe and Bike Hire, 2 km north of the Punakaiki DOC information centre on Highway 6, ☎ (03) 731 1870.

—Description—
Punakaiki Canoe Hire is based on the banks of the Pororari River, almost where it meets the coast. After hiring a canoe and donning a wetsuit and booties you can launch from there and set a course for anywhere upstream.

The river is usually very calm in the lower reaches and gradually becomes rougher further up. The beauty of this is that you become accustomed to the canoe on an easy stretch of water and eventually, when a rapid that you're unwilling to tackle looms ahead, you can simply turn around and paddle back.

You can hire the canoes for any length of time, but to enjoy the really fantastic scenery we recommend you take a packed lunch and your camera (waterproof containers for cameras are supplied) and make a day of it. In the higher reaches you will have to drag your canoe over more and more logs until eventually it's just not worth continuing. The paddle back down is equally rewarding and somewhat more relaxing.

Paddling Down the Pororari River   (Jonathan Kennett)

—Notes— For one single canoe, Punakaiki Canoe and Bike Hire charge $10/$20/$30 per hour/3 hours/ day. They also hire life jackets, booties and camera containers, and have a few Canadian canoes as well. For your interest take Topomap K30 Punakaiki.

12.7 Big River Mountain Biking

Reefton, Victoria Forest Park

For intermediate riders, 3-6 hours one way; 25 km

—Summary— This hilly 4WD track leads riders through lovely native forest to the luxurious Big River Hut. It's worth staying overnight to explore various sidetracks and the abandoned gold workings in the area.

—How to Get There— Reefton is 80 km northeast of Greymouth on Highway 7.

—Description— Ride south from Reefton on Highway 7 and cross the Inangahua River bridge. After 1 km, turn left onto Soldiers Road. This soon becomes a gravel road and climbs up Devils Creek valley for 9 km to the Alborn Coal Mine car park. One hundred metres further the Big River Road (signposted) veers off to the left. The ride continues for another 2-4 hours, through native forest, on a rocky but rideable 4WD track, to Big River. Various sites in this area were extensively mined for gold late last century. Remains of old machinery provide interest for those passing by, while huge piles of mullock (waste rock) stand as testimony to the environmental effects of mining. Big River Hut perches about 50 unrideable metres above the river, overlooking the old township site and surrounding countryside. Remember this is a 4WD track—always give way to those with a smaller brain-to-weight ratio, such as 4WD vehicles.

—Notes— The walking track that continues on to Waiuta, a mining ghost town, crosses fragile pakihi (swamp) vegetation and is not suitable for riding on.

Big River Hut costs $8/night. Refer to Topomaps L30 Reefton and L31 Springs Junction.

12.8 Taipo River

35 km east of Hokitika

For intermediate paddlers, 1-2 river hours.

—Summary— This is one of the West Coast's brilliant hidden spots. A series of playful grade II to III rapids can keep kayakers amused and tubers challenged, making this a great river for an expedition with a mixture of crafts and abilities.

—How to Get There— Drive 35 km east from the coast on Highway 73 (towards Arthur's Pass), to the Taipo River bridge.

—Description— From the Taipo bridge either drive or walk northeast along the highway for 2 km before turning right onto a gravel road (signposted). It takes about an hour to walk over the hill to the Taipo River. It's possible to drive most of the gravel road in a 4WD or rental car. Either put-in as soon as you reach the river or as far upstream as you can be bothered to walk. The main rapids begin where the Taipo River cuts into the hill that you've just walked over. Once you've entered the gorge the only way out is down the river, so you must be a confident grade II+ paddler (or a very good swimmer). All the rapids are best run down the middle. After an hour or so, depending on how many eddies you've caught and stoppers you've surfed on, you'll see the highway bridge in the distance. Jump out here and warm up at the nearby Jacksons Pub.

—Notes— This snow-fed river is c-c-c-cold! Hypothermia is the greatest danger facing keen adventurers, so make sure you wear a good wetsuit, warm footwear and a warm hat under your helmet. The Taipo is a serious proposition in any kind of flood.

Kayaks and equipment can be hired from Topsports in Christchurch, ☎ (03) 365 7585. Topomap K33 Otira is useful.

12.9 Alex Knob

 Franz Josef

For beginner trampers, 6-9 hours.

—Summary— This is an excellent little tramp that, on a fine day, provides fantastic views from the Tasman Coast, right up to the Southern Alps. Franz Josef Glacier and Mt Cook can be clearly seen.

—How to Get There— Walk 1 km up the Franz Josef Glacier Access Road from Highway 6 to a signposted track on your right.

—Description— From the road a well-marked track meanders through lush rainforest to Lake Wombat about 2 km away. The track then climbs steadily through various botanical strata, to golden brown tussocklands on the tops. From the bushline follow the poled route across snow tussock, to Alex Knob (1306 m). Three look-outs en route to the top also provide spectacular panoramas.

—Notes— In winter this is for the experienced only as an ice axe and crampons may be necessary to reach the top of Alex Knob. Ask at the DOC information centre in Franz Josef for up-to-date track conditions. In March 1982 New Zealand's record rainfall event occurred on Alex Knob when 1.81 metres fell in three days. We suggest taking a rain coat. Topomap H35 Franz Josef is useful but not essential.

12.10 Barn Bay Bike or Hike

South Westland, 70 km south of Haast

For experienced riders or intermediate trampers, 4-8 hours one way.

—Summary— Technically difficult riding on bush-covered tracks leads to the breathtaking coastline around Barn Bay. There is a wilderness magic about this region that defies description. More than just fantastic scenery, it has a distinctly enticing atmosphere. Those who embark on a decent exploration of the area are seldom rewarded with less than the adventure of a lifetime.

—How to Get There— Travel southwest from Haast for 60 km to the road end at Martyr Homestead. It's a good quality gravel road often enclosed by beautiful podocarp forest. Great riding. If you have to drive, park 200 metres before Martyr Homestead, avoiding boggy ground.

—Description— From Martyr Homestead, follow an obvious 4WD track across farmland to the Cascade River. If the river is low, cross on foot at the wide shallow ford reached via the track. At normal to high flows, we suggest floating across on tractor tubes close to where the track first meets the river. This river is your main obstacle and shouldn't be attempted when in flood.

Pick up the 4WD track (Barn Bay-Cascade 'Road') on the other side and follow it into the bush. Aim for the gates and red buoys hanging from trees at the edge of the paddock. Once in the bush, the track improves at first but then deteriorates progressively towards the coast—two large streambeds provide rocky challenges. Soon after the slippery and hilly 'Miracle Mile', you'll reach a spacious hut owned by Ken Landaus. It is open to the public free of charge, so make sure you look after it well. From the hut, the track is unrideable so you may as well leave your bikes and walk. After 200 metres you'll reach Hope River. Its wide gravelly bed provides easy walking to Barn Bay. However, if it's in flood, take the seldom used but marked track through thick bush to the coast. Both routes take half an hour. There is a house hidden amongst bush near the base of a tall radio mast and plenty of good camping sites in the vicinity. Once at Barn Bay you'll probably want to stay and explore the area, for at least a day or two. It's a fantastic part of the country.

—Track Conditions— 90% 4WD track, 10% unrideable single track or semi-rideable river bed.

—Notes— The accompanying map for this section is the most up to date available, however, Terrainmap 12 Mt Cook is also useful. There are plans afoot to smash a Highway from here through to Milford. We're hoping it never happens, but just in case, you should get down there and enjoy this beautiful area before it gets 'carved up'.

12.11 Other Adventures

Honeycomb Cave

Kahurangi National Park includes a magnificent area of

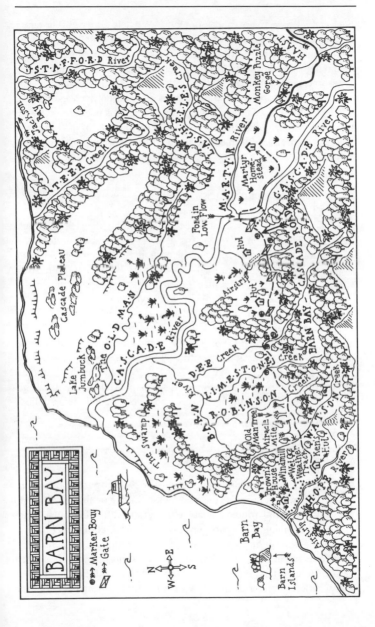

bush, tablelands, rivers, and mountains. What is less well known is that beneath this vast tract of wilderness exists an equally impressive underground world. The Honeycomb Caves offer an easy introduction to caving in this region. Amongst other features is an impressive limestone arch, reputedly the largest in the Southern Hemisphere. Last Resort in Karamea (the northernmost town on the West Coast), ☎ (03) 782 6617, run daily trips to the caves. This beginner's caving trip costs $60 per adult and $30 per child (group size of 4-6). It takes 6 hours return from Karamea and includes transport, refreshments and a guide.

Wangapeka Track

For those who are still keen after walking the Heaphy Track (see 11.1 The Heaphy Track), the Wangapeka Track provides the opportunity to cross back over to the east side of Kahurangi National Park. This historical 76 km track passes through beech-forested river valleys and over two subalpine saddles. Most parties complete the west-east traverse from Little Wanganui River to Wangapeka River in 3-4 days. The track is maintained to a good standard, suitable for intermediate trampers. There are five main huts along the way and several minor ones. Transport can be arranged to/from both ends of the track through several operators. Two of these are North-west Nelson Trampers Service, ☎ (03) 528 6332, Motueka; and Karamea Taxis, ☎ (03) 782 6757, Karamea. Topomaps M28 Wangapeka and L27 Karamea are essential. There is also a specific Trackmap called, surprisingly, Wangapeka Track.

Charleston

A line of metamorphic seacliffs, 29 km south of Westport beside Highway 6, provides the best rock climbing on the coast. There are well over 100 routes (most below grade 20), offering a huge variety of climbing. The sparse protection on some climbs encourages top-roping, thus giving you a chance to concentrate on your climbing technique rather than the Tasman Sea crashing against the rocks below. Be careful when walking around the cliffs during high seas. The Charleston motorcamp, a few hundred metres from the crag, has an up-to-date list of the climbs and offers special rates to climbers staying for a while. Tim Wethey's *Canterbury Rock* (see Further Reading) is an excellent guide to this popular crag.

Kayaking Mecca

The New Zealand Kayak School runs excellent whitewater paddling courses based from Murchison. For more information see chapter 13, section 13.8.

Maruia River

Thirty kilometres southwest of Murchison, the Maruia River branches away from Highway 65 as it disappears behind the densely forested Mt Rutland. It provides experienced kayakers and rafters with a fantastic 18 km long stretch of river. Expect to take all day on tubes—commercial rafters take up to 7 hours depending on the river flow. A third of the way down, there are some bouldery grade III rapids that need to be scouted out and possibly portaged. To reach the put-in site, drive 10 km north of Maruia (just a few buildings and a name on the map) on Highway 65, and turn left onto Creightons Road. After a few kilometres stop at the Warwick River bridge, from where you can paddle, float or grovel 300 metres down the Warwick River to the Maruia River. The take-out site is near Ruffe Creek, where the river meets Highway 65. For more information contact DOC in Reefton or Murchison. In the summer months this river can be too low to tube comfortably. Topomap L30 Reefton is useful.

Mt Rolleston

Rising just west of Arthur's Pass, Mt Rolleston (2275 m) provides excellent climbing for less-experienced mountaineers. A rewarding time of year to climb Mt Rolleston is from winter to early summer, when the whole area is covered in snow. The Otira Slide is the easiest and most frequently climbed route. Even so, basic mountaineering knowledge, especially well-developed skills with both crampons and ice axe, is essential for a safe trip.

From the car park next to Highway 73, it's 2-3 hours' walk up Otira Valley to the base of Mt Rolleston. From there ascend the Otira Slide, an easy snow slope to your left, which leads up to Goldney Ridge. Follow this to your right, up to the Low Peak of Mt Rolleston (2212 m). From Low Peak you have to negotiate the narrow and exposed ridge to High Peak, about 500 metres away. It may be wise to start belaying here—simply tripping on a crampon could be fatal. Depending on conditions, it is usually easier to sidle the middle section to the south of the ridge. For more experienced climbers, Rome Ridge is the classic route up Mt Rolleston. It's exactly the type of winding arête you dream about, so take your camera. The usual descent route for both climbs is the Otira Slide. But beware, it can be very avalanche prone—especially in warm, soft snow conditions. For more information, contact Arthur's Pass National Park Headquarters, ☎ (03) 318 9211. Topomap K33 Otira is essential.

Three Passes

The Three Passes trip in Arthur's Pass National Park can be done from Lake Kaniere on the West Coast. For more information see Chapter 13 (section 13.2), The Three Passes.

Okarito

The turn-off to Okarito village is about 20 km north of Franz Josef on Highway 6. Here, one of New Zealand's most beautiful and wild coastlines awaits you. This relaxing area has some splendid day walks and offers serene kayaking in the lagoon. Kayaking is undoubtedly the best way to explore the calm, mysterious waters of Okarito Lagoon and its surrounding magnificent native rainforest beneath a backdrop of the central Southern Alps. If you're lucky you may spot one of the beautiful kotoku (white heron).

Kayaks can be hired from Okarito Nature Tours, ☎ (03) 753 4014. A 2-hour trip costs $20 per person, a full day trip to the delta is $30 and an overnight trip is $50. All of these must be timed with the tide, and bookings are essential for the overnight option. Also, make sure you have enough time to walk up to Okarito Trig. On a fine day you'll be treated to a stunning mountains-to-the-sea panorama. The track leaves from directly opposite the Youth Hostel Association warden's house, and takes 1-2 hours return. On the way another track branches off to Three Mile Lagoon—it's also worth exploring. During low tide you can return via the coast.

Guided Glacier Walks

The Fox and Franz Josef Glaciers grind down through the Southern Alps, almost reaching the Tasman Sea. This is one of the few places in the world where such massive rivers of ice extend to the level of temperate rain forest—and they are still advancing! Walking amongst the incredible ice formations at the glacier terminals is a fascinating and unforgettable introduction to New Zealand's alpine world. Independent travellers can walk right up to the glaciers, but to actually climb onto them safely, contact one of the guiding companies based in the Fox or Franz Josef townships.

Mt Tasman

At 3498 metres, Tasman is New Zealand's second highest mountain. Since the huge rock slide off Mt Cook in 1991 and its subsequent instability, there has been a marked increase in the number of ascents of this spectacular peak. It is, however, a longer and more difficult climb than Mt Cook. Considered a mountaineer's mountain, its icy white spire is equal in beauty to Mt Aspiring. Mt Tasman is most often climbed via the North Shoulder, from the isolated Pioneer Hut west of the Main Divide. This is a long demanding route graded 3+ (see Grading Systems). Merely to reach the base of the ridge you must first traverse Mt Lendenfeld (3142 m). The ridge beyond the North Shoulder is steep and exposed—classic ice climbing.

Welcome Flat Hot Pools

Hidden amongst the spectacular mountain scenery of the Copland Valley are several large, steaming hot pools. They are 5-8 hours' walk from the West Coast Highway on a well marked track. The track starts at the Karangarua River bridge 25 km south of Fox Glacier. All the major side streams are bridged and there is a comfortable 30 bunk hut, 50 metres from the hot pools. Most people tramp back the same way, but those with mountaineering experience sometimes continue up and over the rugged Copland Pass to Mt Cook Village—see Chapter 13 (section 13.7), The Copland Pass.

Maruia Falls

Maruia Falls are beside Highway 65, about 15 km south of Highway 6 and the Buller River. The rock shelf on the true right, a few metres from the edge of the falls, is a good place to leap from (if there is such a thing!). The true left side has logs recirculating in the pool at the bottom—don't jump there unless you need a log enema. During your 10 m fall, try to look out at the horizon rather than the water below. This helps to keep you feet first and your nose free of water. For a smooth entry into the water it's important to keep your arms by your side, otherwise you risk injury and a difficult swim back. We recommend wearing a wetsuit and a well fastened life jacket. Before jumping check there are no logs or branches floating around the landing site. If you're worried about safety—don't do it!

Leaping off Maruia Falls　　　(Malcolm O'Neill)

13. Canterbury

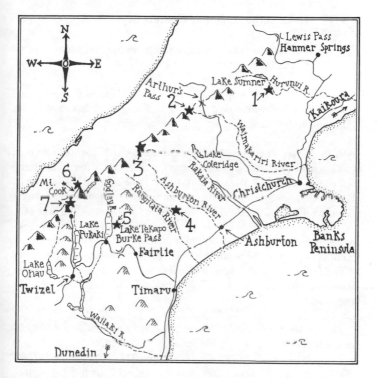

13.1 The Hurunui River

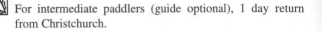

Lake Sumner, North Canterbury

For intermediate paddlers (guide optional), 1 day return from Christchurch.

—**Summary**— The upper section of the Hurunui is one of Canterbury's best recreational rivers. This 8 km stretch has some great II+ rapids to fool around in and sharpen up your skills.

—**How to Get There**— Drive 60 km north of Christchurch before turning west onto Highway 7, just south of Waipara. After 15 km turn left and drive through Waikari. Follow the Lake Sumner road through Hawarden and over Jacks Saddle into the Hurunui Valley. After driving up the valley for a few kilometres you'll pass the take-out point, where the Seaward River joins the Hurunui. Have a good look at the river here so you will recognise the site on the way down. About 5 km after crossing the south branch of the Hurunui River you will see a small 4WD track leading to a camping area and toilet on your right (about 200 metres past a small swingbridge). This is the Jolly Brook put-in site.

—**Description**— It takes 2-3 hours to kayak or raft this scenic stretch of grade II+ water.

Scramble down a small track to the river. There is a great rapid for playing in here, it's about 200 metres long and ends just before the swingbridge. If you want to avoid this rapid then put-in at another common spot about 50 metres downriver from the swingbridge. You can also leap off the cliff a short distance upriver from the footbridge (on the true right).

There are a couple of short gorges before the take-out. Most rapids are best run down the centre, and beginners will probably find the trickiest bits are where the river corners into a couple of bluffs. The river generally runs next to the road, allowing for an easy exit if needed.

Immediately below Seaward River the Hurunui becomes more serious. If you are a competent grade III paddler and can avoid holes, then try kayaking Maori Gully. Allow 2-3 hours for this lower section. The take-out site needs to be scouted before paddling the river. On the drive in, as soon as the road almost meets the river after passing Jacks Saddle, stop at a car parking area near a cattle stop. Follow a small track down to the river and memorise the scene.

—Notes— For $38 per day you can hire a kayak and all the extra gear you need from Top Sports in Christchurch, ☎ (03) 365 7585. They can also arrange a guide. The Hurunui River is warm in late summer, but if there is a howling nor'west wind, consider paddling elsewhere. Refer to Topomap M33 Waikari or Terrainmap 11 Kaikoura.

13.2 The Three Passes Tramp

Arthur's Pass National Park

For experienced trampers, 4 days.

—Summary— This popular trip crosses east to west over the Southern Alps. It is a serious alpine tramp along a route originally used by Maori to take greenstone from the Arahura River on the West Coast to Canterbury. There are excellent views from the passes and beautiful bush scenery in the valleys.

—How to Get There— The trip starts at Klondyke Corner (2 km north of the Waimakariri River bridge), which is 8 km southeast of Arthur's Pass township. Arthur's Pass is 150 km northwest of Christchurch on Highway 73 and is served by the Coast to Coast Bus Service, ☎ 0800 800 847, which runs between Christchurch and Greymouth. The trip finishes at the southern tip of Lake Kaniere, on the West Coast (25 km inland from Hokitika).

—Description—
Klondyke Corner to Carrington Hut; 4-6 hours
The Waimakariri River is typical of Canterbury rivers—wide, flat and seemingly never ending. In dry weather conditions you can walk up the river bed from Klondyke Corner. Start at the end of the gravel road

that branches off Highway 73 near Klondyke shelter on the true left. In wet conditions take the slightly longer wet-weather track on the true right. Anti Crow Hut is a good place for lunch and can easily be seen from the river. The next hut marked on the map is Greenlaw Hut; it's a scungy hole which DOC are planning to remove. Aim to spend the night at Carrington Hut (36 bunks).

Carrington Hut to Park Morpeth Hut; 6-8 hours
The next day walk up the White River for 1 km and either ford the river or cross on the Clough Cableway (at the time of writing this cableway was unusable due to earthquake damage—contact DOC to see if it's been repaired yet). From here climb up the steep bouldery river in the Taipoiti Gorge to Harman Pass (1320 m). Towards the top of the valley, sidle right around the bluffs before following an easy track up to the pass, which is marked by a cairn. Whitehorn Pass can be seen at the head of the unnamed glacier-scoured valley to the southwest. Drop off the pass and head up the valley and over Whitehorn Pass. Take care in the descent to Cronin Stream, as it is steep and can be prone to avalanches.

The Cronin Valley has cathedral-like rock walls rising hundreds of metres from the valley floor. A kilometre before the Wilberforce confluence, take the marked route on the true right to Park Morpeth Hut (6 bunks). Any gear left outside the hut at night should be considered as an offering to the local kea, an extremely mischievous parrot.

Park Morpeth Hut to Harman Hut; 4-5 hours
The next day head up the valley on the true left to the Clough Memorial, before zigzagging your way to the Keas' Head Office at Browning Pass. You'll notice as you cross from east to west on the main divide that the bush changes into west coast rainforest.

Harman Hut to Lake Kaniere; 6-8 hours
From Harman Hut (6 bunks) sidle up to and over the gentle Styx Saddle on a well-marked track, and down into the Styx Valley about 2 hours away. A 5 hour walk down the valley takes you to Upper Kokatahi Road, just south of Lake Kaniere.

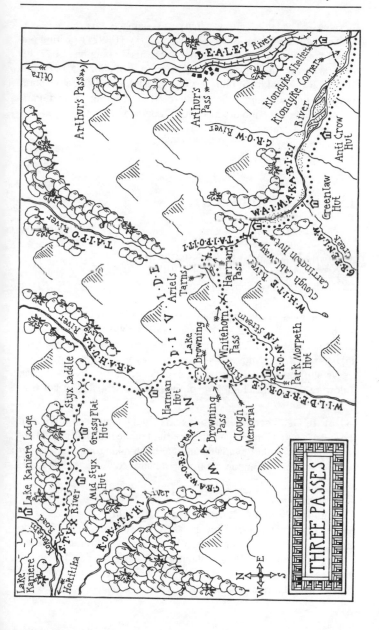

THREE PASSES

—**Notes**— This is a serious alpine trek—always take an ice axe. Contact Arthur's Pass Visitors Centre, ☎ (03) 318 9211, to find out about the current snow conditions because crampons may be necessary even in summer. Pete's Place in Hokitika, ☎ (03) 755 8845, and the Hokitika Taxi Service, ☎ (03) 755 8437, transports trampers to and from Lake Kaniere. Both Carrington and Park Morpeth Huts have mountain radios. Topomaps K33 Otira and J33 Kaniere are essential.

13.3 Whitcombe Pass

130 km west of Christchurch

For fit experienced trampers, 5-7 days.

—**Summary**— Whitcombe Pass is one of the lowest crossing points on the Central Southern Alps but it is still very isolated. While this means it's a great wilderness experience—chances are you won't see another soul during your trip—it also means you're on your own if the brown stuff hits the fan. Tramping experience, especially good track following skills, and a high level of fitness are essential for a safe trip.

—**How to Get There**— This trip starts from Glenfalloch Station, at the end of the road running up the true right of the Rakaia River. There is no public transport available and the hitch-hiking is terrible. Your best bet is to bribe someone from Christchurch to drive you out there.

—**Description**—
Glenfalloch Station to Reischek Hut; 7-10 hours
Stop in at Glenfalloch Station and ask for permission to continue up the valley. At the same time casually ask for advice on crossing the Rakaia River (try to do this without giving them the idea that you're just the sort of greenhorns who will have to be rescued in a couple of days time). The river changes from year to year and is usually the

main obstacle on this crossing. From late summer to winter the river level is generally lowest during the early morning when snow melt is minimal.

From Glenfalloch follow a farm track up valley and around the left of the Whales Back to Lake Stream. Unless you plan to cross the Rakaia here, the quickest route up valley is actually round the back of Prospect Hill (follow a fenceline and then a farm track). Then try and follow an intermittent 4WD track in and out of the river bed and around clumps of matagouri (unmistakeably thorny shrub) all the way to Reischek Hut (6 bunks). This is by far the nicest hut in the valley but it is a long way to walk in one day and unlucky route finding decisions are common.

Also, as it is snow fed, the river will be at its lowest in the early morning and this is the most common (although possibly not the best) crossing point. In any case there are plenty of good places to camp en route.

Louper Biv to Neave Hut; 6-8 hours

The next day try to cross the river to Louper Biv (2 bunks). If it is too deep or swift then look for another crossing spot or just wait for the river to drop.

Assuming you make it across OK, walk up Louper Stream. There is a lot of boulder hopping required as the route follows the streambed, but you should aim to reach Whitcombe Pass for a late lunch. Here you turn your back on the dry barren foothills of Canterbury and enter the lush wild rainforest of the West Coast.

Descend from the pass, across the gravel outwash from Sale Glacier Stream and the tussocky flats beyond. The route then follows the river bank for a few kilometres. You should definitely have picked up a track before entering 'The Gateway', beyond which lies Neave Hut. This is a common destination for the second night.

Neave Hut to Prices Flat; 7-9 hours

From Neave Hut the track continues down the true right of Whitcombe River and podocarp forest takes the place of subalpine vegetation. After about 2 hours you'll reach the historic rock bivvy 'Cave Camp' where there are views of Mt Evans, the highest mountain in the region. A little further downriver, there's a turn-off which leads to a swing bridge and Wilkinson Hut. Unless you need a rest day, just continue on the true right of the Whitcombe River. From here the track sometimes follows the riverbed but mainly sidles in the bush, crossing many slips and sidestreams en route. Cataract Creek and Price Flat Huts are about 5-7 hours from Cave Camp.

Price Flat to Frews Hut; 4-7 hours
There are two huts at Price Flat, the newer one is on a terrace above the old one. The track from here to Frews Hut is fraught with difficulties. It crosses many sidestreams (some of which are impassable in flood) and slips and you will often have to hunt around to find the track again on the other side of these obstacles. This sort of track is far more familiar to most New Zealand trampers than the corridor-type paths that typify the Great Walks.

Frews Hut to the road end; 4-6 hours
From Frews Hut the track alternates between riverbed travel and sidling in the bush. Within an hour you will cross to the true left of the Whitcombe River and follow similar terrain to Rapid Creek Hut about another 2 hours away. Just before the hut you must cross Rapid Creek which is impassable when in flood.

It is another 2-3 hours from Rapid Creek to the old road-end hut and once again the track provides a few challenges, but it's generally good travel. From the road-end hut you will have to walk another few kilometres along what is usually an undriveable section of 4WD track before hopefully being picked up at a prearranged rendezvous.

—**Notes**— As several side streams are uncrossable during heavy rain you should plan to enjoy one or two 'pit days' stuck in a hut eating, reading and listening to rain pounding on a tin roof. You are also well advised to take a mountain radio with you (see Clubs and Contacts). Topomaps J33 Kaniere, J34 Whitcombe, and J35 Arrowsmith are essential.

13.4 Rafting the Rangitata

Peel Forest, 150 km southwest of Christchurch

For all adventurers (guided), 3 hours on the river.

—Summary— This is one of the toughest sections of commercially rafted grade V water in New Zealand. The river pounds through a rocky gorge dotted with house-sized boulders. There's plenty of action along the way, dodging huge rocks, shooting through side channels and plummeting over large cascades.

—How to Get There— Contact Rangitata Rafts in Christchurch, ☎ (03) 366 9731 or at their base on ☎ (03) 696 3735. They arrange transport from Christchurch to the base, which is 35 km upriver from the Rangitata highway bridge, and 8 km beyond Peel Forest.

—Description— The photo display at Rangitata Rafts shows swamped rafts, ripped rafts, upside-down rafts, and sandwiched rafts: the river is full of surprises!

After an early lunch, the guide eases everybody's nerves as you squeeze into wetsuits and get levered into the bus for a short drive to the top of the Rangitata Gorge.

Soon after launching your raft you'll discover muscles you never knew existed, as you back paddle, spin and ferry glide through the practice rapids. At grade II, Glacier Rapid shouldn't be a problem after all your training. Pencil Sharpener (grade III-IV) and Tsunami are long rapids, which give rafters their first serious challenge. Rooster Tail is the first grade V rapid. It's a long full-on chute that finishes with a series of huge stopper waves. The final rapid to look forward to is the Pinch. It requires hopping out, being told how you'll navigate it then, if the river level is low, going down one raft at a time for safety's sake. In high river levels all rafts run it at the same time. It's made up of two excellent drops and sweeping bends that require considerable skill.

A little further downstream, once everyone's pulled themselves together, you'll be introduced to cliff jumping. At 10 metres high, the drop may prompt you to let your guide jump first (just in case...). The take-out is a short distance downriver.

—Notes— The trip costs $105 all inclusive. Showers and hot food are provided before the drive back to Christchurch. The season lasts from September to May. Accommodation is available for $10 per night at Rangitata Rafts' comfy lodge.

13.5 Ski-Touring on the Two Thumb Range

 Lake Tekapo

For all adventurers (guided), 2 or 5 days.

—Summary— Cross-country or telemark-style skis are becoming increasingly popular for alpine travel in New Zealand. During winter this type of long skinny ski is excellent for exploring the rolling hills and stepped plateaus of the Two Thumb Range. Accompanied by a mountain guide and based out of a private hut at 1300 metres, this trip gives a good introduction to cross-country skiing. The varied terrain also provides plenty of challenges for the experienced skier.

—How to Get There— Contact Alpine Recreation Canterbury Ltd, in Lake Tekapo township, ☎ (03) 680 6736, or fax (03) 680 6765.

—Description— After a 30 minute drive along the eastern side of Lake Tekapo, you'll reach a 4WD track leading up through tangled matagouri scrub. In snowy years you can skin up on skis all the way from lake level to Rex Simpson Hut at 1300 metres. Otherwise you'll get there by driving, walking and, finally, skinning up on skis. The winter snows rarely recede beyond the hut.

Once at the comfortable and well supplied alpine hut, there is time for a quick bite before an afternoon cruise. A 5 km sidle to the south illustrates what is involved in efficient cross-country skiing—namely technique rather than brute force.

The skis have a fish-scale textured section moulded into the mid section of the sole. As you stride forward, this part of the ski is compressed into the snow and the scales grip. When you un-weight the ski it slides forward easily. This system works fine on mild gradients but on uncooperative snow or steeper slopes, such as climbing up to the hut, ski skins need to be temporarily attached. Originally seal skins, nowadays synthetic skins are used to resist backsliding. More effective than fish-scales, they also slightly reduce your forward motion. This is why they are not used on gentler slopes.

Cross-country Skiing above Lake Tekapo   (Malcolm O'Neill)

Subsequent days are spent exploring the snow covered peaks and valleys of the Two Thumb Range. Thousands of years of grinding glacier action have sculpted odd lines and basins, leaving a variety of slopes suitable for all skiing abilities. Excellent and patient ski instruction is given, and downhill skiers who persevere will soon pick up the graceful telemark-style turn.

On fine evenings, skinning up to the ridge behind the hut will give you grand views of Mt Cook National Park. Mounts Cook, Tasman and Malte Brun are focused into silhouettes as the sun slips west. In fading light, the soft snow forms a hard crust—not the best conditions for learning telemark turns. Long traverses joined by kick turns will eventually return you to the warm hut.

The steep return to the road can sometimes be accomplished on skis; otherwise it's an entertaining afternoon stroll as you watch those who thought they had sufficient skill to ski back, gently somersault their way down.

—Notes— Trips cost $350 for a weekend and $875 for 5 days. Ski gear, food, hut accommodation, and a mountain guide are included. Average fitness is required.

13.6 Climbing Mt Cook

 The central Southern Alps

For experienced climbers or fit guided beginners, 4-6 days.

—Summary— At 3753 metres, Aoraki (the cloud piercer) stands head and shoulders above all other New Zealand mountains. It was first climbed in 1894 by three self-taught New Zealand climbers, Tom Fyfe, George Graham, and Jack Clarke. Nowadays there are over 30 different routes to the top, but it is most often climbed via the Linda Glacier. Because it is New Zealand's highest mountain, people commonly believe that it is extremely difficult to climb and requires exceptional mountaineering skills and/or suicidal tendencies. In fact, in fine weather, with the aid of a qualified guide, Mt Cook is within the capabilities of most fit beginner mountaineers.

—How to Get There— A daily Mt Cook Line bus connects Christchurch with Mt Cook Village. Flying from Christchurch is also an option.

The 'lost world' of Mangapu Cave, Waitomo

South Island high country

Rangitata High Country Safaris

Tramping in South Westland

Grant Singleton

Mt Taranaki, as seen from the Round-the-Mountain Track

Chris Prudden

Whitewater sledging on the Rangitaiki River

Adventure Photography

Crossing the Cascade River on the way to Barn Bay

Tubing the Otaki River

Rock climbing at Whanganui Bay, Lake Taupo

Mt Aspiring from Colin Todd Hut, and Mt Cook Lily

A 'pop-out' on the Tongariro River—now what?

Jane Shearer

Sailing sea kayaks

Exploring Queen Charlotte Sound

—**Description**— Mt Cook is usually climbed via the Linda Glacier from Plateau Hut, which is half way up the mountain on the edge of a huge snowfield called the Grand Plateau. You can either fly or walk to the Plateau. We walked in, via the Tasman Glacier and up Haast Ridge, and found it to be as long and demanding as the climb from Plateau to the summit.

Most guides will suggest you cut the climb in half by flying in—it means you're fresh for climbing and more likely to get good weather (partly because you can only fly in during good weather).

From Plateau Hut to the summit and back takes 12-24 hours, longer if you get caught out in bad weather. Exactly how long depends on several factors. Your fitness and ability to acclimatize to high altitudes make a big difference. Mt Cook is not quite high enough for altitude sickness to be a serious problem, but some people, especially those who fly in, do feel a bit breathless towards the top.

Unless your guide decides you should bivvy on Linda Glacier, to get a head start the next day, you'll be staying at Plateau Hut (30 bunks) for the night. After practising a few climbing techniques on the slopes near the hut, you should try to get as much sleep as possible.

Midnight: Clamber into all your gear, force breakfast down and rope up. Aim to be heading out the door and across the Plateau by about 1am.

If the snow is soft, plugging steps across the Plateau and up the Linda Glacier is a grind. Late in the season (January to February) you must negotiate a tiring and frustrating maze of long, wide crevasses, plunging hundreds of feet down into dark icy depths. This is where a guide is invaluable. If the snow has frozen then travel will be fast and you should reach the Linda Shelf at the head of Linda Glacier just at dawn.

The summit rocks loom above. Not for the first time your guide will prove his or her worth by leading up each of the seven pitches (rope lengths) to the top of the rocks. Climbing up the rocks is relatively easy, unless they are covered in ice. The 1000 metre drop below gives a sense of exposure that cannot help but encourage safe climbing techniques.

Above the rocks the summit icecap leads to the top. Its 40° slope is often iced up with sastrugi—clear ice fingers formed by the wind that break off under your crampons to tinkle their way down the slope. Sometimes this can be more serious when larger pieces of ice shatter and break away, taking your foothold with them. This is called dinner-plating. As this is the most exposed place in New Zealand, the weather is critical. Strong icy winds can blow up from nowhere and foil an attempt at the last moment.

Standing on the summit in fine weather is a fantastic experience. Looking down on the bushclad West Coast; Mt Tasman and the Tasman Glacier; the vast and barren Mackenzie Country; and, running south off the summit, New Zealand's 'highest mile'—you really do feel like you're on top of the world. But don't relax yet, as the descent is often the most difficult part of a climb. The avalanche-prone Linda Glacier has claimed many lives this century. A particularly notorious section near the top of the glacier, called the Gun Barrel, should be avoided in late afternoon when it's often quite active.

Most climbers walk out from Plateau Hut, either over Cinerama Col or down a snow gully next to Haast Ridge. Both routes are far easier and more enjoyable than the walk in, but involve difficult route finding. It takes 5-10 hours to reach Ball Road end (12 km from Mt Cook Village).

—Notes— If you're doing a trip with a guide, and aren't held up by bad weather, then you have a very high chance of reaching the top. If you manage to climb Mt Cook and still have some time left, have a go at Mt Dixon. It's also a fine climb. Guided trips cost between $2000 and $2600, and last for up to six days. For more information contact DOC at Mt Cook Village, ☎ (03) 435 1819. Topomap H36 Mt Cook is essential.

13.7 The Copland Pass

 Mt Cook and Westland National Parks

For experienced alpine trampers (guide optional), 3-4 days.
—Summary— The Copland Pass is a spectacular and challenging route across the Southern Alps. During the crossing dramatic differences between the South Island's dry east coast and its wet west

coast are experienced at first hand, as the barren crumbling landscape of Mt Cook gives way to lush Westland rainforest.

—How to Get There— A daily Mt Cook Line bus connects Christchurch with Mt Cook Village. Flying from Christchurch is also an option.

—Description—
Mt Cook Village to Hooker Hut, 3-4 hours
From the White Horse Hill camping ground, follow the well marked track up the Hooker Valley. After crossing two bridges over the Hooker River, the view of Mt Cook ahead dominates the scene.

Now and again thundering icefalls tumble down Mt Sefton's precipitous east face. In mid-summer the Hooker Valley is covered with Mt Cook lilies (Ranunculus lyalli), which are the largest ranunculus plants in the world. Their delicate flowers seem to defy the harsh alpine environment. Hooker Hut (12 bunks) is reached soon after passing through the signposted avalanche zone (not a good picnic site). Subsidence of the moraine below the hut, caused by the receding Hooker Glacier, means this hut will have to be relocated some time soon.

Hooker Hut to Douglas Rock Hut, 8-12 hours
The next 500 metre section of track changes from year to year. Check at Mt Cook National Park Headquarters for the most up-to-date description of the route from Hooker Hut to the Copland ridge.

The ridge itself is made up of 'weetbix' rock (technically referred to as shattered greywacke), which is prevalent throughout the region. Try not to dislodge rocks onto people below you (rockfall is a major cause of accidents in the mountains). Pick and weave your way up the narrow rocky ridge until after three hours or so it flattens out somewhat. No, that's not a large discarded beer can ahead, it's the Copland Emergency Shelter (2 bunks). About here the permanent snow and ice begins—sometimes you need to wear crampons even before you reach the shelter.

From Copland Shelter follow the steepish snow slope to the right under the rock ridge. This slope is often very icy and late in the summer a few crevasses appear. Once you've crossed the divide (there are actually about five different places you can cross), scramble down a short rocky section for about 50 metres to the gentler slopes on the west. Further down, a well-cairned track follows a creek on the true left down to the 'zigzag' track at the head of the Copland Valley. As you wander along, spare a thought for the pioneers who constantly got hung up by their swags as they bush-bashed through this very same subalpine scrub. Douglas Rock Hut (12 bunks) is named after New Zealand's most famous West Coast explorer, Charlie Douglas.

Douglas Rock Hut to State Highway 6, 7-10 hours
From Douglas Rock, it's a pleasant 2-3 hours' walk through thick forest to Welcome Flat Hut (30 bunks, gas stove). There are several camp sites nearby including a huge rock bivvy. More importantly there are several large hot pools of varying temperatures. In 1987 the old warden's hut was partially swept away by a huge mud slide. The warden had to escape out the window.

Allow 5-6 hours to walk down the river valley to the road. The Copland River is typical of many West Coast rivers, with its crisp blue water cascading between large boulders into deep pools. The milky blue colour is caused by suspended glacial silt. At the track end there is a small bus shelter. Buses are used to picking up smelly trampers who wave them down. The coast is not renowned for its hitchhiking.

—Notes— The Copland Pass has claimed several lives. The main dangers are rockfall on the ridge up to Copland Shelter and slipping on the hard ice near the pass.

Parties should be well equipped for alpine conditions with ice axes, crampons, rope, and the experience needed for their use. All the huts have a mountain radio.

Mountain Guides can be hired to help groups across the alpine section and they also hire out ice axes and crampons. Contact DOC in Mt Cook Village, ☎ (03) 435 1819, to find out more. Depending on the size of the group, guides cost from $150-$240 per person per day. Topomap H36 Mt Cook is essential.

13.8 Other Adventures

Kayaking Mecca

Based in Christchurch and Murchison, the New Zealand

Kayak School provides the best opportunity for paddlers of all levels to gain more whitewater skills. The school attracts the country's top professional instructors and this shows in its ability to teach new paddling skills very quickly and safely.

Well-priced courses are run frequently in summer and booking ahead is essential. Introductory and intermediate courses are held from Murchison and Christchurch. Advanced 4-day courses are only held from Murchison and take advantage of some of the big water on the Buller, Matakitaki and Matiri Rivers. Special courses can be arranged for groups.

For more information contact Janette Kear, 2 Kruse Place, Christchurch, ☎ (03) 352 5786, or Mick Hopkinson, 95 Mt Pleasant Road, ☎/fax (03) 384 3206.

Waiau River

The Waiau River provides relatively safe grade II kayaking with the added bonus of a long soak in the Hanmer Springs hot pools afterwards. The trip can be done in two half-day sections. The first put-in site is at the picnic area beside the road bridge which crosses the Hanmer River, 3 km after turning off Highway 7 to Hanmer Springs. The first take-out, or put-in for the second section, is at Marble Point quarry. The biggest challenge in the second section is a grade III rapid, called Sharks Tooth, opposite the highway bridge over Stinking Stream. The last take-out is at the irrigation intake where the road to Leslie Hills branches off Highway 7. This river is snow-fed, so wear a wetsuit. Kayaks and all equipment can be hired from Topsports in Christchurch, ☎ (03) 365 7585.

Cave Stream

Cave Stream is an excellent caving adventure for anyone with a torch and a smidgen of common sense. From Christchurch travel towards Arthur's Pass on Highway 73 for almost 100 km. Carry on for 15 km past Porters Pass to Cave Stream Scenic Reserve. Cave Stream is signposted on the right-hand side of the road.

Take some warm gear and your torch, then continue down the track to Cave Stream, 5 minutes away. The cave mouth is huge and inviting.

However, do not enter the cave if it's raining heavily or the stream is swollen—it floods rapidly. Always enter from the downstream end, because it's easier to retreat going downstream if necessary.

It takes 40 minutes to go right through the 360 metre long cave to the other end where a track leads back to the car park. There is a small cliff at the exit (upstream) where some people may require the aid of a rope.

If you're looking for a challenge, try making it through without getting wet or not using your torch for some of the way. No permission is required to enter the land, which is administered as a reserve by DOC. The local Maori people have spiritual claims to Cave Stream, so please respect the area.

Castle Hill

Well known for its great scenery, fine weather and balancy friction moves (rather than 'grunt and crank'), this is one of New Zealand's best rock climbing areas. A series of large limestone boulder fields have hundreds of good climbs for the beginner and expert alike.

Castle Hill is 100 km northwest of Christchurch on Highway 73 (the road to Arthur's Pass). Two kilometres after crossing the Porter River, a long straight section of road runs past the most popular boulder field (on your left), known as The Homestead.

Park on the side of the road, next to a gate where a line of trees leads towards the hills. The rocks are to the west, a short walk of about 1 km, and can be seen from the road.

There are so many climbs it's hard to know where to start. The next best thing to a personal guide is Tim Wethey's *Canterbury Rock* (see Further Reading). Most of the routes are bolted but don't fit standard hangers, so take wires instead. Take a square of carpet to clean your boots—good friction is essential.

Port Hills Mountain Biking

Why take the gondola when you can ride and have ten times as much fun?! This popular beginner's ride takes about two hours.

From the end of Rapaki Road in Opawa, Christchurch, climb up the

The First Ascent of Gone With the Wind, Castle Hill   (Steve Williams)

smooth Rapaki Track to the Summit Road on the Port Hills. Take in the excellent views of Christchurch before turning right and cycling along the Summit Road for about 1 km. Turn right at Bowenvale Park and follow the signposted Bowenvale mountain bike track down to Bowenvale Ave in Cashmere. You will only need a street map of Christchurch to get to and from the road ends. Bikes can be hired from Summit Cycles, ☎ (03) 355 7017 or Trail Blazers, ☎ (03) 366 6033.

Port Hills Paragliding

The Port Hills, overlooking Christchurch, are ideal for paragliding instruction. They have reliable winds and you can drive to most of the good launching spots. Christchurch-based paragliding instructors offer tandem jumps, 1-day courses and longer PG1 and PG2 courses.

In a 1-day course, costing around $140, you learn how to take off and land, and complete between two and five memorable flights. No previous experience is needed and all equipment is provided. To find out more about paragliding on the Port Hills, contact Nimbus Paragliding, ☎ (03) 3288 383 or ☎ 025 324 874, or Phoenix Paragliding, ☎ (03) 384 3131.

Banks Peninsula

The rugged coast around Banks Peninsula is a great spot to explore either by sea kayak or on foot.

Sea kayaking can be done either independently or with a guided group. There are lots of camping sites and a fair bit of wildlife to see as you paddle from Lyttelton to Akaroa. Top Sport in Christchurch, ☎ (03) 365 7585, run trips and courses year-round and also hire out boats to competent paddlers. Guided trips cost from $30 for an evening's paddle to $385 for a 4 day tour.

To explore on foot there's a choice of two privately-run tracks. The best is the Banks Peninsula Track, which starts and finishes at Akaroa, takes two to four days and provides comfortable huts by the coast every night. A variety of terrain is covered on this moderately easy tramp and there is plenty of time for swimming or fishing en route. Costs are $100/60 per person for the 4-day/2-day trip. For more

Taking Off on the Port Hills

(Malcolm O'Neill)

information or bookings (which are essential) phone ☎ (03) 304 7612
(Box 50, Akaroa) or contact Outdoor Recreation Centre,
Christchurch.

Ice-skating on Lakes Ida and Lyndon

Ducking in and out of bays, avoiding overhanging trees, and tripping
over snow drifts are all part of the experience of exploring a naturally
frozen surface. Two popular places for ice-skating in this region are
Lake Ida and Lake Lyndon. Lake Ida is 35 km northwest of the Rakaia
River road bridge on Highway 72. Lake Lyndon is 3 km west of
Porters Pass on Highway 73. Seekers Communications, in
Christchurch, ☎ (03) 379 2720, can give you up-to-date information
on ice conditions, and skates can be hired for $8 per pair from Arthur
Sparrow, ☎ (03) 366 0603. The ice is usually in condition for 4-8
weeks in June and July. Always be cautious when testing the surface
of a frozen lake.

 Hanging Rock

This large limestone boulder field in South Canterbury has
easy access, good views, a swimming hole, and dozens of excellent
climbs. Most of them are bolted and many start with pocky overhangs
that lead up to smooth slopes, demanding delicate footwork.

The crag is 150 km southwest of Christchurch. From Pleasant Point
(20 km northwest of Timaru) drive northwest on Opihi Road for 11
km, before turning left onto Gays Pass Road. After another 1 km turn
right down a gravel road. Park next to the barn at the top of the hill, a
few kilometres further on. As this crag is on private property you must
respect the farmer's wishes: sign the logbook on the way in, don't
litter, and leave gates as you find them. Access is closed for lambing
from mid-August to mid-October.

There is free camping a few kilometres further down Opihi Road,
next to the bridge that crosses Opihi River (1 km downstream from
the crag). For more information read Tim Wethey's *Canterbury Rock*
(see Further Reading).

Meuller Hut

This fine alpine trek from Mt Cook Village up to Meuller Hut (1830 m) and back can either be done in one longish day, or, if you would like to spend a night at the hut, two easy days. Start the trip from the DOC information centre in the village so that you can get a weather forecast and update on snow conditions. The trip should only be done in summer and autumn and you will need to have some alpine experience. Crampons and ice axe may be needed. The trek takes 4-5 hours and finding the hut in low cloud conditions can be difficult.

The track starts from the Hermitage, leads past White Horse Hill camping area and up to the hut via Seally Tarns. A tremendous mountain panorama will unfold long before reaching the hut. The shorter walk to Kea Point (3 hours return) is also worthwhile. Topomap H36 Mt Cook shows these and many other walks in the park.

Tasman Glacier Mountain Biking

This 34 km ride takes 3-6 hours return. Ride out of Mt Cook Village on the main road for one kilometre before turning left onto the signposted glacier road. The next 10 km to Celmisia Flat are easily rideable. However, because of glacial slips and water erosion, the road from there to Ball Shelter deteriorates into a single track—most people choose to hide their bike behind a rock and walk the last few kilometres.

The track continues past the shelter for another 400 metres before stopping at the edge of the moraine wall.

Tasman Glacier is impressive in its ugliness, but be careful when cycling/walking close to the edge of the moraine wall—it's 150 metres straight down to the glacier! Also, the keas will steal or destroy anything they can lay their beaks on. Bikes can be hired from Mt Cook Guides in the village.

The Ball Pass Crossing

As New Zealand's highest guided trek, this 2-3 day loop

takes you as close as it's possible to get to Mt Cook without mountaineering experience.

The route, which crosses the Mt Cook Range, gives spectacular views of New Zealand's highest mountains, and the Tasman and Hooker Glaciers.

On the first day you climb from the Tasman Valley up Ball Ridge to a private hut at 1830 m directly opposite the dramatic Caroline Face of Mt Cook.

The second day is spent climbing up towards Ball Pass (2130 m) and ascending an adjacent peak before returning to the same hut.

On day three you cross the pass and descend into the Hooker Valley, home of the famed Mt Cook lily. The hut is well stocked so only light packs need to be carried.

The trip costs $580 per person and includes a guide, food, gear, hut accommodation and transport from Lake Tekapo or Mt Cook Village. Discounts are available for groups of three or more.

Contact Alpine Recreation Canterbury Ltd in Tekapo, ☎ (03) 680 6736, or fax (03) 680 6765.

 Tasman Glacier Ski-Touring

New Zealand's longest glacier grinds its way for almost 30 km down the battered Tasman Valley lined by the highest peaks of Mt Cook National Park.

Various mountain guides run regular 2-5 day trips for fit and competent downhill skiers. After flying or skinning up to Kelman Hut (2600 m) and exploring the Tasman Glacier névé, you can climb peaks such as Hochstetter Dome and Elie de Beaumont—time, weather and experience permitting. The descent home along the Tasman Glacier is a breathtaking end to the trip.

Trips cost $415-950 per person depending on group size, trip length and whether glacier access flights are included or not. Two operators offering this trip are Southern Alps Guiding in Mt Cook, ☎ (03) 435 1890, and Alpine Recreation Canterbury Ltd in Tekapo, ☎ (03) 680 6736. Alpine Recreation supplies ski-mountaineering skis; Southern Alps Guides have hinged bindings that pop into your own downhill skis. In both cases you will need your own ski boots.

Mountaineering Course

The fastest and safest way to develop truly excellent mountaineering skills is to do a course with a professional guide. Week-long courses are offered by various guides in this region and cover all the essentials, such as rope handling, crevasse extraction, map reading, bivouacs, abseiling, and belaying.

If the weather permits, a couple of peaks are usually climbed as well. A reasonable level of fitness is required as you may have to carry a heavy pack for 6-8 hours.

The cost ranges from $1000-2000 per person, depending on the length of your course and size of the group.

For more information contact the New Zealand Mountain Guides Association, PO Box 10, Mt Cook or refer to the numerous pamphlets at any climbing shop.

Buildering

Buildering is rock climbing on buildings. There are plenty of tricky little buildering problems to solve in the cities. Try traversing around a building a safe distance from the ground. Climbing higher on most buildings requires committing moves, odd-shaped bits of climbing equipment, and an expedition-style assault.

Unfortunately, climbing all over the architectural features of a building is illegal unless you have the owner's permission. If you don't, and reaching the top of the building is your only objective, wear something you want to be photographed in and be prepared to pay a contribution to the running of our legal system.

Breaking anything off a building can be lethal to others and if it is a foothold it's likely to be lethal to yourself as well. Try not to leave black scrape marks all over the walls from your rock climbing boots.

Keep an eye out for builderers, especially in the court reports. Nelson's Column in London, Sydney's Centrepoint Tower and even Wellington's BNZ building (as illustrated here) have all been climbed by dedicated builderers.

First & Only Ascent of the BNZ Building, Wellington   (Dave Moss)

14. Southern Lakes

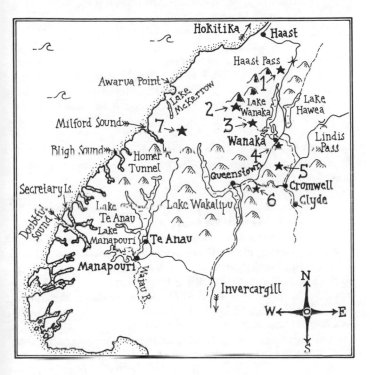

14.1 Gillespie Pass Tramp

 Makarora, Mt Aspiring National Park

For intermediate trampers, 3-4 days.

—Summary— This popular summer trip takes trampers up the Young Valley, over the impressive Gillespie Pass and down the Siberia and Wilkin Valleys. These three beautiful bushclad valleys are hidden amongst some of New Zealand's most spectacular mountain scenery.

—How to Get There— The trip starts and ends at Makarora, 65 km north of Wanaka on Highway 6. There is a daily Intercity bus passing through Makarora.

—Description—
Makarora to Young Hut; 7-9 hours
If the Makarora River level is low you can cross it at the Young River confluence—ask at the DOC visitor centre in Makarora about the safest crossing point. From the other side there is a good track leading up the true left of the Young River to the North and South Young forks, 3-4 hours away. If the Makarora River is running high you'll have to take a jet boat up the first section of river. A jet boat trip can be arranged at the Makarora tearooms.

At the forks, cross the North Branch on the new swing bridge and continue, on a marked track, up the true left of the South Branch. Young Hut (10 bunks) is at the head of this valley 20 minutes above the treeline on the other side of the river. This is the best place to stay for the night, although in summer it may be full. There are good camping sites nearby.

Young Hut to Siberia Hut; 6-8 hours
From the hut, walk up the valley for about 1 km to a signpost. You should fill your water bottles up here as there is usually no water further on. The track follows snow poles and climbs steeply through alpine tussock to Gillespie Pass (1490 m). From here there are spectacular views of the surrounding snow-capped mountains, and

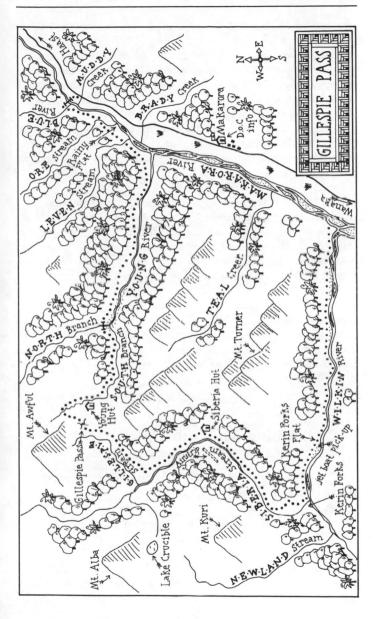

especially of Mt Awful (2202 m). If the weather is calm and clear, there is no finer lunch spot.

From the pass continue following snow poles southeast along the ridge for a kilometre, before dropping down to a tussocky basin. Sidle through a tongue of bush to the bottom of the basin. From here a marked track leads down the true left of Gillespie Stream to the large open valley of the Siberia River.

It takes one hour of easy walking down the true left of the valley to reach Siberia Hut (20 bunks). This is an exceptionally beautiful area, well worth exploring further if you can spare the time. For starters you could follow the marked track to Lake Crucible, 2-3 hours away.

Siberia Hut to Makarora; 7-9 hours walking the whole way
From Siberia Hut it takes about 3 hours to walk to Kerin Forks. Most trampers arrange to have a jet boat from Makarora pick them up at the grassy Kerin Forks Flat, 2 km further downstream. Otherwise continue down the farmed river flats for 16 km to Makarora. Do not attempt to cross the Makarora River in high flows.

—Notes— Only those with mountaineering experience should attempt to cross Gillespie Pass in winter. For your own safety, sign in at the DOC visitor centre in Makarora, ☎ (03) 443 8365, before you start your trip and ask for up to date information about track, river and snow conditions (don't forget to sign out). Topomap F38 Wilkin is essential.

14.2 Climbing Mt Aspiring

Mt Aspiring National Park, 50 km northwest of Wanaka

For experienced mountaineers (grade 2+), 4-6 days.

—Summary— Mt Aspiring (3027 m), or Tititea (peak of glistening white), stands high above the surrounding peaks and glaciers, It is one of New Zealand's most beautiful and dramatic mountains. Although it is not technically difficult to climb, it is remote, and there are a few sections that require extreme care.

—How to Get There— Drive west out of Wanaka on the Wanaka-Mt Aspiring Road. It's 50 km to the car park at the Matukituki Valley road end. Several fords in the last 10 km may be impassable after heavy rain.

If you don't have transport contact the Bus Company, ☎ (03) 443 8775, or Mt Aspiring Express, ☎ (03) 443 7414. Failing that, try one of the backpacker hostels.

—Description—
Road end to French Ridge Hut; 6-9 hours
The walk up the West Branch of the Matukituki River to the grand old Aspiring Hut (30 bunks) takes 2-3 hours from the car park. The valley is wide, with easy walking initially on grassy flats and further up in open beech forest.

Much to the discredit of DOC, they still allow stock to trample and graze this valley. At Pearl Flat (2 hours from Aspiring Hut) you have to cross the Matukituki River (use Pearl Flat Bridge just upstream if the river is up) before climbing steeply up French Ridge through beech forest to alpine tussock. French Ridge Hut (12 bunks) is a welcome sight after the 3-hour grind.

French Ridge to Colin Todd Hut; 4-8 hours
From French Ridge Hut, just below the permanent snowline, there are two ways to reach the Bonar Glacier. The safest is up French Ridge onto the Quarterdeck. In late summer, large schrunds and crevasses can close this route or necessitate a close traverse on the cliff edge of Gloomy Gorge. The alternative route is via the Breakaway below Mt French. It is quicker, but exposed to icefall and avalanches.

The walk across the Bonar Glacier to Colin Todd Hut takes 3-6 hours, depending on snow conditions. You'll need to be roped up for glacier travel and in late summer pick an intricate route through the crevasses. Leave early in the morning when the surface is frozen; plugging steps across the Bonar in the afternoon can be very demoralising. In misty conditions the glacier requires careful navigation—take a compass bearing.

The Ocean-like Bonar Glacier   (Malcolm O'Neill)

Colin Todd Hut sits in an excellent position on Shipowner Ridge with big sunbathing rocks and fantastic views. In 1996, a new 12- person hut was flown in to replace the old hut.

Colin Todd to the Summit return; 6-12 hours

Leave early to climb Mt Aspiring. The usual route to the summit is via The Ramp and the North-west Ridge. From the hut sidle up the gentle slopes to the bottom of The Ramp. There is usually a bergschrund to negotiate at the bottom to get onto The Ramp proper.

Although not technically difficult, The Ramp has claimed many lives. It requires concentration both on the way up and down. There is a small col where The Ramp meets the North-west Ridge, which is an excellent spot for a rest stop. From there it's a relatively easy 2-hour climb to within 100 metres of the top.

The last section is not much steeper, but it has long drop-offs on both sides. There are stunning views in all directions from the top of this magnificent peak.

To avoid The Ramp on the descent some people continue down the full North-west Ridge or drop east onto the Therma Glacier. From the bottom of The Ramp you can retrace your steps to Colin Todd Hut. There are many different routes up Mt Aspiring; the more difficult South-west Ridge is also a classic climb. Small peaks like Mt Bevan and Mt French are excellent warm-up climbs, and the larger more challenging Rolling Pin and Mt Avalanche are worth attempting if time and weather permit.

If avalanches are at all prevalent while you are in the area then Bevan Col, a possible route from the Bonar Glacier to the Matukituki Valley is likely to be one big horrendous avalanche chute. We recommend heading out via French Ridge.

—Notes— For more information about climbing in the area, read Graham Bishop's *The Mount Aspiring Region*. To climb Mt Aspiring you need to be an experienced and well-equipped mountaineer. Several companies offer guided ascents of Mt Aspiring (contact DOC in Wanaka, ☎ (03) 443 7660, for more information). Don't forget to sign in (and out) at the DOC headquarters in Wanaka. The trip is totally weather dependent. Topomap E39 Aspiring is essential and F39 Matukituki is recommended.

14.3 Matukituki River Kayaking

Wanaka

For beginner paddlers (guide optional), 1 day from Wanaka.

—Summary— This is an excellent introduction to whitewater kayaking on a relatively safe grade II river. While gliding down the calm stretches you can see the snowy mountains, crevassed glaciers and tumbling waterfalls of Mt Aspiring National Park. In between these mellow sections, wide open rapids provide a good challenge for most beginners.

—How to Get There— Drive west out of Wanaka on the Wanaka-Mt

Aspiring Road. After 45 km you'll pass a swing bridge; from here, it's only 5 km to the put-in site at the road end. There is a car parking area and DOC toilet opposite the put-in site. Several fords in the last 10 km may be impassable after heavy rain.

—Description— Those who have never been kayaking before should try to pick up as many skills as possible before being swept down the first rapid. If you're one of the 30% who do tip out, don't panic—there are good runouts after every rapid. The record for capsizing is an incredible 23 times in one trip! If you're unsure of your ability, just paddle as fast as possible. This was the first river Jonathan ever paddled and that's what he reckons kept him upright.

Guided groups stop for a halfway cuppa just down from the swing bridge. If you only want to do a short paddle then this is a good place to get out. Otherwise carry on for the same distance again to a good take-out beach just south of Mad Cow Flat. This lower section is a tad more relaxing.

Mad Cow Flat is a grassy picnic spot with a stone fireplace, just upstream from the stretch of road jammed between the river and bluffs. According to kayaking legend, a mad cow once ate the pants that a paddler, called 'Kymbra the Kid', left lying on the grass. Twenty steps later the deranged beast barfed them up again.

—Notes— This trip is run commercially by Alpine River Guides in Wanaka, ☎ (03) 443 9422. For $95 they drive you, and all the kayaking gear imaginable, from Wanaka to the put-in site. Qualified instruction is given on the way down. If this gets you hooked on kayaking, then try the nearby grade II+ Makarora River the next day.

14.4 Wanaka Paragliding

Wanaka

For beginner adventurers (guided), 1 day.

—Summary— Without a doubt, paragliding is one of the easiest ways to fly. Within a matter of hours, absolute beginners can be silently gliding above the hills, performing graceful 180° turns and then landing perfectly. Mt Iron, overlooking Lake Wanaka and facing towards the snowcapped peaks of Mt Aspiring National Park, is one of the most spectacular places in New Zealand to learn this exciting sport.

The winds are steady and there are often long periods of settled weather, especially in the winter. After a day's practical instruction you may be ready to do a 1000-feet flight off the nearby Treble Cone skifield.

—How to Get There— Contact Wanaka Paragliding, ☎/fax (03) 443 9193 or (025) 838 860.

—Description— After a general talk covering the theory of paragliding, students are driven to Mt Iron, just out of Wanaka, where there is a well set-up practice hill. There's usually a steady wind blowing up the hill off Lake Wanaka. A large paddock at the bottom makes a perfect landing site.

Experienced paragliders like your instructor have an uncanny ability to read the wind. They can observe a far off rustling leaf and predict when the next gust of wind will reach you. By the third practice take-off you should be airborne—it's as easy as that. Your instructor will communicate with you through a radio built into your helmet. It's hard to believe that you're actually flying free through the air.

Each flight begins a bit further up the hill than the last one. There's a great feeling of anticipation as you bundle up your paraglider and trudge up to the next take-off site. Before you realise it, half the day will have gone and you'll be about to launch yourself for a 300-feet flight from the summit of Mt Iron.

After a day at Mt Iron you may be ready to paraglide off Treble Cone. This 1000-feet jump lasts 5-6 minutes (a long time for beginner paragliders) and gives breathtaking views of the surrounding area.

—Notes— The complete introduction day costs $156. A three to five day student licence course costs $440. And for those with only half a day, a Tandem flight ($108) from Treble Cone with an instructor lets you take control and pilot the paraglider down on your first big flight.

14.5 Nordic Skiing on the Pisa Range

 Cardrona Valley south of Wanaka

For all adventurers, 1 or more days.

—Summary— The Waiorau Nordic Ski Area on the rolling hills of the Pisa Range has a number of groomed trails for cross-country skiing. The safe terrain, relaxed atmosphere and fresh-baked muffins the size of footballs make a day or two's skiing at Waiorau well worthwhile.

—How to Get There— From Wanaka drive south for 25 km on Highway 89. The Waiorau Nordic Ski Area is well signposted.

—Description— Nordic skiing may feel strange to downhill skiers at first—the skis are long and thin, the boots very comfortable and the poles reach up to your armpits. Skiers new to the sport will be shown the basics by a cross-country ski instructor.

There are over 20 km of groomed trails waiting to be explored. The trails have two sets of parallel grooves cut in them to guide your skis. Having stepped into the tracks, you'll spend some time learning the kick and glide technique for moving forward, and the fall-on-your-bum technique for stopping.

On a fine day beginners can do the 'River Run', stopping at Meadow Warming Hut for lunch before returning via Loop Trail. There are stunning views of the Southern Alps along the way. If you need a rest from skiing, check out the huge basin that has been groomed especially for tobogganing on truck inner tubes.

Keen skiers can try the run to Bob Lee Hut, well clear of the main field. This and other huts are set up for skiers to stay in overnight. On clear nights skiing by the light of the moon across the monochrome landscape is a magical experience.

—Notes— A pass to the field costs $20 and gear hire is $15. Introductory lessons cost only $5 and a 1 hour lesson costs $15. The southern end of the Pisa Range, is a good area for experienced ski-tourers to explore. For more information contact Waiorau Nordic Ski Area, ☎ (03) 443 7542.

14.6 Surfing the Kawarau River

 Queenstown

For all adventurers (guided), 3 hours.

—**Summary**— Using 1-metre boogie boards to execute 'rad' surfing manoeuvres on the grade IV Kawarau River rapids while wearing nothing but a fluoro wetsuit, helmet and flippers, puts this trip in the adrenalin-plus category.

—**How to Get There**— Contact Serious Fun in Queenstown, ☎ (03) 442 5262.

Going Nowhere Fast on the Kawarau.   (Jon Imhoof)

—**Description**— Once at the riverside you'll carry your boogie board down a steep bank to the water. Overhead, 6-metre rafts whistle down on a flying fox to carry the continual busloads of tourists that ply the river by more conventional means. Before you get in the water the surfing guides spend 10 minutes demonstrating the basics of control, concentrating on relaxing and working with the current, rather than against it.

Smiths Falls is the first rapid and it's here that you realise river surfers are really on to something. Because you're in the river rather than on it, the perspective is totally different to other river sports.

You'll pass under the bungy bridge, glad that your challenge lasts longer than 10 seconds. At the second major rapid there are huge stoppers and the guides do their best to show you the basic skills, with varying degrees of success. Most of all, though, they impress you with their ability to pop up beside you when help is required. The rapid called 'Do Little Do Nothing' looks like a non-event, but the guides are able to pull off 10-metre squirts. A squirt involves diving into the eddies and whirlpools and travelling under the water before being spat out downstream.

The massive grade IV Chinese Dog Leg rapid is a real howler. It is one of the longest commercially rafted rapids in the Southern Hemisphere. After an easy start where you can try your new skills, it becomes extremely hectic—Malcolm and Greg held on in a death grip all the way to the finish.

—**Notes**— This trip costs $95, including all the gear and transport to and from Queenstown. The Danes, ☎ (03) 442 7318, also offer river sledging down the Kawarau which is quite similar.

14.7 The Hollyford Track

100 km north of Te Anau

For intermediate trampers, 4 days.

—**Summary**— The historic Hollyford Track passes through lush Fiordland rainforest on its way to the rugged, remote West Coast at Martins Bay. The forest is rich in birdlife and on the coast you'll often see seals, Fiordland crested penguins and the occasional dolphin.

—**How to Get There**— From Te Anau head north on Highway 94 (the road to Milford Sound) for 87 km before turning right onto Lower Hollyford Road. From here it is 16 km to the road end and the start of the track. There is a campground at Hollyford (Gunns Camp).

—**Description**—

Road end-Lake Alabaster, 5-6 hours

From the Hollyford road end a well-marked track passes through magnificent rainforest on the true right of the emerald Hollyford River. It takes a couple of hours to reach Hidden Falls Hut (20 bunks) on the northern side of Hidden Falls Creek, just past Sunshine Hut (private). Hidden Falls are a few minutes up the creek from the bridge. From the hut gradually climb up to Little Homer Saddle (158 m), the track's modest high point.

Across the valley you'll get glimpses of the awesome Darren Mountains—solid, immovable granite. Joined contour lines that look like brown smudge marks on the map are no misprint. Descend back to the Hollyford Valley floor past Little Homer Falls, a grand 60-metre cascade. Parts of the track have been washed away by the river but alternative routes are marked. Pyke Lodge (private) is at the confluence of the Pyke and Hollyford rivers. Continue up Pyke Valley for half an hour, past the Pyke River swingbridge to Lake Alabaster Hut (20 bunks).

Lake Alabaster Hut-Demon Trail Hut, 4-5 hours

A short backtrack takes you to the impressive swingbridge over the Pyke River. After a couple of hours' tramping through dense forest, you re-emerge beside the Hollyford River. An hour later, McKerrow Island appears at the head of Lake McKerrow. There is a route across the flood channel to McKerrow Island Hut (20 bunks).

If it rains heavily you'll be the proud inhabitants of your own inaccessible island. The main Hollyford track continues on the true right to Demon Trail Hut (12 bunks). There are excellent views across Lake McKerrow to the Darran Mountains beyond.

Demon Trail Hut-Hokuri Hut, 5-6 hours

The track sidles above the lake through thick forest. Birds are more often heard than seen as their calls resound around the lake. Hokuri Hut (20 bunks) is a welcome sight after 5-6 hours of rocky, undulating track and several wire bridges.

Hokuri Hut-Martins Bay, 4-5 hours.

Hokuri Creek is 10 minutes on from the hut. If it's not in flood then cross at the mouth and wander along the lake shore. Otherwise walk 15 minutes upstream to the wire crossing. After a kilometre or so along the lake shore, you'll come to what's left of Jamestown—an overgrown 19th century settlement.

From Jamestown the track winds along the shores of Lake McKerrow until returning into lowland forest. Dolphins and seals are sometimes seen in the lake. After 1-2 hours you'll pass a couple of airstrips and private lodges, including Martins Bay Lodge. From here the track follows the river, parallel to the coast, for an hour to the new Martins Bay Hut (20 Bunks) near the Hollyford River mouth. There is good camping around here and penguins and seals can be seen around Long Reef. To return to civilisation you can tramp back the way you came, or leave by jetboat or aeroplane.

—Notes— The creeks on the Demon Trail section can rise quickly. Jet boat transport as far as Little Homer Saddle costs $65 per person (minimum of four people) and can be arranged with Hollyford Valley Tours, ☎ (03) 442 3760 or ☎ (03) 249 8012. Transport can be organised before you leave or at the Pyke or Martins Bay Lodges. Flights can be arranged through Air Fiordland, ☎ (03) 249 7505, and cost $265 per flight (holds up to four people). Trackmap 03 Hollyford is essential.

14.8 Other Adventures

 Rob Roy

This excellent day tramp, amongst the peaks of Mt Aspiring National Park, leads up to an alpine basin at the head of Rob Roy Valley. Within a stone's throw of the shattered faces of Rob Roy Peak, exposed beneath massive icefalls, this is an awe-inspiring place to spend a hot summer's day.

For directions to the Matukituki road end, where the tramp starts, see section 14.2 Mt Aspiring. From the car park follow the track alongside the Matukituki River for 800 metres before crossing a swingbridge to the true left. The track then continues up to Rob Roy Stream about 1 km away. From there the track follows the true left of the stream up through a gorge to the alpine basin. You can explore further or simply find a comfortable spot to enjoy lunch in the sun. This trip is one of the most spectacular day walks in the region and takes 4-6 hours return. Take Parkmap 02 Mt Aspiring.

Canyoning

Canyoning is the art of exploring steep and confined river gorges using a variety of techniques including abseiling, jumping, climbing and even sliding down waterchutes. It's sort of like caving without the cave. Canyoners descend through stone chasms draped with ferns and moss. Rumbling waterfalls diving into clear green pools present the main challenges of the day.

Deep Canyon Experience in Wanaka, ☎ (03) 443 7922, run guided trips down three local canyons, all of different character and levels of adventure. Water confidence is an advantage and abseiling instruction is provided if necessary. Just bring a swimsuit and a pair of outdoor shoes. Trips cost $145 per person.

Wanaka Outlet Track

This is a pleasant 18 km run or ride from Wanaka Township. Head 7 km out of Wanaka to Albert Town via Highways 89 and 6. Turn left off Highway 6, onto Alison Ave (signposted) and follow it to the 'Outlet Track' at the end of the avenue. Hop over the gate and follow the signs along a narrow track to the lake outlet.

From the end of this track, follow a few kilometres of gravel road before turning onto another single track which starts next to the Penrith Motor Camp, then leads to Bremmer Bay and is also signposted.

At the end of this track, follow the road, either straight ahead or to the right, back to Wanaka township. If you turn right through the pines you'll connect with another short section of singletrack.

Wanaka Rock Climbing

The present rock climbing boom around Wanaka is centred in the spectacular Matakitaki Valley, 20 km from town on the Mt Aspiring Road. At the time of writing there were 130 climbs of grade 12 to 30, with more being put up all the time. Some climbs use natural protection while others are bolted. All climbs have bolted top chains. A guidebook compiled by the Wanaka Rock Climbing Club is available locally with all proceeds going to pay for bolts and chains. Out on a Thread, ☎ (03) 443 9418, are based in Wanaka township and offer qualified guides to show out-of-towners the climbs, whether they be absolute beginners or experienced rock jocks. They also offer instruction to suit all abilities and can provide all necessary safety equipment including rock boots. A one-day rock climbing tour costs $85. It begins with extensive safety instruction and ends when you can't climb anymore!

Note that camping is a sensitive issue in the Wanaka rock climbing area so discretion is required. Farmers and their property should be treated with respect. If the weather is bad check out the Wanaka Rock Climbing Gym at 155 Tenby Street.

  ### Macetown

It takes beginner riders about 2 hours to cycle along a 10 km 4WD track to the abandoned gold mining town of Macetown. There are many points of interest en route which are described in a 'self guide' brochure available at local information centres. As you have to cross at least 40 fords on the way from Arrowtown (20 km from Queenstown) to Macetown we suggest you only do the trip in summer when it's hot. Topomap F41 Arrowtown shows the route. This is also a good run/walk/horse ride.

Adventure Queenstown Style

Queenstown is the adventure tourism capital of New Zealand. Those looking for almost any type of adrenalin fix will love this scenic yet bustling town. Rafting, bungy jumping, mountain biking, skiing, tramping, kayaking and climbing. Almost every activity is catered for, usually by more than one company, and nearly every tourist in the country passes through Queenstown. While some may find the hype and commercialism a little nauseating, there is no doubt that most people who go to Queenstown with money in their pockets have a great time. We haven't bothered to mention every adventure on offer at Queenstown because they're all very obvious once you get there— just take a walk down the main street.

Exploring the Tracks around Queenstown   (Jonathan Kennett)

Skippers Canyon

For an excellent day ride with lots of variety and brilliant scenery, try Skippers Canyon. Head out of Queenstown on Arthurs Point Road and ride up to Skippers Saddle (930 m). From there you can take the old pack track to the right of the road.

It's a neat little single track that rejoins Skippers Road about a third of the way to Skippers Bridge. At the bridge you can watch bungy jumpers plummet 71 metres into the canyon. Over the bridge and 1 km further on is a picnic and camping area with drinkable tap water.

From there several adventurous day trips can be done. All you need are a couple of maps (Topomaps E40 and E41) and a keen urge for exploration.

To hire mountain bikes in Queenstown drop in to Alpine Cycles, 45 Camps Street, or Redges Bike Hire on Beach Street. They can also provide information on good trips just out of town.

 ### Shotover River Rafting

The Shotover is the most commercially rafted river in the South Island. The commonly rafted section is from Deep Creek in Skippers Canyon to Arthurs Point.

With medium to high river flows, it's an excellent grade IV rafting trip. At low flow, however, it's not what the marketing videos would have you believe. Following the Mother Rapid, the final thrill is rafting through the pitch black Oxenbridge Tunnel—an old gold mining water race.

The river is run by every rafting company in Queenstown. Just wander down Shotover Street to get an idea of who offers what in terms of trips and prices. The approximate cost is $95 for a 2-hour trip.

 ### Skippers Bungy Jump

Towering 71 metres above the Shotover River, the view from Skipper Canyon Bridge will probably fill you with dread rather than joy (unless you're just spectating of course). Ten years ago leaping from this colossal height with nothing but a high tech rubber band tied around your ankles would have turned up in our lunatic category.

With an insane cheerfulness your name is called and your feet are attached to the end of that famous umbilical cord. Any irrational urge you may have had to throw yourself from such a suicidal height soon disappears completely.

Madly hoping that thoughts are the only thing about to go through your head, you inch your way out on the little board extending from the bridge.

Peer pressure is a baffling thing, and very soon you'll notice that your brain has told your body to leap. Whistling air is followed by relief as you realise, with the courage of hindsight, that the secret behind its success is making something that is completely safe appear utterly lethal.

The jump costs anywhere from $90 upwards, depending on your choice of transport to the bridge (vehicle, jet boat or helicopter). There is a higher 102-metre bungy jump further up river at the 'Pipeline', and A J Hackett Bungy still run jumps from the world's first bungy site at Kawarau Bridge (43 m). Book through any adventure office in Queenstown.

Tandem Paragliding & Hang Gliding

A tandem paraglider or hang glider enables two people to fly together. Absolute beginners can fly with an instructor, riding the thermals above Queenstown or Wanaka for an unforgettable experience. Hang gliding company Sky Trek in Queenstown, ☎ (03) 442 6311, takes people for flights of up to 20 minutes for $125, and paragliding flights cost from $100 and last up to 45 minutes.

There are several paragliding companies in the area and most offer tandem flights. Explore your options at one of the local information centres.

? The Secret South Safari

Departing from Queenstown weekly, this 10-day nature safari explores the lesser known wilderness areas from the lakes district to the southern coast of the South Island and up to Christchurch. As the title suggests, we can't tell you too much about this eco-adventure.

It probably involves lots of wilderness hiking and wildlife investigation, possibly in areas like Fiordland National Park, Port Craig, the wild Catlins coast, Otago Peninsula and Mt Cook National Park.

And maybe you'll hike through incredible forest, past beautiful lakes and along breathtaking coasts to see creatures like the Hectors dolphin, Yellow Eyed Penguins, Royal Albatross, Tuatara and more. Perhaps this is the best trip in the country for adventurous nature lovers; we don't really know.

To find out for sure contact NZ Nature Safaris, ☎/fax (04) 563 7360, Wellington. This trip costs $650 per person. For more general information on NZ Nature Safaris, refer to Chapter 7, section 7.8.

 ### Rees-Dart Track

A popular intermediate tramp in the Queenstown area is the 4-6 day (70 km) Rees-Dart track. After walking up the Rees Valley you cross over Rees Saddle (1506 m), and descend into the headwaters of the Dart River. From here the track follows the Dart River down valley, amongst spectacular scenery.

There are four huts, plenty of secluded camping spots and several rock bivouacs. From the shelter of the bush deep within the mountains, keen trampers can do some great day trips. On a good day you could zip up to Cascade Saddle for some great views, checking out the Dart Glacier on the way.

This area has more than its share of sandflies. The road ends, 20 km drive from each other, are well serviced by public transport from November to April. For more information contact DOC in Queenstown, ☎ (03) 442 7933. Topomaps E39 Aspiring and E40 Earnslaw are essential.

 ### Routeburn Track

The historic Routeburn Track was once part of the route connecting Queenstown with the now-defunct settlement of Jamestown on Fiordland's west coast. In recent times it has become one of the country's most popular alpine walks.

Most trampers take 2-3 days to cover the 40 km track across Harris Saddle (1280 m) between the head of Lake Wakatipu and the Milford-Te Anau Road. This high quality track slips through some dramatic alpine country as it crosses over the main divide to the rainforested Hollyford Valley in the west. From Harris Saddle there are stunning views across to the Darren Mountains.

This section of track is also exposed to the full brunt of any foul weather, so go well equipped.

You may find some solitude if you wander off on side trips (such as Conical Hill) but if you want to avoid crowds, go elsewhere. Try the Greenstone or Caples valleys, they're not so crowded and there are plenty of camp sites.

From November to April there is plenty of public transport servicing both ends of the track. A winter crossing requires alpine equipment and skills. Camping within 500 metres of the track is prohibited. A booking system for huts and campsites was introduced in 1995, and is similar in its operation to the Milford system. For more information ask DOC in Queenstown, ☎ (03) 442 7933. Take Trackmap 02 Routeburn & Greenstone—it has a good trip write-up on the back.

The Greenstone & The Caples

Both these tracks provide great tramping routes from the end of the Routeburn back to Queenstown. Both tracks are well marked, take 2 days to walk and have huts every few hours along the way. The two combined also provide an excellent round trip.

From Greenstone Wharf on the edge of Lake Wakatipu, where the tracks end, you can either drive or boat back to Queenstown. For more information buy Trackmap 02 Routeburn & Greenstone.

The Kepler

With panoramic views and superb forests this 'Great Walk' easily lives up to most people's expectations. This 4-day round trip from the southern end of Lake Te Anau is on a high quality track and has three palatial huts. As with all the tracks in this region it is likely to be unwalkable at times during winter because of snow.

Either walk from Te Anau township around to the Control Gates (1 hour) or catch the boat across the lake to Brod Bay and start from there. Trackmap 09 Kepler has all the information you could possibly need to do the trip.

Fiordland: Sea & Lake Kayaking

As well as tremendous lakes, mountains, forests and valleys, Fiordland National Park, as the name suggests, contains an ample number of large fiords. As a result, kayaking, sometimes combined with tramping or mountain biking, is a great way to explore the area.

Increasingly popular options include paddling up Lake Te Anau to the start of the Milford Track or down Lake Manapouri at the completion of the Dusky Sound Track. Mountain biking over Percy Pass or Wilmot Pass can also be combined with kayaking on Lake Manapouri or Doubtful Sound.

Just paddling around the wonderfully scenic Lake Manapouri or Lake Te Anau can take from 1-5 days, or longer. Both lakes are set within towering glacial landscapes, and have more than 50 islands scattered around their crystal clear waters. There are plenty of remote sandy beaches on which to camp or just relax.

The famous Milford Sound, is comparatively small and best suited to day trips only. Doubtful Sound, on the other hand, extends 40 km inland and has several other arms or sounds branching off it.

It is home to a resident pod of approximately 70 Bottlenose dolphins, with fur seals and Fiordland Crested penguins adding to the marine wildlife of this attraction, famed as 'the sound of silence'. To fully explore this huge and diverse waterway takes about 9 days by kayak.

The inaccessibility of Doubtful Sound (a 30-km boat trip across Lake Manapouri, followed by a 20-km drive over Wilmot Pass) has meant that this has remained a pristine wilderness area. Generally the only people setting foot on the land are kayakers who stop to rest or camp overnight.

Regular guided kayaking trips are available in the sound, most commonly for 2 or 3 days in duration. This is often followed by 2 or 3 days paddling back independently down Lake Manapouri. Groups with experienced paddlers may undertake independent rentals in Doubtful Sound.

For more information contact Fiordland Wilderness Experiences, 66 Quintin Drive, Te Anau, ☎/fax (03) 249 7700.

Milford Track Hike 'n' Paddle

The Milford Track, in Fiordland National Park, connects the head of Lake Te Anau with Milford Sound. Its international fame, combined with magnificent beauty, has made this trip so popular that it became the first of New Zealand's tramps to need restrictions on the number of walkers. This has stopped the place being trampled to death and gives walkers more space to enjoy themselves.

The walking season extends from around November 1 to April 18. Book well in advance through the Tourist Hotel Corporation—March to April is the quietest time, and high season prices start around $200. Kayaking from the end of the track across to Milford can be done at any time of year and normally costs $55 per person.

Out of season the weather is more likely to be bad, but it's much cheaper then (only $98 for a sail, hike, kayak package, plus $4 per night for the huts). For more information on this and other hike 'n' paddle options in the area, contact Rosco's Milford Sound Sea Kayaks, ☎ (03) 249 8840.

During winter, transport to Milford is scarce and avalanches are a danger. Camping within 500 metres of the Milford Track is prohibited. For more information on the track contact DOC at Te Anau, ☎ (03) 249 7921 or get hold of Trackmap 01 Milford.

 ## Percy Pass

Percy Pass, just southwest of Lake Manapouri, is one of the most scenically awesome and challenging mountain bike routes in New Zealand. From Manapouri township catch the tourist boat to the West Arm of the lake. Then simply follow the pylon track, under the power station transmission lines, to the top of Percy Pass.

The track ends here, and to continue you must carry/drag your bike through dense native forest on a very basic trail for $1^1/_2$ kilometres. If you get lost, use the transmission lines above as a guide and eventually you'll pick up another pylon track that leads southeast to Monowai.

From there it's about 40 km back to Manapouri. The whole trip takes about two days and there is good camping at the South Arm of Lake Manapouri.

The day trip from West Arm over to Doubtful Sound and back again is also very rewarding. Refer to *Classic New Zealand Mountain Bike Rides* for more details (see Further Reading). Take Terrainmap 16 Invercargill.

Night Riding

Why ride at night? Because the days are too short during winter, you want to ride a banned track without causing a ruckus, you got lost during a day ride, or because it makes a familiar track seem completely new. Whatever the reason, it's a creepy experience that really helps heighten all your senses.

Although powerful 'Night Sun' type lights are manufactured specially for the job, you can use any old torch that has a halogen bulb and tape it to your handle bars or helmet. During a full moon you may not need a torch at all. The less powerful your light, the more lunatic the ride will be! To night ride during the day simply put a paper bag over your head and carry on as usual.

Boiling the Billy   (Grant Singleton)

15. The Far South

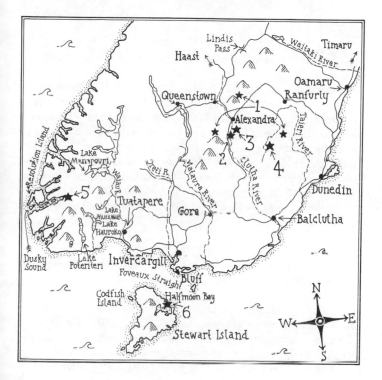

15.1 Back Country Ski-Touring

Central Otago

For intermediate skiers with alpine experience, 1-7 days.

—**Summary**— In a good season there are hundreds of kilometres of snow-covered terrain to explore on Central Otago's flat-topped mountains. We have identified three of the more reliable ski-touring areas in this region. They may just look like hills but are actually up to 2000 metres high, and are the best place in New Zealand for intermediate cross-country skiers to let loose. However, snow conditions can vary tremendously—blue ice, wind-scored crust and deep powder may be found within a few metres of each other; the weather also changes rapidly and skiers must be prepared for all conditions.

—**Description**—
The Old Man Range, Old Woman Range and Garvie Mountains; 25 km southwest of Alexandra.

This huge wilderness is arguably the best area in Otago for ski-touring. There are places on top of this polar-like plateau where the white expanse of snow extends to the horizon in every direction. Clear still skies can create 10-20 cm of frost-dried powder. However, wind often shrieks across the flat barren tops, and sheltered valleys are few and far between.

There are three public huts (Pattersons, Fraser and Fraser Basin) on the route between Nevis Road and Symes Road, and plenty of places to dig snow-caves elsewhere. A week can easily be spent exploring from hut to hut. Three public roads give access to the ranges. The Nevis road (southwest of Cromwell) leads to Duffers Saddle on the northern end of Old Woman Range and provides the best access because it is regularly cleared of snow. Two other options are Symes Road (up to the transmitter) and Waikaia Bush Road, which both climb up the eastern side of Old Man Range off Highway 8, south of Alexandra. Walking is usually necessary to reach skiable snow.

Topomaps F42 Kingston, G42 Alexandra, F43 Garvie, and G43 Roxburgh are essential. Grid references for the public huts are: Pattersons Hut 013 482 (F42 Kingston); Fraser Hut 078 349 (F42 Kingston); Fraser Basin Hut 112 326 (G42 Alexandra).

Dunstan Mountains; 25 km north of Alexandra.

This smaller area has less reliable snow but is still good for cross-country trips. Thompsons Saddle (991 m) provides access to the more commonly skied southwestern end of the range. After a steep climb to 1222 metres the ridge becomes more gentle, taking you to Leaning Rock (1617 m), 15 km away. To reach Thompsons Saddle drive 25 km northeast of Cromwell on Highway 8 before turning east onto Ardgour Road and then Thompson Gorge Road, which leads to the saddle. Access to the east of the range is via Omakau, 30 km north of Alexandra. Take Topomap G41 Cromwell.

Back-Country Skiing (Greg Carlyon)

Rock and Pillar Range; 60 km east of Alexandra.

This is a slightly lower range but covers a large area between 1200 and 1400 metres that is regularly skiable. Once the site of an early downhill skifield, the Rock and Pillar Range is a popular destination for Dunedin cross-country skiers.

The main access onto the range is off Highway 87, 9 km north of Middlemarch. A 4WD farm track leads to two tramping club huts that used to be ski lodges. Take Topomap H42 Waipiata and H43 Middlemarch.

—**Landowners**— All of these ranges are on private farmland. Permission is needed to cross grazed land to reach the snow—you will be extremely unpopular if you unwittingly push stock up onto the exposed tops. If a public road takes you well into the snow you're unlikely to bother stock. If you're unsure, ask at a local information centre.

—**Notes**— This gentle terrain suits cross-country skis, which are good for covering large distances as they are light and fast. Downhill skis with ski-mountaineering bindings are better for steeper slopes and nasty snow conditions. Whatever skis you have, you will find skins useful—wax and fish-scales don't always grip adequately. Mountain Works in Queenstown, ☎ (03) 442 7329, and The Wilderness Shop in Dunedin, ☎ (03) 477 3679, hire out all manner of ski-touring equipment.

Because of the gentle slopes and broad summits, sheltered valleys may be a long way away. Local ski-tourers take the weather very seriously, and so should you. Always take food, drink, warm and windproof clothes, and tell someone where you are going. Taking a snow shovel is also a good idea in case you have to dig an emergency shelter. White-out conditions are common and make route finding very difficult on these featureless plateau tops; always take a map and compass. Some of the roads used for access to the ranges are muddy and snow-covered—snow chains are essential, mainly for the mud.

15.2 Roxburgh Gorge

Alexandra to Roxburgh

For beginner paddlers (guide optional), 1 day.

—**Summary**— After paddling around the first bend of the Clutha River, you leave modern civilization behind and enter the remote Roxburgh Gorge. During the next 30 km you'll discover one of New Zealand's most isolated and well preserved 19th century mining settlements.

Canoeing on Lake Roxburgh   (Johnny Mulheron)

—How to Get There— Contact Canoe Adventures in Alexandra, ☎ (03) 448 8048 during the day and on ((03) 448 6360 after hours.

—Description— It doesn't take long after paddling away from the Alexandra boatshed to become familiar with the stable 5-metre long Canadian canoes. If you're worried about tipping out, two canoes can be lashed together to form an untippable cata-canoe.

As you paddle past numerous claustrophobic rock shelters built into the steep gorge walls, it's hard to imagine how the inhabitants managed to survive here. The formidable and barren landscape is intensely hot in summer yet often snow covered in winter.

After paddling through the gorge for a couple of hours, you'll easily make out Doctors Point ahead. Back in the 1880s it was the centre of the Roxburgh Gorge mining community—you'll land here to get a close look at the stone huts, tailraces and rusted machinery. Crawl down caves that were dug by desperate miners following veins of gold, test the old winch or try your luck at gold panning. After a couple of hours you'll have to continue paddling to beat the strong headwind that picks up each afternoon. There's still more to be explored downriver.

Near the end of the trip little outboard motors are attached and you can relax for the last hour as you putt across Lake Roxburgh to the dam.

—Notes— The trip costs $42 per person for a group of six, ranging up to $95 per person for a group of two. All gear, food and transport is supplied. We had our bikes driven down to the dam and cycled back via the Knobby Range after the canoeing (see section 15.3, Coronary Classic). It was a long day, but excellent fun.

Canoe Adventures also run a kayak course for beginners that starts with a swimming pool session and ends with a trip down the upper Shotover River—highly recommended.

15.3 Coronary Classic

Alexandra

For intermediate riders (guide optional), 5-10 hours.

—Summary— This summer ride traverses a desolate rocky ridge, called Knobby Range, on The Old Coach Road—a fast 4WD track. An impressive Central Otago panorama is laid out on either side. This is BIG country—the hills are the size of mountains and the valleys are huge wide plains.

—Description— From Alexandra cycle south over the main bridge, and down Highway 8 for 33 km to Roxburgh Dam. Cross the dam and cycle south towards Roxburgh East for almost 3 km, then turn sharp left onto Knobby Range Road. Before you lies the hill that gave this ride its name!

After 14 km of dry dusty gravel road there is one last, lung-bursting climb onto the Knobby Range. At the top take the first gate on your left. If you reach two gates next to each other on a flat spot then you've cycled 100 metres too far. Look back over your left shoulder and you'll see the gate you should go through. The gravel ends here and a 4WD track leads north along Knobby Range. Look across the valley to your left at the Stonehenge-like rocks on top of Old Man Range—the largest, Obelisk, is 25 metres tall.

This part of the ride is on farmland, so stay on the track (don't take any more left turns) and slow down for stock. After 15 undulating kilometres the track drops down on your right beside a gate with two old markers attached. From here the shortest way back is to carry on straight ahead before veering left to freewheel down to the bottom of Graveyard Gully, just out of Alexandra.

An even better alternative is to hop over the gate with the two old markers and take the 4WD track down to Little Valley Road. Turn left and cycle up this gravel road for $1^1/_2$ km to a gateway on your right at the crest of a hill. Cycle through this gateway and you'll soon reach a jumble of tracks that weave their way around to the left, back to Alexandra a few kilometres away. Amongst the maze are challenges such as the Big Dipper, Roller Coaster and The Wall. They're great fun—just like a gigantic BMX course.

—**Notes**— If you haven't got the fitness or time to tackle the coronary hill then contact Richard Bailey, ☎ (03) 448 8048 or (03) 442 7329. For $30 a rider, he'll take a vanload of you and your bikes from Alexandra practically to the top of the hill. He's a competent mountain biker and knows the track well. He also hires out bikes.

Remember, Central Otago hills are dry and weatherbeaten so take at least two water bottles and extra warm clothes. In winter take a pair of skis instead of your bike. Take Topomaps G42 Alexandra and G43 Roxburgh.

15.4 Dunstan Trail

Dunedin to Alexandra

For intermediate riders, 2-4 days, 172 km.

—**Summary**— The historic Dunstan Trail was the route originally used by goldminers in the 1860s to travel from Dunedin to the goldfields in Central Otago. Nowadays it's no easier to find gold on the trail than it was 150 years ago. In fact, just finding the trail is hard enough in places.

—**Description**— To leave Dunedin by the shortest possible route, cycle straight up Stuart Street from the Octagon and veer right onto Taieri Road, which turns into Three Mile Hill Road. Soon after crossing Silver Stream, turn right onto Milner Road. Carry straight on and you'll reach Highway 87 a few kilometres north of Mosgiel. It's mostly uphill cycling, northwest on Highway 87, to Clarks Junction about 30 km away.

The Old Dunstan Road turns off to the left here, and you head into an isolated and barren Central Otago landscape. From Clarks Junction, it is 48 km of up and down (but mostly up) to Paerau, called

'Styx' by the locals, where there is a camping area and a few old buildings. The jail, which has almost fallen down, has a fireplace that may be useful if it is raining or snowing. There are also stables that provide some shelter.

From here, it's a hard 71 km day to Alexandra with a lot of up hill and heaps of down hill. Cycle north on the Styx-Patearoa Road for 1_ km. A fence leads to the left just before the telephone lines meet the road. An 800 metre section of the old trail, on the north side of the fence, has been ploughed up. If you cycle to the end of the fence on the southern side, two historic cartwheel ruts in the grass should be easy to pick up. They are marked on the map as a 4WD track and will lead you to a derelict house on Linburn Runs Road, 7 km away. From here, turn north for 300 metres before turning west on another 4WD track, which is also the original Dunstan Trail. After 3 km it meets up with the Old Dunstan Road. Route finding from here to Alexandra is relatively easy.

—Track Conditions— 35 % sealed road, 45 % gravel, 20 % 4WD.

—Notes— DOC in Alexandra may have completed a pamphlet on the trail by now. This area can experience extremes of weather any time of year, so go well prepared. Topomaps H42 Waipiata and H43 Middlemarch are essential to follow the Dunstan Trail proper, because the existing road diverts from it twice.

15.5 The Dusky Sound Track

 Fiordland National Park

For experienced trampers, 6-10 days.

—Summary— Fiordland is New Zealand's largest, wettest and most remote national park. Crammed in between countless rugged ranges, huge U-shaped valleys lead through rich green forest to fiords as deep as the mountains are tall.

Set in the heart of this vast wilderness, the Dusky Track offers trampers a complete Fiordland experience. From Lake Hauroko to Lake Manapouri, 84 km away, it traverses huge hanging valleys, crosses over two spectacular mountain ranges and takes you to Supper Cove in Dusky Sound.

—How to Get There— The Spitfire bus service leaves from Te Anau daily at 8.30am and from Invercargill daily at 1pm. It takes the southern scenic route to Tuatapere, the self-proclaimed Sausage Capital of the South. From Tuatapere, Lake Hauroko Tours, ☎ (03) 226 6681, run people to the head of Lake Hauroko. They leave at 9.30am on Mondays and Thursdays and charge $45 per person. You can also charter the boat any time of the week for $350—it holds 10 people.

—Description—
Hauroko Burn Hut to Halfway Hut; 4-6 hours
The trip starts with a pleasant 45-minute boat trip, across New Zealand's deepest lake, to Hauroko Burn Hut (12 bunks). From there a good quality track follows Hauroko Burn (river) up to Halfway Hut (12 bunks). Because the boat runs only twice a week the huts are often packed, so you should consider taking a tent (make sure it's insect-proof).

Halfway Hut to Lake Roe Hut; 3-5 hours
The next day continue up Hauroko Burn for 5 km, fording it twice, before climbing up to Lake Laffy and Furkert Pass. Lake Roe Hut (12 bunks) is perched on the edge of the bush, above the eastern shores of Lake Laffy. It's well worth spending the afternoon exploring the beautiful lakes and spectacular granite tops in the area. Lake Roe is 20 minutes away; the Merrie Range another hour.

Lake Roe Hut to Loch Maree Hut; 4-6 hours
From Furkert Pass the poled route climbs west, nipping in between Lake Horizon and Lake Ursula. It then climbs over the Pleasant Range before dropping down a steep ridge to the Seaforth River. On fine days there are fantastic views of Dusky Sound and the surrounding mountains.

A long three-wire bridge crosses the Seaforth to Loch Maree Hut (20 bunks), on the opposite bank. When Johnny and Jonathan were there in summer, the Seaforth River was in flood and they had to wade through waist-deep water just to reach the bridge. The day before,

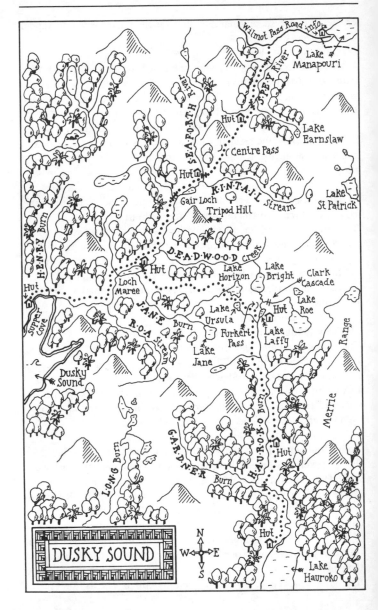

the bridge and most of the track beside the river, had been underwater.

Loch Maree Hut to Supper Cove return; 2 easy days

Allow a day each way for the tramp to Supper Cove in Dusky Sound—there's heaps of exploring to do when you get there. This section of track was built by a Public Works road gang in 1903, when jobs were scarce. Some of their abandoned tools still lie beside the track below Loch Maree. In low tide you can walk around the coast at Supper Cove, but the normal route is via the track through the bush.

There is a dinghy at Supper Cove Hut (20 bunks) so take a fishing line and row out into the appropriately named cove. Don't go too far, as conditions can change for the worse very quickly. Back in 1909, 10 rather unlucky moose were brought over from Canada and 'liberated' at Supper Cove. They haven't been seen since.

By this stage you'll be fitter and your pack a lot lighter, so the walk back to Loch Maree should be relatively easy.

Loch Maree to Upper Spey Hut; 9-11 hours

The next day continue up through beech forest beside the Seaforth River (the track can be difficult to follow if the river is in flood). After 4-5 hours you'll reach the turn-off to Kintail Hut, 5 minutes away. Cross the bridge over the Seaforth River and tackle the 770 metre climb to Centre Pass. The views from the pass of Tripod Hill and the Seaforth Valley are superb. Taking a bad photo from here is a real challenge. There is a poled route over the tops, from where you follow a steep track down through bush beside Warren Burn to Upper Spey Hut (20 bunks). This is a long day but can easily be split into two by staying at Kintail Hut for a night.

Upper Spey Hut to Lake Manapouri; 4-6 hours

From Upper Spey Hut the track follows the Spey River through lush beech forest and across grassy clearings to the Wilmot Pass Road. It's another 6 km along the road to Lake Manapouri and the Manapouri Power Station. There is an information centre 50 metres from the jetty. If you arrive too late in the day to catch one of the tourist boats across to Manapouri township then stay in the hut 200 metres east of the information centre. From Manapouri township a connecting bus takes you to Te Anau.

—Notes— As there is such a high potential to be delayed on this track (because of flooded rivers and tracks) you should take at least 2 days' spare food and fuel, and plan to have a rest day somewhere. During winter the track is impassable because of deep snow and avalanche danger. Take heaps of insect repellent—the sandflies are keen.

A shorter trip can be done by flying into, or out of, Supper Cove. Flights are weather dependent and cost $149 per person. Contact Waterwings Airways in Te Anau, ☎ (03) 249 7405.

It is a good idea to take a mountain radio with you (see Clubs & Contacts). Topomaps NZMS1 S148 Wilmot and S157 Heath are essential.

15.6 The North West Circuit

 Stewart Island

For fit intermediate trampers, 8-12 days.

—Summary— Stewart Island, known in Maori legend as 'te Punga o te Waka a Maui' (the anchor of Maui's canoe), remains mostly an untracked, forested wilderness. The North West Circuit is a popular tramping track that has many well-spaced huts.

Much of it winds through native forest but it is the beautiful beaches that most people remember. Seals are often seen basking in the sun while penguins and oyster catchers go about their business. The island is well known for its widespread population of Stewart Island kiwi but there is also a great variety of other birdlife, including kakariki (parakeet), tui and albatross. Trampers should allow as much time as possible to explore this unique island.

—How to Get There— From Bluff it takes an hour to cross Foveaux Strait to Halfmoon Bay (Oban) by catamaran and costs about $74 return. Contact Foveaux Express on ☎ (03) 212 7660.

From Invercargill it takes 20 minutes to fly and costs about $130 return or half that on a standby flight if you have a student or Youth Hostel Association (YHA) card. Contact Southern Air on ☎ (03) 218 9129.

—Description—
Halfmoon Bay to Port William; 4 hours
From Halfmoon Bay follow the road north for 5 km to the start of the track at Lee Bay. The first hut (30 bunks) is at Port William, used as a sealing base early last century. One kilometre before the hut the popular Rakiura Track (see section 15.7) to North Arm branches off on the left.

Port William to Christmas Village Hut; 8 hours
There is a hut (20 bunks) at Big Bungaree Beach (3 hours from Port William), which is an excellent place to explore. From here it takes 5 hours to reach Christmas Village Hut (20 bunks), passing the golden Murray Beach along the way.

It's hard to believe you're in the subantarctic rather than the tropics—if you're unsure, go for a swim.

Christmas Village to Mt Anglem return; 6 hours
From Christmas Village you can do a 6-hour return trip to Mt Anglem (980 m), the highest point on the island. On a clear day the view from the summit across Ruggedy Flat is spectacular; and to the north, the Fiordland mountains are also visible.

Christmas Village to Yankee River; 6 hours
The next day the track meets the coast only once (at Lucky Beach) before winding along to the sluggish peat-stained Yankee River where there is a hut (20 bunks) and good camping at the beach.

Yankee River to East Ruggedy; 7-10 hours
A few kilometres further away there are some more good camp sites at each end of the wild Smoky Beach. From here the track weaves and winds inland again before reaching Long Harry Bay (4-6 hours from Yankee River). The excellent little hut (6 bunks) sits atop a cliff, looking out to the Bishop and Clerks Islands.

The track then alternates between mud, sand and coastal boulders before leading inland from East Ruggedy Beach to East Ruggedy Hut (20 bunks, 3-4 hours from Long Harry Bay). A track branches off to the right going down to the seldom visited West Ruggedy Beach, which has a camping cave at the northern end.

East Ruggedy to Hellfire Pass; 7-hours

The North West Circuit then turns inland for 2-3 hours before crossing the Ruggedy Mountains and dropping to Waituna Bay. Hellfire Pass Hut (16 bunks) is 4 km further.

Hellfire Pass Hut to Mason Bay; 7 hours

From Hellfire Pass the new track follows southeast along the ridge to Little Hellfire Beach. Continue south over a small ridge to Mason Bay. Walk 5 km down the beach to Duck Creek where a track leads inland to Mason Bay Hut (16 bunks), 10 minutes away. Mason Bay is home to a large population of screeching Stewart Island kiwi who stomp around as if they own the place. There are also some amazing sand dunes that are well worth climbing.

Mason Bay to North Arm; 7-10 hours

From Mason Bay Hut it takes 3-4 hours to reach Freshwater Hut (12 bunks) just after the footbridge, on the true left of Freshwater River. It may seem strange that there's a jetty this far inland, but boats frequently come up this way. From Freshwater it takes another 5-6 hours to reach North Arm Hut (30 bunks).

North Arm to Halfmoon Bay; 5 hours

On your last day the track traverses above North Arm, around to Sawdust Bay and on to Kaipipi Bay a stone's throw from Halfmoon Bay.

—**Notes**— At Halfmoon Bay there is a general store, campgrounds, backpacker accommodation, and a DOC office, ☎ (03) 219 1130. Since the maps have been published many of the tracks and huts on Stewart Island have either changed or been removed. The East Ruggedy Beach to Freshwater Landing track, across the boggy Ruggedy Flat, is now a route only. You can also arrange to be dropped off and picked up by a water taxi—book before you leave Halfmoon Bay. The Holidaymaker Stewart Island map is useful but Topomaps E48 Halfmoon Bay and D48 Ruggedy are essential.

The Hoiho or yellow-eyed penguin (the world's rarest penguin) lives on the coast. They are a shy bird so please keep away from them and their nests. If you plan to supplement your diet with seafood then remember that fish numbers are declining around Stewart Island. Contact DOC to find out what the minimum allowable sizes are and take only what you need.

15.7 Other Adventures

Nevis Valley

The isolated Nevis Valley offers a classic cycle touring short cut, from Cromwell to Garston (near the southern tip of Lake Wakatipu). For intermediate riders the 100 km trip on gravel roads and 4WD tracks takes 1-2 days. Terrainmap S14 Te Anau covers the route.

From Cromwell, cycle south through Bannockburn and up Nevis Road to the 1300 m high Nevis Saddle. Fly down the other side, past Craigroy Station, across the Nevis River, and veer south on Nevis Road. It's generally a good quality gravel road that follows the Nevis River, passing the occasional stone hut that remains from the gold-rush days of last century, and includes numerous stream crossings.

After 40 km there is another smaller hill to be tackled when the road climbs out of the valley. The ride to Garston finishes, as all rides should, with a long downhill.

Ice-skating on the Lower Manorburn Dam

When this reservoir freezes over in winter it provides Central Otago adventurers with an opportunity to skate, play curling or just fool around. The whole area has a distinct 1950s feel about it, with its lifesavers' pill box and background rock'n'roll music from the nearby rink.

There are skates for hire at the artificial ice-skating rink by the car park, where you can also find out if the lake is safe to skate on— always be wary of thin ice. To get there, head 4 km northwest of Alexandra on Highway 85, then turn right and follow the signposts to the Lower Manorburn Dam, 4 km from the main road.

The Old Man Range

This 1-2 day cycling trip is an awesome way to ride from Central Otago to Southland. However, these mountains are subject to extremely fast and severe weather changes, and navigation in the mist requires considerable skill.

In 1863 an unknown number of miners died trying to climb over the range to avoid starving at their claims near Campbell Creek. Unless it rains or snows, there is no water on the range. This is a great place for ski-touring in winter (see 15.1 Back Country Ski-touring).

If you just want to do a day trip onto the range then cycle up from Fruitlands (15 km south of Alexandra on Highway 8), explore the Obelisk and howl back down the same way. The 1400 m climb from Alexandra up to the rocky moonscape of the Old Man Range makes this one of the most challenging (and rewarding) workouts this side of the galactic hub. If continuing over to Southland, turn west at the southern end of the range. Follow an unrideable boggy 4WD track down to the Waikaia River.

Once you start descending, the track improves untold, and the ride through the bush to Piano Flat is simply superb.

 ### Dunedin Paragliding

Pro-Pacific in Dunedin, ☎ (03) 476 2371, offer a variety of paragliding courses. For a 1-day fun course that instructs you how to pilot the wing, from launching to landing, they charge $164. Wear sturdy footwear and hard-wearing clothes. The flying sites are chosen on the day as they vary depending on the weather conditions.

  ### Swampy Summit Bike or Hike

For great views of the Otago Peninsula try a 2-4 hour walk, ride or run to the top of Swampy Summit. The Dunedin information centre has pamphlets on this area and mountain bikes can be hired from Browns for Bikes, on Stuart Street, ☎ (03) 477 7259.

Head out of Dunedin on Stuart Street and then Three Mile Hill Road. Turn right onto Flagstaff Whare Flat Road (1 km past Halfway Bush) and continue up to the Bull Pen carpark. From the carpark take the gravelly 4WD track leading east uphill. At the Y-intersection veer left as indicated by the 'Swampy Ridge Track' sign. Half an hour later you'll reach another intersection—veer left again towards Swampy Summit. Once you reach the summit plateau follow the ridge road along to the Doppler radar, which looks like a UFO. Runners and walkers may want to go back the same way or take the Pineapple Skyline Walkway (no cyclists allowed). Cyclists should change into top gear and enjoy the downhill. After about 4 km the road is blocked by a steel gate with spikes. Climb over it and coast down to an intersection by the Whare Flat Pottery. Veer left and follow Whare Flat Road back up to the Bull Pen carpark.

 Catlins Coast Exploration

The Catlins Forest Park (90 km south of Dunedin) contains the largest tract of native forest left on the South Island's east coast. The area is well known for its laid back atmosphere, rustic craft shops and abundant animal life.

Native birds inhabit the forest and marine animals, including the rare Hoiho penguin, sea elephants and Hectors dolphins, live along the ragged coast. There are also spectacular sea-carved caves and numerous short walks to these and other points of interest. Just about all the information needed to explore this area is clearly laid out in the 'Catlins Walks and Tracks Information' booklet, available for a few dollars at DOC offices in Dunedin, Owaka or Invercargill. The route from Dunedin to Invercargill via the coast is a very popular cycle touring pilgrimage, and as the distances involved are not large, a bicycle is certainly the best means of transport.

There are several camping grounds and a few hostels scattered throughout the Catlins. Bikes can be hired in Dunedin, and cyclists often catch the train back from Invercargill. Take Terrainmap 17 Dunedin.

 Rakiura Track, Stewart Island

For beginner trampers or those pressed for time, the Rakiura Track 'Great Walk' is a better option than the North West Circuit (see 15.6). It takes 2-3 days and completes a loop from Halfmoon Bay (Oban) to Port William, then runs via the Rakiura Track to the North Arm of Paterson Inlet before returning to Halfmoon Bay. The area is well known for its beautiful coast, native bush, abundant birdlife (especially around North Arm) and huge stretches of boardwalk. You can either stay in Port William Hut (30 bunks) and the new North Arm Hut (30 bunks) along the way, or choose between the three camp sites at Maori Beach, Port William, and Sawdust Bay. There is a very informative track pamphlet available from DOC at Halfmoon Bay.

 Stewart Island Coast

For a truly remote southern adventure, try sea kayaking around the bays and inlets of Stewart Island. Seals and penguins often accompany kayakers who paddle these crystal clear southern waters. The huts within Paterson Inlet provide excellent accommodation; there are also plenty of good spots to camp. A classic trip is to paddle up Paterson Inlet, and then Freshwater River, to Freshwater Landing Hut. From there you can do an overnight tramp to Mason Bay on the west coast and go kiwi watching.

If you have some paddling experience, kayaks can be rented for around $40 a day. Otherwise, for a fun introduction to sea kayaking try a one day guided trip ($60). For more information contact Innes Dunstan Backpackers in Halfmoon Bay (Oban), ☎ (03) 219 1080.

Bridge Swinging

Bridge swinging involves connecting yourself to the centre point of a bridge with a long climbing rope (not too long!) and walking back along the bridge before leaping off and doing a giant adrenalin-crazed swing. Bridge swingers need to be fully aware of the numerous technical limitations of their climbing equipment, especially of how quickly a sharp or abrasive edge can cut through ropes running over them.

What to do once you are at the bottom of a rope, spinning at 45 rpm above an eel-ridden river, is the type of problem you should try to anticipate before jumping. Once you start using longer ropes and higher launch points, the forces involved become much greater—wise lunatics always test the system with a full pack of gear rather than themselves.

You may conclude, like most, that paying for a proper bungy jump instead, will give just as good a thrill with a lot less hassle. If you haven't got the skills needed for reasonably serious lead climbing then don't even think about setting up a bridge swing. And by the way, this is illegal on public road and railway bridges.

Jonathan

Greg

Malcolm

ˊ Jonny

Wilderness Nightmares

Every year the following nightmares become reality for a number of unlucky or unwary people. Do not treat the advice given here as a substitute for any of the excellent instruction manuals or outdoor courses available.

Totally Lost in the Bush

"I have never been lost, but I was bewildered once for three days."
(Daniel Boone)

You've failed to back-track to your last known point, don't recognise any prominent landmarks (or can't see any) and don't have Daniel Boone with you. Stop and have a snack and something to drink. This gives you a chance to consider the situation carefully and rationally. Search and Rescue teams check huts, tracks, rivers, and ridges first. If you have left your trip details with a DOC visitors centre or someone reliable at home, then Search and Rescue (SAR) will come looking for you one or two days after you are due out. Make the job easier for them by leaving obvious markers around and get a smoky fire going. If you're in a good spot, stay put—a person on the move is much harder to find. If you haven't told anyone where you were going then you're on your own—to survive you must walk out. Carefully consider the local topography when deciding whether to travel on a ridge, in a stream or beside a river.

Benighted

If you're stuck out in the bush for a night and the weather is bad, try to find a sheltered spot out of the wind and rain. Think about making an improvised shelter out of branches and fern fronds. Start a fire if you can and keep it going all night if necessary. Other ways of staying warm are: build a big bed of ferns and crawl into it; huddle together; wear all your clothes and put your legs into your pack; or, if it's really cold, jog on the spot. If you can spare the food then keep eating.

Caught in an Avalanche

Discard your pack and ice axe (or skis and ski-poles) immediately and swim frantically towards the surface (a quick panic attack doesn't do any harm). Just before the avalanche stops moving, hold one hand in front of your mouth to create an air pocket and thrust the other one upwards towards the surface. Rescuers may see your hand, but the best way to be found is by wearing an avalanche transceiver (Pieps). These can be hired from the Mountain Safety Council (see Clubs & Contacts) and some climbing shops.

Swept Down a Swollen River

If you're wearing a pack then undo your waist belt and sternum strap immediately (they should always be undone before crossing a river anyway), otherwise the pack's buoyancy may force your head under water. Keep hold of your pack, tube or kayak because they provide excellent flotation.

When being swept through rapids, try to keep your feet in front of you and as high as possible to avoid wedging them between rocks. As soon as you can, try to use the force of the current to swim to the bank. Always choose a crossing site that has a safe run-out. Refer to the *Bushcraft Manual* (see Further Reading) for more information.

Sliding Down an Icy Snow Slope

If you don't have an ice axe then simultaneously punch your hands and feet into the snow, as if doing a high speed press-up. If you do have an ice axe, self arrest (dig in the pick) as soon as possible. Once you gather speed it's almost impossible to stop.

Blown Out to Sea in a Gale While Kayaking

Stay with your boat no matter what. Try to face your boat directly into the oncoming waves. If people are in danger of capsizing then raft together. For stability it may be necessary to lean right over and onto the kayak next to you. Attempt to steer the kayaks using a paddle. If you can see no sign of land when the storm has passed, start collecting rainwater, rationing food, and fishing. Cheer up—people have been known to survive at sea for months.

Out of Control while Skiing Down a Hill

If you're certain that you can't keep it together, then lay yourself down sideways. Keep both skis below you (downhill) and across the slope, digging your edges in to brake. If this happens to you often, then consider wearing a helmet.

Stuck in a Squeeze While Caving

Whatever you do, don't panic: you'll start hyperventilating and your chest will expand, jamming you in even more. You got in, so you can get back out.

Caught Out in a Snow-storm

It can be very dangerous to continue climbing or skiing in poor visibility (white-out). If bad weather sets in, consider building a snow cave (or snow shelter) and staying put until the storm clears. Keep the cave entrance and ventilation holes clear of snow. Wriggle your hands and toes to keep the blood circulating to stave off frostbite. Sleep on your rope (if you have one), stick your feet inside your pack and huddle together. Ration food if you have any.

Abseiling to the End of a Rope (without having reached the ground)

If you can't prusik back up the rope, because you forgot your prusik cords and no one can pass you any, then yell for help and wait. It is virtually impossible to climb hand-over-hand up a full length of climbing rope. Always have a spare prusik sling tied to your harness. Many climbers tie a knot in the end of their rope before abseiling to avoid the danger of abseiling straight off the end of the rope.

Grading Systems

Use guidebooks for just that: as a guide only. Let the conditions and your common sense tell you what you're capable of. We stress that all gradings vary depending on the conditions at the time. Variables such as weather, snow, ice, loose rock, length of the trip and river levels must be taken into consideration.

Mountains

Mountaineering gradings run from 1 to 7. They take into account technical difficulty, objective danger, length, and access. Even though grade 1 (Easy) climbing is usually straightforward, it still falls into our 'experienced' category. The easiest route on Mt Cook is grade 3 (Mildly difficult) and Mt Aspiring is grade 2+ (Moderate). Grades 4-7 (Difficult to Extremely Difficult) involve steep ice and/or rock and possibly a difficult access route. Mountains of all grades are unpredictable and dangerous, and as the weather and snow and ice conditions change from day to day, season to season, so do the grades.

Rock

New Zealand's rock climbing grades run from 8 to 32 and apply to bouldering, rock climbing and some rock pitches in mountaineering. This grading system was developed in Australia in the 1960s. To give travellers a rough idea, we've made the following approximate comparisons with grades from other parts of the world.

—NZ 8 to 11, American 5.0 to 5.3, European (France, Switzerland, Italy) 3 to 4, British Easy to Very Difficult.
—NZ 12 to 16, American 5.4 to 5.8, European 4+ to 6a, British Hard Very Difficult to Very Severe.
—NZ 17 to 21, American 5.8 to 5.10c, European 6a to 7a, British Very Severe to Extreme E2.
—NZ 22 to 29, American 5.11a to 5.12, European 7a to 8b, British E3 to E6.

Grades 12 to 16 are good for beginners, with definite handholds on every move, generally on moderately sloping rock. Grades 17 to 21 are intermediate and grades 22 to 29 are advanced with what appears to be a lack of holds and the requirement to dyno (leap) on some pitches. Grade 30 and up are for those who can climb upside-down, inside-out and back to front.

Rivers

The gradings for rivers run from I (for flatwater) to VI (for extremely dangerous conditions). Grade II rivers are excellent for beginners to learn skills. They have few obstacles, small rapids and safe run-outs. Grade III, IV and V indicate the degree of technical competence and experience required to run increasingly difficult rivers. The amount of water flowing down a river dramatically changes the grade. Some rivers become more difficult in high flows others become tricky in low flow.

Overseas Information Sources

New Zealand Tourism Board Offices Overseas

AUSTRALIA
– Sydney
Level 8, 35 Pitt Street
Sydney, NSW 2000
PO Box R1546, Royal Exchange,
PO 2000, Sydney
☎ (02) 247 5222
Fax (02) 241 1136

– Melbourne
Level 6, 60 Albert Road
South Melbourne
Victoria 3205
☎ (03) 9698 4800
Fax (03) 9698 4811

– Brisbane
Level 12, 145 Eagle Street
Brisbane, Queensland 4000
GPO Box 2634, Brisbane,
QLD 4001
☎ (07) 3831 8315
Fax (07) 3831 5337

CANADA
Suite 1200-888 Dunsmuir St.
Vancouver
BC V6C 3K4
☎ (604) 684 2117
Fax (604) 684 1265

GERMANY
Friedrichstrasse 10-12
60323 Frankfurt am Main
☎ (069) 9712 11 0
Fax (069) 9712 11 12

HONG KONG
1501 Universal Trade Centre
3 Arbuthnot Road, Central
☎ (852) 2526 0141
Fax (852) 2524 1811

SINGAPORE
391 Orchard Road, #15-01,
Ngee Ann City, 15th Fl, Tower A
Singapore 0923
☎ (65) 738 5844
Fax (65) 235 2550

JAPAN
–Tokyo
Shinjuku Monolith 21st Floor
2-3-1 Nishi Shinjuku
Shinjuku-ku, Tokyo 163-09
☎ (03) 5318 6331
Fax (03) 5381 6327

– Osaka
Meiji Seimei Sakaisuji Honmachi Building,
2nd Floor, 1-7-15 Minami Honmachi, Chuo-ku, Osaka-shi 541
☎ (06) 268 8355
Fax (06) 268 8412

SOUTH KOREA
Room 1608, Sunwha Building
502 Sunwha-dong, Chung-ku, Seoul
☎ (02) 777 9282
Fax (02) 777 9285

TAIWAN
New Zealand Commerce & Industry Office
Rm 2512, 25F International Trade Building, 333 Keelung Road, Section 1, Taipei 10548
☎ (02) 757 9514
Fax (02) 757 6114

THAILAND
ITF Tower 11
14th Floor, Unit 14D,
140/26 Silom Road
Bangkok
☎ (02) 231 6456
Fax (02) 231 6451

UNITED KINGDOM
New Zealand House, Haymarket
London SW1Y 4TQ
☎ (0171) 930 1662
Fax (0171) 839 8929

USA
– Los Angeles
501 Santa Monica Blvd #300
Santa Monica, CA 90401
☎ (310) 395 7480
Fax (310) 395 5453

– New York
780 3rd Avenue
Suite 1904
New York, NY 10017-2024
☎ (212) 832 8482
Fax (212) 832 7602

– Chicago
1111 North Dearborn Street
Suite 2705,
Chicago, Illinois 60610
☎ (312) 440 1345
Fax (312) 440 3808

New Zealand Clubs & Contacts

The following list includes central 'umbrella' organisations for each outdoor activity. Contact them to find your closest club.

Clubs

Federated Mountain Clubs (FMC)
PO Box 1604, Wellington
☎ (04) 384 2448

NZ Alpine Club (NZAC)
PO Box 3040, Wellington
☎ (04) 384 4413

NZ Canoeing Association (NZCA)
PO Box 3768,
Wellington

NZ Hang Gliders Association
(NZHGA),
PO Box 817,
Wellington

NZ Mountain Bike Association
(NZMBA), PO Box 361, Timaru
NZ Speleological Society (NZSS)
PO Box 18, Waitomo Caves
☎ (07) 878 7640

NZ Underwater Association
(NZUA)
PO Box 875, Auckland 1
☎ (09) 849 5896
Fax (09) 849 7051

The Diving Network
PO Box 38023, Auckland
☎ (09) 367 5066
Fax (09) 576 2993

Other Contacts

The Department of Conservation
Head Office
PO Box 10 420, Wellington
☎ (04) 471 0726
(or contact the Park
HQ/Information Office for your
destination)

NZ Alpine Guides Association
PO Box 10, Mt Cook Village

NZ Mountain Safety Council Inc.
PO Box 6027, Te Aro,
Wellington
☎ (04) 385 7162

Royal Forest & Bird Protection
Society of New Zealand
PO Box 631,
Wellington
☎ (04) 385 7374

Mountain Radio Services

The following Mountain Radio Service contacts hire out mountain
radios to those heading into the hills. At specific 'sched' times each
evening they provide a mountain weather forecast, take details of your
day's progress and can relay messages. In the event of an emergency
a mountain radio can be a life saver.

- Taupo
John Head: ☎ (07) 378 9194

- Central North Island (Turangi)
Graham Brebner: ☎ (07) 386 6163

- Napier
Ron Ward: ☎ (06) 844 2797

- Waipawa
Lyell Wallace: ☎ (06) 856 5877

- Wanganui
Darryl Greeks: ☎ (06) 344 4416

- Palmerston North
Hugh Wilde: ☎ (06) 356 9450

- Masterton
Collin Coutts:
Home ☎ (06) 377 0426

- Hutt Valley
Bob Sewell: ☎ (04) 564 6929

•Wellington
Morris Perry: ☎ (04) 476 6010

•Christchurch
Paul White: Home ☎ (03) 332 5846; Work ☎ (03) 366 5241

•Dunedin
Ron Kingston: ☎ (03) 454 4664

•Westport
John Griffiths:
Home ☎ (03) 789 8399
Work ☎ (03) 789 7259

•Invercargill
Dick Sheehan: ☎ (03) 215 9713

Local Information Centres

Department of Conservation (DOC) Information Centres

(An abridged list, north to south. These centres provide information about the local DOC estate and the activities available in the area.)

Northland Forest Park
Waipoua
☎ (09)439 0650

Bay of Islands Maritime & Historic Park
Pitt Street, Russell
☎ (09) 403 7685

Hauraki Gulf Maritime Park
Corner Karangahape Rd & Liverpool Streets, Auckland
☎ (09) 307 9279

Coromandel Forest Park
Kauaeranga Valley
☎ (07) 868 6381

Urewera National Park
Highway 38, Aniwaniwai
☎ (06) 837 3803

Whirinaki Forest Park
Highway 38
☎ (07) 366 5641

Egmont National Park
Egmont Road, Inglewood

Pembroke Road
Stratford
☎ (06) 765 5144

Dawson Falls
Upper Manaia Road

Tongariro National Park
Mountain Road, Ohakune
☎ (06) 385 8578

Kaimanawa Forest Park
Turangi Place, Turangi
☎ (07) 386 8607

Whanganui National Park
68 Ingestre Street, Wanganui
☎ (06) 345 2402

Mt Bruce Wildlife Centre
Masterton-Woodville Highway
☎ (06) 375 8004

Rimutaka Forest Park
Catchpool Valley
Coast Road, Wainuiomata
☎ (04) 564 8551

Marlborough Sounds Maritime
Park
Auckland Street, Picton Foreshore
Picton
☎ (03) 573 7582

Abel Tasman National Park
Corner King Edward & High
Street
Motueka
☎ (03) 528 9117

Kahurangi National Park
1 Commercial Street
Takaka
☎ (03) 525 8026

Nelson Lakes National Park
View Road, St Arnaud
☎ (03) 521 1806

Paparoa National Park
Main Road, Punakaiki
☎ (03) 731 1893

Hanmer Forest Park
Corner Amuri & Jacks Pass Road
Hanmer Springs
☎ (03) 315 7128

Arthur's Pass National Park
Arthur's Pass
☎ (03) 318 9211

Westland National Park
Main Road, Franz Josef
☎ (03) 752 0727
or ☎ (03) 752 0796

Main Road
Fox Glacier
☎ (03) 751 0807

Mt Cook National Park
Mt Cook Village
☎ (03) 435 1819

Mt Aspiring National Park
Ardmore Street,
Wanaka
☎ (03) 443 7660

Fiordland National Park
Lakefront Drive, Te Anau
☎ (03) 249 7921

Catlins Forest Park
Corner Campbell & Ryley Streets
Owaka
☎ (03) 415 8341

Stewart Island
Halfmoon Bay
Main Road, Stewart Island
☎ (03) 219 1130

Tourist Visitor Information Centres

An abridged list, from north to south. These centres provide regional information about activities, travel, accommodation and points of interest. In recent years these centres have become more like advertising agencies for regional tourist companies, and small adventure companies may not be mentioned.

—The North Island—

Kaitaia
Northland Information Centre
Jaycee Park, South Road
☎/fax (09) 408 0879

Paihia
Information Bay of Islands
Marsden Road
☎ (09) 402 7426
fax (09) 402 7301

Whangarei
Whangarei Visitors Bureau
Tarewa Park, Otaika Road
☎ (09) 438 1079
fax (09) 438 2943

Dargaville
Dargaville Information Centre
65 Normanby Street
☎/fax (09) 439 8360

Auckland
Auckland Visitor Centre
299 Queen Street
☎ (09) 366 6888
Fax (09) 358 4684

Auckland
Arataki Park Visitor Centre
Scenic Drive
Centennial Memorial Park
Titirangi, the Waitakeres
☎ (09) 817 7134

Waitomo Caves
Museum of Caves Information
Centre,
Main Street
☎ (07) 878 7640
fax (07) 878 6184

Opotiki
Opotiki Information Centre
Corner St John & Elliott Streets
☎ (07) 315 8484
fax (07) 315 8664

Gisborne
Eastland & Gisborne District
Information Centre,
209 Grey Street
☎ (06) 868 6139
fax (06) 868 6138

Tauranga
Tauranga Information Centre
The Strand
☎ (07) 578 8103
fax (07) 577 6268

Rotorua
Tourism Rotorua Travel & Visitor
Centre,
67 Fenton Street
☎ (07) 348 5179
fax (07) 348 6044

Taupo
Information Taupo
13 Tongariro Street
☎ (07) 378 9000
fax (07) 378 9003

Turangi
Turangi Information Centre
Ngawaka Place
☎ (07) 386 8999
fax (07) 386 0074

Mt Ruapehu
Whakapapa Visitor Centre
Highway 48,
Whakapapa Village
☎ (07) 892 3729
fax (07) 892 3814

Ohakune
Ruapehu Visitors' Centre
54 Clyde Street
☎ (06) 385 8427
fax (06) 385 8427

Napier
Napier Visitor Information
Centre
Marine Parade
☎ (06) 835 7579
fax (06) 835 7219

Wellington
Wellington Visitor Information
Centre, 101 Wakefield Street
☎ (04) 801 4000
fax (04) 801 3030

—The South Island—

Picton
Picton Information Centre
Severn Street
☎ (03) 753 8838
fax (03) 573 8858

Nelson
Nelson Visitor Information Centre
Corner Trafalgar & Halifax Streets
☎ (03) 548 2304
fax (03) 546 9008

Kaikoura
Kaikoura Information Centre
236 High Street
☎ (03) 319 5641
fax (03) 319 5308

Hanmer Springs
Hurunui Visitor Information
Centre, Corner Amuri Avenue &
Jacks Pass Road
☎ (03) 315 7128

Arthur's Pass
Arthur's Pass Visitor Centre
Clyde Street
☎ (03) 318 9211
fax (03) 318 9271

Christchurch
Christchurch/Canterbury Visitor
Centre
Corner Worcester Street & Oxford
Terrace
☎ (03) 379 9629
fax (03) 377 2424

Mt Cook
Mt Cook National Park Visitor
Centre, Bowen Drive
☎ (03) 435 1818
fax (03) 435 1895

Wanaka
Wanaka Visitor Information
Ardmore Street
☎ (03) 443 1233
fax (03) 443 9238

Queenstown
Queenstown Travel & Visitor
Centre
Corner Shotover & Camp Street
☎ (03) 442 4100
fax (03) 442 8907

Te Anau
Te Anau Fiordland Travel
Information Centre
Te Anau Terrace
☎ (03) 249 8900
fax (03) 249 7022

Dunedin
Dunedin Visitor Centre
48 The Octagon
☎ (03) 474 3300
fax (03) 474 3311

Invercargill
Invercargill Visitor Information
Centre, Queens Park
☎/fax (03) 218 9753

West Coast

Westport
Buller Visitor & Information
Centre, 1 Brougham Street
☎ (03) 789 6658
fax (03) 789 6658

Punakaiki
Punakaiki Visitor Centre
Highway 6
☎ (03) 731 1895

Greymouth
Greymouth Information Centre
Corner Mackay & Herbert Streets
☎ (03) 768 5101
fax (03) 768 0317

Hokitika
Westland Visitor
Information Centre,

Weld Street
☎ (03) 755 8322
fax (03) 755 8026

Franz Josef Glacier
Franz Josef Visitor Centre
Highway 6
☎/fax (03) 752 0796

Fox Glacier
Fox Glacier Visitor Centre
Highway 6
☎ (03) 751 0807
fax (03) 751 0858

Haast
South Westland World Heritage
Visitor Centre, Highway 6
☎ (03) 750 0809
fax (03) 750 0832

Stewart Island

Stewart Island Visitor Centre
Main Road, Halfmoon Bay
☎ (03) 219 1218
fax (03) 219 1555

Backpacker Hostels
Some backpacker hostels have almost as much information as official
information centres. They are often more up-to-date and provide specific details
for young-at-heart travellers in their area.

Further Reading

Instruction Manuals

Bushcraft, Mountain Safety Council Manual 12.
Department of Internal Affairs, Wellington, New Zealand.

Mountaincraft, Manual 20, Lyndsay Main.
New Zealand Mountain Safety Council, Wellington, New Zealand.

The New Zealand Tramper's Handbook, Grant Hunter.
Heinemann Reed, Auckland, New Zealand.

Outdoor First Aid, Manual 14, Bev Abbott and Wayne Mullins.
New Zealand Mountain Safety Council, Wellington, New Zealand.

Outdoor Pursuits in New Zealand, Graeme Dingle.
Reed, Wellington, New Zealand.

Safety in the Mountains, Field Guide, Federated Mountain Clubs
of New Zealand (FMC). FMC, Wellington, New Zealand.

Guide Books

Canterbury Rock (and updates), Tim Wethey.
Tim Wethey, Christchurch, New Zealand.

Central North Island Rock, Pete Manning.
NZ Alpine Club, Wellington, New Zealand.

Classic New Zealand Mountain Bike Rides, The Kennett Bros.
PO Box 11 310, Wellington, New Zealand.

Guide to the Whanganui River.
NZ Canoeing Association. Auckland, New Zealand.

New Zealand Travel Survival Kit.
Lonely Planet Publications, Melbourne, Australia.

Tramping in New Zealand
Lonely Planet Publications, Melbourne, Australia.

Mobil New Zealand Travel Guides, (North Island & South Island volumes), Diana and Jeremy Pope.
Reed Methuen, Auckland, New Zealand

The Mount Aspiring Region, Graham Bishop.
NZ Alpine Club, New Zealand.

New Zealand Cycle Touring Adventures, The Kennett Bros.
PO Box 11 310, Wellington, New Zealand.

New Zealand's North Island Rivers: A Guide for Canoeists and Rafters, Graham Egarr. 1989.
David Bateman, Auckland, New Zealand. (Available at libraries only)

New Zealand's Top Ten Tracks, Mark Pickering.
Reed, Auckland, New Zealand.

Quarry Climbs, Rick McGregor. 1983.
URGA, Auckland, New Zealand

Tramper's Guide to New Zealand's National Parks; A, R Burton and M Atkinson.
Reed Methuen Publishers, Auckland, New Zealand.

Taupo Regional Mountain Bike Guide, The Kennett Bros.
PO Box 11 310, Wellington, New Zealand.

Wellington Regional Mountain Bike Guide, The Kennett Bros.
PO Box 11 310, Wellington, New Zealand.

Whitewater River Running in New Zealand, Graham Egarr. 1988.
Reed Methuen Publishers, Auckland, New Zealand (Available at libraries only)

101 Great Tramps in New Zealand, Mark Pickering and Rodney Smith.
Reed Books, Auckland, New Zealand

General Reading

Great Peaks of New Zealand, Hugh Logan.
John McIndoe, Dunedin, New Zealand. 1990.

Land of the Mist, the Story of Urewera National Park.
The Department of Lands and Survey, Gisborne, New Zealand. 1983.

New Zealand Adventure
Christchurch, New Zealand. Quarterly magazine.

New Zealand Wilderness
David Hall Publishing Ltd, Auckland, New Zealand. Monthly magazine.

The Lorax, Dr Suess.
Collins, 1994.

Other Sources

FMC Bulletin, published quarterly by the Federated Mountain Clubs of New Zealand (FMC, Wellington, New Zealand), is free to members of affiliated clubs or available on subscription. The Royal Forest & Bird Protection Society of New Zealand publishes the quarterly magazine, *Forest & Bird*, and charges $45 yearly for membership, including the magazine. Information Centres and DOC offices have displays chock-a-block with brochures and pamphlets on tracks, trips and adventures. The Department of Lands and Survey publishes the National Park and Forest Park guidebook series; and the New Zealand Canoeing Association (NZCA) publishes numerous canoe guides.

Glossary

Abseil (or **rappel**): to descend a rope with the aid of a friction device such as a 'figure of eight'.

Anchor: a sling, bolt, snow stake, ice screw or any other piece of equipment that climbers use to attach themselves to a mountain or rock face.

Arête: steep narrow ridge.

Belay: a climber is 'on belay' when roped up to a climbing partner who is anchored to the mountain.

Bivvy: (i) the act of camping out, usually without a tent, and often unexpectedly; (ii) a small two-bunk hut.

Bomb-proof: extremely strong; often said to reassure nervous climbing partners that the anchors they are using are fail-proof.

Bony: a rocky and often shallow section of river.

Bouldering: rock climbing on boulders without the need for ropes, as opposed to scaling huge scary rock faces.

Buildering: climbing on buildings, see Chapter 13, section 13.8, Buildering.

Bush: New Zealanders refer to native forest as 'bush'

Bushline: same as treeline; where trees/bush stop and alpine tussock begins.

Cairn: small pile of rocks that marks a route.

Canadian canoe: common term in New Zealand for an open-top canoe.

Crag: rock climbing area.

DOC (Department of Conservation): government department that manages most public recreation areas, including national parks and marine reserves.

DOSLI (Department of Survey and Land Information): government department that produces and sells Topomaps, Terrainmaps, etc.

Eddy: swirling back-current in a river.

Edging: using the edge of your foot to stand on a small foothold.

Eskimo roll: technique used by kayakers to right themselves after capsizing.

4WD track: any track negotiable by a 4WD vehicle but not a standard car—usually two parallel wheel ruts.

Face Plant: (i) any cycling manoeuvre that ends up looking like an attempt to hypnotise an earthworm, or (ii) any vegetation growing between chin and hairline.

Ferry Gliding: technique used by kayakers and rafters to move across a river by paddling diagonally against the current.

Glissade: to ski without skis, a controlled slide down a snow slope on your boots.

Gnarly: rugged, rough.

Grid Reference: the grid line coordinates on a topographical map used to pinpoint a location (for example, 754 428). All DOSLI Topomaps explain how to use a grid reference.

Great Walks: a group of the most popular tramping tracks in New Zealand. Users must buy a 'hut and campsite pass' in advance.

Hills: 'the hills' is a common term for forested and tussock covered mountain ranges.

Karabiner: strong alloy link used to connect a climbing rope to anchors and harnesses.

Lead Climbing or **Leading**: the person who climbs first, putting in protection as he/she goes (much scarier than top-roping).

Map Stop: a face-saving way of asking for a rest. You can never have too many map stops.

Moraine: huge piles of rocks transported by a glacier.

Névé: snowfield at the head of a glacier.

Objective Danger: what the environment throws at you, for example, avalanches, lightning and rock falls. See subjective danger.

Paper Road: a legal road that has been drawn on a surveying map, but may no longer exist or indeed never have been built. Many of these are 4WD tracks suitable for riding.

Parkmap: a DOSLI map that covers a state forest or national park.

Pitch: the distance between two belay points—up to the length of your rope.

Podocarp: native conifer trees, such as, rimu, totara, kahikatea.

Portage: to carry your kayak, tube or raft. Usually done to avoid a dangerous rapid.

Primus: the name commonly given to a portable stove (more specifically a Swedish brand of stove).

Protection (**runner**, **pro**): when used in climbing circles refers to an anchor that the rope passes through.

Put-in: the place where you start a river trip.

Queen's Chain: strip of land, 20.1 metres wide, that follows New Zealand's coastline, estuaries and waterways, and allows public right of way. Some farmers deny its existence.

Run-out: (i) area below you on a river or mountain; (ii) when you climb a dangerous distance above your last piece of protection.

SAR: Search and Rescue.

Self Arrest: to stop oneself from sliding down a snow slope. It is best done with an ice axe, and as quickly as possible.

Sidle: a route around or along the side of a hill.

Ski Skins: see Chapter 13, Ski-touring on the Two Thumb Range.

Snake Bite (or **pinch puncture**): a double puncture caused by hitting a rock so hard that the rim pierces the tube. To avoid snake bites on rocky trails, pump your tyre pressures up to 50 PSI.

Spur: a small ridge that leads from a valley up to a main ridge.

Stopper: a wave spiralling back on itself; named thus because of its ability to stop canoeists or rafters when paddling down a river.

Subjective Danger: danger caused by your judgement, fear and decisions. See also objective danger.

Take-out: the place where you end your river trip.

Tarn: Small mountain lake, often found on flat ridges.

Terrainmap: 1:250 000 scale maps produced by DOSLI.

Togs: swimming clothes.

Tops: 'the tops' is a common term for areas above the treeline.

Topomaps: 1:50 000 scale maps produced by DOSLI. The South Westland area, where these maps have not yet been produced, is covered by the older NZMS1 'inch-to-the-mile' series.

Top-roping: rock climbing technique when the climber is belayed from the top of the climb, and therefore shouldn't fall any distance.

Trackmaps: maps produced by DOSLI that cover specific tracks, and have excellent information about the area and track times.

Traverse: (i) Moving horizontally across a slope; (ii) following the top of a ridge.

True Left: the left side of a river when facing downstream.

True Right: (i) political anachronism describing free market philosophy, or (ii) the right side of a river when facing downstream.

Index

CONVERSION TABLE

To convert	Multiply by
inches to millimetres	25.4
millimetres to inches	0.0397
inches to centimetres	2.54
centimetres to inches	0.397
feet to metres	0.304
metres to feet	3.28
miles to kilometres	1.609
kilometres to miles	0.621
square feet to square metres	0.092
square metres to square feet	10.76
square miles to square kilometres	2.59
square kilometres to square miles	0.386
ounces to grams	28.35
grams to ounces	0.035
pounds to grams	453.6
grams to pounds	0.0022
pounds to kilograms	0.453
kilograms to pounds	2.205
pints to litres	0.568
litres to US gallons	0.26
US gallons to litres	3.79
litres to imperial gallons	0.22
imperial gallons to litres	4.54
°Celsius to °Fahrenheit	1.8 and add 32
°Fahrenheit to °Celsius	subtract 32 then multiply by 0.55

— CLIMATE CHART —

H=High L=Low (average) °C/°F R= rain days		WINTER (Jun, Jul, Aug)	SPRING (Sept, Oct, Nov)	SUMMER (Dec, Jan, Feb)	AUTUMN (Mar, Apr, May)
AUCKLAND	H	15/59	18/64	24/75	20/68
	L	9/48	11/51	12/53	13/55
	R	15	12	8	11
BAY OF ISLANDS	H	16/60	19/66	25/77	21/69
	L	7/44	9/43	14/57	11/51
	R	16	11	7	11
CHRISTCHURCH	H	12/53	17/62	22/71	18/64
	L	3/37	7/44	12/53	8/46
	R	7	7	7	7
QUEENSTOWN	H	10/50	16/60	22/71	16/60
	L	1/33	9/43	10/50	6/42
	R	7	9	8	8
ROTORUA	H	13/55	17/62	24/75	18/64
	L	4/39	7/44	12/53	9/48
	R	13	11	9	9
WELLINGTON	H	12/53	12/53	20/68	17/62
	L	6/42	6/42	13/55	11/51
	R	13	13	7	10